TERESA OF AVILA
DOCTOR OF THE SOUL

Teresa of Avila

Doctor of the Soul

Peter Tyler

B L O O M S B U R Y
LONDON • NEW DELHI • NEW YORK • SYDNEY

First published in Great Britain 2013

Copyright © Peter Tyler, 2013

The moral right of the author has been asserted

No part of this book may be used or reproduced in any manner whatsoever without written permission from the Publisher except in the case of brief quotations embodied in critical articles or reviews. Every reasonable effort has been made to trace copyright holders of material reproduced in this book, but if any have been inadvertently overlooked the Publishers would be glad to hear from them.

A Continuum book

Bloomsbury Publishing Plc
50 Bedford Square
London WC1B 3DP

www.bloomsbury.com

Bloomsbury is a registered trade mark of Bloomsbury Publishing Plc

Bloomsbury Publishing, London, New Delhi, New York and Sydney

A CIP record for this book is available from the British Library.

ISBN 9781441187840

10 9 8 7 6 5 4 3 2 1

Typeset by Fakenham Prepress Solutions, Fakenham, Norfolk NR21 8NN

Printed and bound in Great Britain by CPI Group (UK) Ltd, Croydon CR0 4YY

Contents

Introduction: Woman Beyond Frontiers...

'All those books I read in order to understand Teresa of Jesus...'
Baltasar Álvarez (Teresa's Confessor) to Francisco de Ribera[1]

'I salute you, Teresa, woman without frontiers, physical, erotic, hysterical, epileptic, who makes the word, who makes flesh, who undoes herself while being beside herself, waves of images without pictures, tumults of words, cascades of explosions... night and light, too much body and without body... quickly searching for the Beloved who is always present without ever being there... Teresa, Yes, my sister, invisible, ecstatic, eccentric, Yes, Teresa, my love, Yes!'
Julia Kristeva, *Thérèse mon amour*[2]

'Why write, if this too easy action of pushing a pen across paper is not given a certain bull-fighting risk and we do not approach dangerous, agile and two-horned topics.'
José Ortega y Gasset, *On Love: Aspects of a Single Theme*[3]

Five hundred years after her birth in Avila, Spain in 1515, Teresa of Avila continues to court controversy. The life and writings of this remarkable woman erupt into the world's consciousness in the middle of the troubled sixteenth century and they have never left us. One of her latest interpreters, the French post-structuralist, feminist and psychoanalytic writer Julia Kristeva, describes her in her latest 'love letter' to Teresa, *Thérèse mon amour* (Kristeva 2008), in the words quoted above, as an 'ecstatic, eccentric, hysteric', a 'woman without frontiers or boundaries'. How true this is! Stylistically in her works, as in her life, Teresa forever defies categorization. Scholars of literature, psychoanalysis,

---

[1] Ribera 1908: 136.
[2] Julia Kristeva, *Thérèse mon amour*, 2008: 41.
[3] Trans. T. Talbot. New York, Meridian 1957: 121.

mysticism and feminism all try to claim her as their own, yet, as we shall see, she always manages to deftly evade being too easily classified. Some of this arises from the peculiar circumstances within which she grew and developed, circumstances that we shall return to throughout this book. However, a great part of this 'uncategorization', as I will argue in this book, arises from her unique manner of writing. A manner of writing, I will suggest, that owes much to the medieval tradition of 'mystical theology' to which she was heir and which would be transformed and revivified by her work. Accordingly, this book, the third and final part of a 'mystical trilogy' begun in 2009 with my *John of the Cross* (Continuum 2010) and followed by *The Return to the Mystical – Teresa of Avila, Ludwig Wittgenstein and the Western Mystical Tradition* (Continuum 2011) will have the following aims.

First and foremost I want to explore the enigma that is Teresa by concentrating on the style and manner of her mystical writing and how it relates to the great medieval tradition of *theologia mystica*. In doing this I have aimed to revivify the ancient Christian tradition of mystical writing by exploring the process involved in the writing itself. In *The Return to the Mystical* I argued that this was a conscious and deliberate method of writing that had flourished in the medieval period and would be used by Teresa of Avila when she embarked upon her own writing career, as a middle-aged woman in difficult circumstances. I shall expand and deepen the lessons learnt in the earlier book in the present volume as I continue this exploration through 'listening to the voice' of Teresa, primarily through her own writings. As we celebrate the 500th anniversary of her birth in 2015 I am aware that there will be many coming afresh to Teresa's writing and context. Consequently, I have tried as far as possible to contextualize her writings in the special and unique circumstances within which they were conceived.

In these books I have also wanted to show how the two great Spanish mystics, Teresa of Avila and John of the Cross, inherited this tradition and used it to their own ends. In the *Return to the Mystical* I argued that Teresa's training in mystical theology came from her reading of the early sixteenth century master of the art, Francisco de Osuna, modified and developed by her contact with other such luminaries as Bernardino de Laredo. In this final book I will continue this process by concentrating on Teresa's own mystical style and drawing out some implications for our contemporary reading of her work. This shall be enhanced by a study of her reception in the English-speaking world in the five centuries since her death, paying particular attention to her own unique 'language of the soul' and how her English interpreters have coped with the demands of her style.

However, in addition to the need to elaborate the nature and ambit of the mystical style, I have had another aim before me throughout this writing. According to many commentators, the twentieth century saw the death crisis of modernism when the great project of the modern world begun, arguably, in the sixteenth century crucible of the Renaissance and Reformation hit the buffers of the crises provoked by two world wars, the rise of Communism and Fascism and the collapse of the 'great narratives' that had dominated world thought for so long. The ushering in of the 'postmodern world' has led thinkers to regard our period as a new era of 're-birth' when new forms and expressions of the human spirit will thrive. One form this new culture has taken is in the twenty-first century 'turn to the spiritual', or, as it has been called, 'the return to the religious' (see Tyler and Woods 2012). For me, this return to the religious is the point where our pre-modern guides, especially Teresa and John, enter into conversation with our 'postmodern' world. It is no coincidence, I believe, that writers such as Kristeva can find such depth and resonance in Teresa's work. Her studied ambiguity and transgressive texts are once again finding a new audience among those who are seeking to make sense of the self and its expression in a world where the boundaries of religion are once again, as they were in the sixteenth century, being stretched and morphed into new and unforeseen patterns.

In *The Return to the Mystical* I gave Teresa a striking contemporary conversation partner, the Austrian philosopher Ludwig Wittgenstein. For her anniversary year I thought it would be appropriate to end my trilogy by allowing Teresa to take centre stage, to give her her own voice as it were. However I shall broaden the conversations of *The Return to the Mystical* in this volume by bringing in two other dimensions of contemporary thought not explored in the earlier one. The first of these will be provided by the psychological discourse of the Swiss psychiatrist Carl Gustav Jung. The second will come from the contemporary dialogue of Christianity and Buddhism, with particular reference to the discourse of 'mindfulness' as practised in pastoral and healthcare settings. In bringing Teresa into dialogue with these two discourses towards the end of this book I aim to show her continued relevance to our post-modern, and possibly 'post-Christian', world and the contribution her works can continue to make to our religious debates today. My concerns at this point in the book will centre on the rediscover of 'soul language' in contemporary psychology as I delineate how

Teresa's own 'language of the soul' may once again find expression in contemporary examinations of the nature of the human person.

As I returned to early translations of her work in the writing of this book, some of which by translators who would have known friends and colleagues of Teresa, and attempted to decipher her notoriously elusive style, I felt like an art restorer gently dabbing away 500 years of accumulated grime to allow the original fresh colours of her prose to shine through. When the original colours of Michelangelo's Sistine Chapel were revealed a few years ago many art critics denounced the exercise as a travesty. Now, as we have got used to the bright colours revealed by the restorers, it is difficult to return to the faded monochromes of the untreated frescoes. So I believe it is the case with Teresa's texts. Over-familiarity has bred, if not contempt, at least a certain indifference to the 'shock and awe' of the original texts. Time and again while working on this volume I have puzzled over difficult passages thinking: 'Did she *really* say *that*?' However, consultation with other scholars and translators has led me to the conclusion that her prose is as challenging as I originally thought. A conclusion, incidentally, shared by most of her translators. Edgar Allison Peers, for example, one of her greatest exponents in the twentieth century, once wrote that 'in everything she wrote, St Teresa's "rough style" (*grosería*, so she herself terms it) is unconventional, disjointed, elliptical, frequently ungrammatical and too often obscure. The general sense of any of her phrases can usually be made out, but about its exact meaning there can often be no kind of certainty, and the guess of any one person conversant with the language, and the Carmelite history, of the sixteenth century will be as good as the guess of any other' (Allison Peers *The Letters of St Teresa of Jesus*: 1). This particular Teresian style has lent a certain challenge, and charm, to the work and I shall miss that distinctive voice when this volume leaves my hands. If, having read this book, you feel inspired to return to her texts with new interest and vigour then I will have fulfilled my task.

I have divided the book into three sections. The first will explore the context of Teresa's life and times. As I wrote this I was aware that much of this territory has been covered by other biographers and excellent commentators. However, for a book such as this the general reader will need to have some context within which to place Teresa's work and, in addition, I felt that recent scholarship has thrown light on certain aspects of Teresa's life and times and that those outside specialist academic circles may enjoy getting acquainted with them. In particular, I have dealt in this section with recent thought on such matters as the origins of Teresa's family, the context of sixteenth century Spanish society and her chosen Religious Order – the Carmelites.

Having covered this ground, in the second part of the book, I shall concentrate on Teresa's writings, looking in particular at her four great texts: *The Book of the Life, The Way of Perfection, The Book of the Foundations* and *The Interior Castle.* I shall survey these texts in the light of the linguistic dynamic presented by Teresa and how this can be interpreted from a contemporary psycho-spiritual perspective. Here I shall be particularly concerned with expounding what I call her 'language of spirit': her unique linguistic approach to this most elusive of discourses. This perspective will be extended in the third part of the book where I shall concentrate on two specific aspects of interpretation of Teresa – from the perspective of the psychological framework illustrated in the work of Carl Jung and within the dialogue presented by the contemporary discourse on mindfulness which itself draws on perspectives from Buddhist thought. In embarking on this conversation my clear aim has been to illustrate the continuing relevance and importance of Teresa and her writings at the time of her 500th anniversary.

Throughout the volume I have tried to give ample justification for my choices of translation, and where I feel my translation may be questionable I have added the translations of other scholars and the original Spanish passage itself so that readers can make up their own minds. In my desire to go back to Teresa's original voice I have worked with the closest edition to Teresa's original, that edited by Efrén de la Madre de Dios and Otger Steggink in the *Obras Completas de Santa Teresa de Jésus* in the series *Biblioteca de Autores Cristianos* (BAC, Madrid 1997). As the first full English translations of her work by Kavanaugh and Rodriguez and Allison Peers rely heavily on the older critical edition by P. Silverio de Santa Teresa, I have also turned to this edition for certain passages as published in *Santa Teresa Obras Completas* edited by Tomás Alvarez in the editon of *Monte Carmelo* (BMC, Burgos 1998). Unless stated all translations of Teresa's works are my own. Some of this work has necessitated returning to facsimiles of the original autographs of Teresa's works and here I have turned to the facsimile editions produced by Tomás Alvarez for BMC and the venerable first photostatic edition of the original manuscript of *The Interior Castle* produced by Archbishop Cardinal Lluch in 1882. Even though at times I may be critical of some editorial decisions made by commentators and translators alike I became throughout the writing of this work increasingly aware of my dependence upon them. Anything achieved in this work is due entirely to five hundred years of painstaking and loving Teresian scholarship conducted by generations of wise interpreters. Only by standing on the shoulders of such giants can we hope to peer into the future. My hope for this book would be that it will pass on that tradition to a new generation of scholars and readers.

Before I end this brief prologue I would like to clarify two matters. In the Spanish speaking world Teresa is normally referred to as 'Teresa de Jésus'. Although the anglicized version 'Teresa of Jesus' is still extensively used it is the other version, 'Teresa of Avila', that has prevailed in the anglophone world and one that I will use within this book. Similarly, the town of her birth, Ávila, is usually rendered in English minus its accent as 'Avila'. Again, I see no reason to stray from this convention and will continue it here. Apart from these two conventions I shall, as far as possible, remain with Spanish spellings of names, places and works, giving the English equivalent where necessary. Where English versions exist (e.g. 'Castile') I will use them.

Once again I would like to set down my sincere thanks to all who helped in the writing of this book in so many ways. I am grateful to the spiritual and intellectual assistance of the Carmelite communities at Boar's Hill, Oxford, the *Centro Internacional Teresiano Sanjuanista* at Avila and at Toledo and in particular Fr Jimmy McCaffrey OCD, P. Javier Sancho Fermín OCD, P. Tito de la Cruz OCD and Joanne Mosley. All of my books with Continuum/Bloomsbury would not have come about without the professional support and friendship of Robin Baird-Smith; to him and his fantastic editorial team, especially Joel Simons and Kim Storry, I owe an enormous debt. My colleagues and students at St Mary's University College, Twickenham have been their usual forbearing selves and I thank them all most sincerely for giving me the time and space to complete this work. I am also most grateful to Federico Filippi and Paul Trafford for their advice on Chapter 8 and, in Federico's case, much needed horticultural therapy! In the final stages of the work conversations within the Mystical Theology Network, especially with Eddie Howells, Terence O'Reilly and Louise Nelstrop were very helpful and I express my thanks to them.

Once again, I extend special thanks to my family and friends for helping me to keep my balance during this difficult task and I thank in particular Julienne McLean, Gwynneth Knowles, Br Patrick Moore, Hymie and Gill Wyse and Ashish Deved to whom this book is especially dedicated.

London
Candlemas, 2013

PART ONE

The Context

1

Teresa and her Interpreters: A Question of Style

Introduction

If we want to learn about the difficulties of interpreting and understanding Teresa of Avila there can be few better people to turn to than the celebrated twentieth century British Hispanist, Edgar Allison Peers (1891–1952), the first person to complete an English translation of Teresa's work in its entirety. In his preface to his *Complete Works of St Teresa of Jesus* (hereafter Allison Peers CW) he cites the difficulties of translating Teresa and her unique style. Allison Peers was the latest in a long line of interpreters who had struggled to make sense of the often rambling, sometimes incoherent, sentences of the sixteenth century Spanish nun. 'Even Spaniards familiar with her books', he suggested, 'are continually baffled when asked the precise meaning of phrases which at first sight may seem perfectly simple' (Allison Peers CW: 1: xviii). Accordingly, he felt that 'one often has frankly to guess at her exact meaning ... and half a dozen people may make half a dozen different guesses.'

This view is shared by Kieran Kavanaugh, her most recent translator, who, in the preface to his translation in 1976, stated that working on her text was like 'working on puzzles' and even he could never be sure that some of these puzzles had been solved (Kavanaugh and Rodriguez CW: 1: 48). She writes, he states, as though 'her thoughts were jostling with each other for position, her sentences often become highly involved with parentheses and digressions, causing her sometimes to lose the thread – which never prevents her from leaping forward quickly and easily to a new thought. Within her sentences ... she shifts back and forth from singular to plural, from first person to third, from past to present, and so on.'

Yet despite (or perhaps because of) this lack of grammatic precision both authors agree that reading Teresa's writing can be both challenging and exhilarating. As Allison Peers puts it, 'if the usage gives the reader a slight shock, that is probably what she often intended' (Allison Peers CW 1: xx). And he bemoans any attempt to try to 'tidy up' her prose, reminding us that 'all the time the translator has to remember that he is dealing with a unique kind of woman – it would be nothing short of tragedy if (the translator) turned her into a writer of text books' (Allison Peers CW 1: xvii).

It was this 'shock and awe' in Teresa's writings that first attracted me to her. Here, I thought, was Christian writing quite unlike the somewhat dry academic tomes I had read in my theological studies. In fact, it was a surprise to learn that theology students were somewhat discouraged from reading Teresa, let alone take her seriously as a 'Doctor of the Church', as declared by Pope Paul VI in 1970 (the first woman to receive this accolade). Part of the reason for this relative neglect (which I think now is coming to an end, no doubt helped by Teresa's anniversary year in 2015) was the mistake of confusing Teresa's somewhat challenging style with lack of thought, coherence or even knowledge of the spiritual path. This is not helped by her unashamed and unabashed tendency to place before us the most intimate details of her spiritual life, including vivid descriptions of what we would now call 'paranormal' or 'supernatural' phenomena. The Anglo-Saxon suspicion of such excesses (at least since the Reformation) has led to her being treated very warily by those from the Reformed traditions. This, however, is not something new to us. Teresa herself in the *Book of Foundations* noted that 'Some people seem to be frightened at the very mention of visions or revelations' and added that she herself 'could not see the source of the alarm' (F: 8.1). As our own era has seen the rise in charismatic phenomena, Pentecostal events and new religious revival across the religions we can turn again to these passages from Teresa with a new eye, perhaps correcting the disdain felt towards her since the Enlightenment move towards a 'rational religion'. For there is no doubt that Teresa understood, like Søren Kierkegaard, that religion was not just another branch of natural sciences like sociology or geology, but there was a craziness, an absurdity about religion, and, as Kierkegaard so correctly pointed out, if we miss that element of religion we miss the point of religion. From Plato onwards the West has sought to balance the craziness of the 'mythic' element of religion with the order of its 'logical' element. The wonderful thing about Teresa's writings is that she explores this interface without timidity or trepidation. For her, religion must be a life choice, a full-on plunging into the embrace of the infinite, or it is nothing at all. As Ludwig Wittgenstein once said: 'A religious question is either a "life question" or (empty) chatter' (Wittgenstein BEE 183:202).[1]

When we work with the texts of Teresa of Avila we are clearly dealing with someone who took 'life questions' seriously and I would go further to suggest that the people who have really *understood* her works, or her mission, are those who have seen her task as that of someone who wants to show us *how to live* rather than *how we should think about life*. Accordingly, when we look at the history of the reception of her texts we can see how she speaks to the 'life question' of each generation over the past five hundred years, up to and including our own. Which is why I contend a study of Teresa is as relevant now as at any time over the past half millennium – and with our recent self-imposed amnesia regarding all things religious, perhaps even more so than ever before.

Fray Luis de Léon

The first, and in many ways most important, of her interpreters recognized this. The Augustinian priest Luis de Léon (c. 1527–91) was no stranger to controversy himself and had in fact been imprisoned by the Inquisition for four years for allegedly promulgating heretical statements, chiefly in his translation and interpretation of the Hebrew Song of Songs. He successfully defended himself against these charges and rose to occupy the highest professorial chairs of the University of Salamanca.[2] Thus, after Teresa's death on 15 October 1582,[3] when her followers, in particular Ana de Jésus and John of the Cross, found themselves in need of someone to edit the unpublished manuscripts, Fray Luis seemed an ideal choice. The state of Teresa's manuscripts at the time of her death was anything but clear. Her first written work, *El Libro de la Vida*

---

[1] My translation. *'Eine religiöse Frage ist nur entweder Lebensfrage oder sie ist (leeres) Geschwätz.'*

[2] Born Luis Ponce de Léon in either 1527 or 1528 in Belmonte near Cuenca of *converso* parents, he entered the University of Salamanca in 1541 at the age of 14 to study Canon Law and joined the Augustinian order in either 1543 or 1544. Becoming Vice-Rector of the University of Salamanca in 1567 he was arrested by the Inquisition in 1572 and imprisoned in Valladolid for four years during which time he worked on his great treatise *Los Nombres de Cristo*. He was released in 1576, later holding chairs of Moral Philosophy, Biblical Studies and Holy Scripture at the University. He died at Madrigal de Las Altas Torres in 1591 aged 64. The best recent exposition of his work in English is Thompson (1988), see also Bell (1925).

[3] Although Teresa died during the night of the Feast of St Francis (4 October), the following day saw the introduction of the new Gregorian reformed calendar. Thus it is that her feast day is celebrated on 15 October.

(*Book of the Life*, hereafter V) written on the advice of her confessors, especially García de Toledo, had disappeared into the hands of the Inquisition shortly after she had finished it in 1575. It was only the persistence of Ana de Jésus, who managed to prise it from the Inquisition in 1588, which gave Fray Luis access to this crucial manuscript. Although her next work, *El Camino de Perfección* (*The Way of Perfection*, hereafter CV, CT or CE as we have three versions of the text – Valladolid, Toledo and Escorial codices respectively), did not find its way into the hands of the Inquisition (it was in fact one of her few works that she explicitly intended for wider circulation and publication), it did suffer from careless editing so that by the time Fray Luis had to make his editorial decisions there were several versions of the text. Interestingly, Fray Luis decided to take the least polished version of Teresa's text (the so-called Valladolid version) for his work, an editorial decision we shall see shortly that he defended vigorously in his preface to her *Collected Works*.

The final two great texts of Teresa's writing career were likewise in need of much attention when Fray Luis took over the job. Her last completed work, *El Libro de Las Fundaciones* (*The Book of Foundations*, hereafter F), remained after her death in Alba de Tormes in 1582. Although Fray Luis received it for publication he decided not to publish it with the other texts and it was not until 1610 that Ana de Jésus and Padre Jerónimo Gracián undertook the first publication, this time in Brussels. Although Fray Luis claimed there was not enough time to edit the *Foundations* it seems more likely that the book describing events, some of which had happened in the past few years and detailing many people still alive, was probably considered too 'near the bone' for the good friar. Even in 1610 Madre Ana and Padre Gracián felt it wise to omit certain sections dealing with events and people still considered controversial. In fact it was not until 1880 when *The Foundations*, along with other key Teresian texts, was presented in photostat version that scholars had access to the original manuscript.

The final, and perhaps greatest, work of the quartet, *Las Moradas* (*The Interior Castle*, hereafter M), was handed over to Teresa's co-worker, Padre Gracián, shortly after it was completed. However Gracián couldn't resist editing the work, including the deletion of several passages, before it reached Fray Luis' hands. This led to a strongly worded rebuke from Teresa's first biographer, the Jesuit Francisco de Ribera (1537–91), who wrote these words on the title page of the *Interior Castle*:

What the holy Mother wrote in this book is frequently deleted and other words are added or glosses are made in the margin. And usually these deletions are done badly and the text is better the way it was first written and one can see how the sentences appeared much better as first written … And since I have read and looked over this work with a certain amount of care, it appears to me advisable that anyone who reads it does so as the holy Mother wrote it, for she understood and said things better, and to pay no attention to what was added or changed unless the correction was made by the Saint herself in her own hand, which is seldom. And I ask out of charity that anyone who reads this book respect the words and letters written by so holy a hand and try to understand her correctly; and you will see that there is nothing to correct. Even if you do not understand, believe that she who wrote it knew better and that the words cannot be corrected well unless their meaning is fully understood. If their meaning is not grasped, what is very appropriately said will seem inappropriate and such is the way that books are ruined and lost.

(Las Moradas: Title Page)

This tendency to tamper with and alter Teresa's writings has thus been the temptation of Teresa's editors from virtually the first moment the pages were written.

Much has been made in recent years, especially by the American feminist scholars Gillian Ahlgren and Alison Weber, of the 'suppressed voice' of Teresa and there is no doubt that from very early on there was something about Teresa's voice that made her editors (usually men) very uncomfortable indeed.[4] Yet, we should be grateful to Fray Luis, for if we were to divide Teresa's interpreters into the 'tamperers' and the 'untouchables', Fray Luis very much fell into the latter category. We do not know for sure whether this arose from his skilled experience in biblical interpretation or his own unhappy encounter with the censoring voice of the Inquisition, but what we are certain of is that he made a definite editorial decision to leave as well alone as possible with Teresa's maddening, convoluted, exhilarating texts. In doing so Fray Luis did *la Santa* a great service which future generations have much to thank him for.

We know that he made this important editorial decision from the dedicatory letter to Ana de Jésus and the nuns of Madrid that he attached to the preface of the first edition of the collected works in 1588. Even today this letter repays careful consideration, and, for the first century or so of Teresa editions, was included with the text. In many ways this letter provides the template for many

---

[4] This point is strongly endorsed by Kristeva (2008). For her, Teresa presents the female voice *par excellence* in its semiotic irruption through the 'phallocentric' web of language.

of the future editorial decisions and conundrums that any reader or interpreter of Teresa must address at some stage and it is worth examining in detail.

'Her Daughters and Her Books'

Fray Luis begins his letter by stating:

> I never knew, or saw, Mother Teresa of Jesus while she lived on earth; but now that she lives in Heaven I do know her, and I see her almost continuously in two living images of herself which she left us – her daughters and her books.
>
> (Allison Peers CW: 3.368)

'Her daughters and her books': from the beginning Fray Luis recognizes that the book, what we see in front of us in ink and paper, is only half the story. The written words show as much as they say. And what do they show? They show us *ourselves, our community and our relationship with the Divine*. For the book is half the story, and we supply the other half, or indeed the living community of Carmel provides the other half.

Thus, from the very beginning Fray Luis recognizes how 'alive' Teresa's texts are and how dependent they are on the 'oral community' of Carmelites that she had created:

> I believe that your reverences are important witnesses, for you are quite similar models of excellence: I never remember reading her works without imagining that I am listening to Your Reverence's voices, nor, conversely, do I ever hear you talk without feeling that I am reading the words of the Mother. Those who have experience of this will know that it is the truth.
>
> (Allison Peers CW: 3.372)

For Luis, Teresa's writings *must* be understood within the context of the oral community. They benefit from being read aloud and strive to repeat the patterns, rests and pauses of speech with which she was familiar. The texts are peppered with *'errs'*, *'umms'* and *'puess'* as she seeks at headlong pace to transcribe the oral to the written. Take, for example, this breathless inter-ruption to the exposition of the 'Prayer of Quiet' in Mansion Four of the *Interior Castle*:

God help the mess I've gotten into! I've already forgotten what I'm writing about as business and poor health have forced me to put this work on one side until things were better, and as I have a bad memory everything will come out confused as I can't return to read it all over again. Perhaps everything I say is confused – that's what it feels like anyway.[5]

(M: 4.2.1)

Writing on Teresa's style in 1941 (and possibly having in mind passages such as the above), the Spanish critic Menéndez Pidal wrote:

St Teresa does not really write, but speaks through writing; thus the excitement of her emotional syntax constantly overflows the restrictions of ordinary grammar.

(Menéndez Pidal 1942: 135)

She is not averse to giving snatches of reported dialogue and will often introduce more than one narrative voice into the text:

O Lord, Lord! Are You our Model and Master? Yes, indeed! Well then, what did Your honour consist of, You who honoured us? Didn't you indeed lose it in being humiliated unto death? No, Lord, but You won it for all.

(CV: 36.5)

She presents us the reader with open questions:

And supposing my Lord that there are others who are like myself, but have not realized this? ... Oh God help me sisters! If we only knew what honour really is and what is meant by losing it!

(CV: 36.3)

Why do we serve the Lord in so doubtful a way ... ? Who is plunging you into those perils?

(CV: 18.9)

---

[5] *¡Válame Dios en lo que me he metido! Ya tenía olvidado lo que tratava, porque los negocios y salud me hacen dejarlo al major tiempo; y como tengo poca memoria irá todo desconcertado,por no poder tornarlo a leer, y an quizás se es todo desconcierto cuanto digo. Al menos es lo que siento.*

She also puts questions in her interlocutors' mouths so that she can answer them:

> But why, you will say, does the Prioress excuse us? Perhaps she would not if she knew what was going on inside us.
>
> (CV: 10.7)

> What do you think His will is, daughters? That we should be altogether perfect, so as to be one with Him and with the Father, as in His Majesty's prayer. See how far we are from attaining this!
>
> (M: 5.3)

As De Certeau suggests,[6] when we read passages such as these later ones from the *Interior Castle* where she has perfected her craft, it is almost as though we can see the sisters round us, pressing nearer to hear what she has to tell us (see also M: 6.4, 3.1, 4.1, 4.2). We do not, suggests Kristeva (2008: 36), go to Teresa's texts for balance and poise, rather, it is in the headlong dash of strangely dislocated phrases that the whole work comes alive. When we engage in reading Teresa, she suggests playing on the French words, we engage in a *co-naissance*. The very act of reading and 'knowing' Teresa invites us to be 'reborn' in the text as we become engaged and enmeshed in the great web of words that Teresa spreads before us. Reading Teresa cannot be a neutral affair – she beguiles us into a new place of embodied self-awareness, as we shall see.

In his dedicatory letter Fray Luis also defended Teresa's habit of 'failing to carry her argument to its conclusion, but introducing other arguments which often break the thread of her sense' (Peers CW: 3.373). Throughout her writings Teresa is not concerned to reproduce the classical Latin style of the new Renaissance humanism. Hers is a 'rough and ready' style whose directness is its appeal. Teresa, like the great medieval masters of mystical theology, frequently employs paradox to shift meaning to the point where it begins to break down.[7] The soul in the third degree of prayer in the *Book of the Life* is:

---

[6] See De Certeau (1992).

[7] My *Return to the Mystical* (Continuum 2011) presents a detailed account of how this language evolved and how it was used by Teresa. I shall return to this theme in Chapter 6 below.

Rejoicing in this agony with ineffable joy ... the state is glorious folly ... a heavenly madness ... delectable disquiet ... So delectable is this distress that life holds no delight which can give greater satisfaction.

(V: 24)

Menéndez Pidal writes of her style in a similar vein as Luis de León:

Her incessant ellipses; confused grammatical arguments; enormous parentheses, which cause the reader to lose the train of thought; lines of reasoning that are never completed because of interruptions, verbless sentences.

(Menéndez Pidal 1942: 135)

It is as though the understanding must be thwarted in order to allow the soul's direct access to God. The tumbling morass of sentences, adverbs, meandering constructions and exclamations only helps to serve that purpose. As Rivers puts it:

She refuses to accept the analytical or linear sequentiality of linguistic discourse, and she strives for simultaneity, for saying everything all at once, as it actually happens, 'writing with many hands'.

(Rivers 1984: 127, see, for example, CV: 20.6)

How It Seems

In an important essay on Teresa's *Interior Castle* published in 1983 (Flasche 1983), Hans Flasche points out the importance of the verb *parecer* – 'it seems, it appears' – in Teresa's writing, especially in the *Interior Castle*. *Parecer*, he writes, 'is one of the most important words in Saint Teresa's lexicon' (Flasche 1983: 447). She uses the verb repeatedly in all her texts creating a deliberate atmosphere of incertitude and provisionality which can only assist in the 'disguising' of Teresa's intentions with regard to her exposition of the 'mystical theology'. Pictures and suggestions are 'offered' to the reader as possible solutions and answers she has found: as we explore her texts in this book we shall become all too familiar with this 'stammering, broken voice' of Teresa. In the *Interior Castle*, for example, it appears frequently: '*Paréceme que aun no os veo satisfechas*' / 'It seems to me that you're still not satisfied' (M: 5.1). '*Paréceme que estáis con deseo de ver qué se hace esta palomica'* / 'It seems to me you have a desire to see what this little dove is doing' (M: 5.4). *'Paréceme que os estoy mirando cómo decís'* / 'It seems to me that I can see you asking' (M: 6.6). Accompanying this studied incertitude is Teresa's continual insistence that as an unlettered *'mujercilla*/little woman' she is not qualified to talk on such lofty matters:

> For the love of God, let me work at my spinning wheel and go to choir and perform the duties of religious life, like the other sisters. I am not meant to write: I have neither the health nor intelligence for it.
>
> (Allison Peers CW: 1.xxxix)

Frequently she tells us she is unqualified and useless to the task:

> God help the mess I've gotten into! I've already forgotten what I'm writing about as business and poor health have forced me to put this work on one side until things were better, and as I have a bad memory everything will come out confused as I can't return to read it all over again. Perhaps everything I say is confused – that's what it feels like anyway.
>
> (M: 4.2.1, immediately followed by a *Parece*: 'It seems to me I have explained the nature of consolations in the spiritual life')

It is notable that these linguistic devices become more evident when Teresa talks of the more 'inexpressible' elements of prayer such as are dealt with in the later Mansions of the *Interior Castle*. The phrase 'little woman' or 'stupid woman' was a typical theological attack on women's inadequacy when it came to questions of doctrine or theology. Bartolomé de Medina had denounced her as *'mujercilla'* saying that her nuns would be better off 'staying in their convents and praying and spinning' (Weber 1990: 36).

As Weber shows in her classic exposition of this tactic, Teresa's defence was to 'embrace stereotypes of female ignorance, timidity, or physical weakness but disassociate herself from the double-edged myth of woman as seducible/ seductive' (1990: 36). For example in *The Book of the Life* 11.14:

> As for a poor woman (*mujercita*) like myself, a weak and irresolute creature, it seems right that the Lord should lead me on with favours (*regalos*), as He now does, in order that I may bear certain afflictions with which He has been pleased to burden me. But when I hear servants of God, men of weight, learning and understanding (*de tomas, de*

letrados, de entendimiento) worrying so much because He is not giving them devotion, it makes me sick to listen to them ... They should realise that since the Lord does not give it to them they do not need it.

As Weber remarks 'With disarming modesty she concedes to women's intellectual inferiority in a way that frees her to explore a new theological vocabulary' (1990: 38):

> I shall have to make use of some comparison, for which I should like to apologise, since I am a woman and write simply what I am ordered to write. But this spiritual language is so difficult to use for anyone who like myself has not gone through studies, that I shall have to find some way of explaining myself, and it may be that most of the time I won't get the comparison right. Seeing so much stupidity will provide some amusement for your Reverence.
>
> (V: 11.6)

As Weber comments:

> In these passages, and in many others, Teresa concedes to women's weakness, timidity, powerlessness and intellectual inferiority but uses the concessions ironically to defend, respectively, the legitimacy of her own spiritual favors, her disobedience of *letrados*, her administrative initiative, her right to 'teach' in the Pauline sense and her unmediated access to scripture.
>
> (Weber 1990: 39/40)

She writes, adds Kristeva (2008: 16), 'in the tonality of the Song of Songs', but 'for the first time from the pen of a European woman'. Teresa, these writers suggest, does nothing less than bring to birth in her writings the suppressed soul of the Western Christian woman.

The Medium is the Message

In Luis de León's letter to Ana de Jésus he points out that he does not feel it is necessary to amend the style with which Teresa presents her writing:

> I have neither amended them verbally nor adopted the considerable changes which copies now in circulation have made in the text of them either through the copyists'

own carelessness or out of presumption or error ... If her critics had a real understanding of Castilian, they would see that that of the Mother is elegance itself. For even
though, in certain passages of what she writes, before she completes the sentence that
she has begun, she contaminates it with other sentences and breaks the train of thought,
often beginning anew with interpolations, nevertheless she inserts her digressions so
skilfully and introduces her fresh thoughts with such grace that the defect itself is a
source of beauty, like a mole on a lovely face.

(Allison Peers CW: 3.373)

As we have seen, Luis, her first editor, recognized at the outset that the meaning
of Teresa's message was inextricably bound up with the medium: that rag-tag
bag of flooding prose full of errors, inconsistencies, *puess*, *buts* and *errs*. The very
same style that makes the whole work come alive for the reader. Exclamations
litter Teresa's text, as do lengthy repetitions and interpolations in the text. In the
Book of the Life in particular the sentences tumble out making it difficult for the
reader, and the translator, to keep up:

At first these things did me harm – so it appeared (*me parece*) -, and it shouldn't have
been her fault, but mine; for afterwards my own wickedness was bad enough, together
with the servants we had, whom for every wrong they were able to assist; that if one had
given me good counsel, to benefit me; rather self-interest blinded them as did desire
me. And because I was never inclined to much wrong – because I naturally abhorred
bad things –, but to the pastime of pleasant conversation; yet, placed in the situation,
I was in the hand of danger, and would be placing my father and brothers in it as well.

(V: 2.5)[8]

---

[8] My translation. This is a very difficult passage to translate and should really be left as it stands: '*Al principio
dañáronme las cosas dichas – a lo que me parece -, y no devía ser suya la culpa, sino mía; porque después mi
malicia para el mal bastava, junto con tener criadas, que para todo mal hallava en ellas buen aparejo; que
si alguna fuera en aconsejarme bien, por ventura me aprovechara; mas el interese las cegava, coma a mí la
afeción. Y pues nunca era inclinada a mucho mal – porque cosas deshonestas naturalamente las aborrecía -,
sino a pasatiempos de Buena conversación; mas puesta en la occasion, estava en la mano el peligro, y ponía
en él a mi padre y hermanos.*' Kavanaugh/Rodgriguez and Allison Peers both give two varying translations
which at times verge on the ungrammatical like my crude translation above. I give both in full to illustrate
the problems and pitfalls of translating Teresa:
    'These things did me harm, I think, at the beginning, and it wasn't her fault but mine. For afterward my
malice was sufficient, together with having the maids around, for in them I found a helping hand for every
kind of wrong. If there had been one of them to give me good counsel, I perhaps would have benefited by
it; but self-interest blinded them as my vanity did me. I was never inclined to great evil – for I naturally
abhorred indecent things – but to the pastime of pleasant conversation; yet, placed, in the occasion, the

Teresa seems to recognize that in order to maintain the vitality of the spiritual world she is trying to convey to her reader she must also retain the rough edged inconsistency of speech in real time. As suggested above, her texts 'show' as much through what they do not say as through what they do. Accordingly, Teresa will often use pictures, metaphors and images to 'disorientate' the discursive intellect and take it to places it would rather not go. We shall return to this idea at a later stage in the book.

As we have seen above, Teresa frequently uses the 'rhetoric of incompetence'. Thus in *Interior Castle* 1.2.7 we find the following passage:

> These interior matters are so obscure for our minds (*tan oscuras de entender*) that anyone who knows as little as I will be forced to say many superfluous and even foolish things in order to say something that's right. Whoever reads this must have patience, for I have to have it in order to write about what I don't know. Indeed sometimes I take up the paper like a fool (*una cosa boba*), for I don't know what to say or how to begin.
>
> (M: 1.2.7)

Following medieval masters of mystical theology such as Jean Gerson and Francisco de Osuna, the 'fool' (or 'little woman') is the one who is wise in the '*theologia mystica*'. Again, Teresa refers to these things '*tan oscuras de entender* / '*so dark to the understanding*' – perhaps a reference to the dark and obscure knowledge of Dionysius' '*theologia mystica*' so central to this tradition (see Tyler 2011)? Perhaps, she implies, all of us, writer and reader alike, must become fools before we can enter the strategy of the 'mystical theology'. For, as we shall see in later chapters, Teresa's discourse relies as much on 'unknowing' as it does on 'knowing'. Indeed, her writings can be seen as a choreography between the two. 'Neither rationalist nor sceptic' writes Kristeva (2008: 36), 'while using knowledge (*connaissance*) as much as not-knowing (*non-savoir*),

---

danger was at hand, and my father's and brothers' reputation was in jeopardy as well.' (Kavanaugh and Rodriguez CW 1.59)

'At first, I believe, these things did me harm. The fault, I think, was not my friend's but my own. For subsequently my own wickedness sufficed to lead me into sin, together with the servants we had, whom I found quite ready to encourage me in all kinds of wrongdoing. Perhaps, if any of them had given me good advice, I might have profited by it; but they were as much blinded by their own interests as I was by desire. And yet I never felt the inclination to do much that was wrong, for I had a natural detestation of everything immodest and preferred passing the time in good company. But, if an occasion of sin presented itself, the danger would be at hand and I should be exposing my father and brothers to it.' (Allison Peers CW 1.15)

the 'I' of Teresa is straightway a co-birth (*co-naissance*) in the love of the Other for the Other.' Her writings will disorientate us and strip away our securities as we are brought closer to the spiritual reality of God as Being.

Humility and Humour

As was attested by many of her contemporaries and is clear from her writing, humour was always an important part of Teresa's armoury in her struggles to establish the Discalced reform. Although examples of this abound throughout her work perhaps the clearest examples are in the *Book of the Foundations*, that somewhat controversial work describing in open fashion the recent events around the founding of her convents in Spain which Fray Luis decided not to include in the first edition. As we have seen, the topics dealt with had to be done so with tact and care as many of the protagonists were still alive and the tension between the Discalced reform and the Carmelites of the Mitigated Rule remained high. She describes her style in the prologue to the book as *tan pesado* ('too heavy') and suffering from too much *grosería* ('coarseness'). Weber describes the history as 'picaresque':

> She slyly reveals that in her determination to do God's work she must rely on her charm, ingenuity, and, at times, deception in order to outwit unenlightened souls, be they landlords, town councilmen, or archbishops.
>
> (Weber 1990: 128)

A few examples will suffice:

In Chapter 31 she describes the difficult foundation at Burgos. Here the Archbishop, Don Cristóbal Vela was initially enthusiastic, encouraging the sisters to come prior to his granting a licence for the foundation.[9] Teresa describes the struggles to get to Burgos, the rivers in full spate and her own illness. Having finally arrived Teresa describes how the Archbishop does not want them there and tells them if they do not have an income and a house of their own they should leave to which Teresa comments: 'The roads of course were charming and it was such nice weather!' (F: 31.21).

---

[9] His uncle was Teresa's godfather, see Allison Peers CW 3.184 fn. 2 and Chapter 5 below.

Chapter 19 describes the foundation of Salamanca with the full vigour of the picaresque. The house they had chosen (which still presently stands on the Plaza de Santa Teresa) had previously been occupied by students and Teresa's description of the first night herself and an elderly sister, terrified of the evicted students returning on Hallowe'en, is a masterpiece:

> When my companion found herself shut up in the room, she seemed to be a little calmer about the students, though she did nothing all the time but look about her fearfully, first in one direction then in another ... 'What are you looking for?' I asked her. 'Nobody can possibly get in here.' 'Mother', she replied, 'I am wondering what you would do all alone if I were to die here.' ... So I said to her: 'Well, sister, I shall consider what is to be done if the occasion arises: now let me go to sleep.'
>
> (F: 19.5)

One of the most interesting depictions of humour occurs in Chapter 6 which begins with Teresa back with her favourite topic of the *Life* and the *Interior Castle* – that is, the spiritual life and how progress can be made in prayer. Almost immediately she reaches the 'point of unknowing': 'I wish I knew how to explain myself here, but it is so difficult that I do not know if I shall be able to do so' (F: 6.2). However in this chapter she touches on the controversial subject of raptures and ecstasies, so easily associated with the *Alumbrados*.[10] The chapter also deals with the controversial topic of the relationship between spirituality and sexuality and the proximity of sensual with spiritual delights. She gives clear guidelines that prioresses should beware these prolonged 'swoons' or 'raptures' and not encourage them in their sisters. To make her point with humour she refers to an incident that took place at Medina del Campo with a choir nun, Alberta Bautista and lay sister Inés de la Concepción (see Allison Peers CW: 3.30 fn. 1). In their desire to experience ecstasy they asked for frequent communion from their confessor: 'the result was such an increase in distress that unless they communicated daily they thought they were about to die' (F: 6.10). Teresa realizes how unhealthy this attachment has become but has to deal with an obdurate confessor who refuses to believe this can cause anything but good for the sisters. Let Teresa complete the story herself:

---

[10] A group of Spanish spiritual seekers condemned by the Inquisition in the early sixteenth century. We shall return to them in the following chapter.

I started to talk to the nuns and to give them many reasons, sufficient, in my opinion, to prove to them that the idea that they would die without this particular help was pure imagination. But the notion was so deeply rooted in their minds that no argument could eradicate it and it was useless to reason with them further. So, seeing that it was in vain, I told them that I had those very desires myself and yet I should stay away from Communion, so that they might realize that they ought not to communicate except when all the nuns did so together: we would all three die together, I said.

(F: 6.11)

Potential heretics, timid and difficult nuns, wavering clerics: Teresa encounters each with humanity and warmth allowing her humour to pepper the narrative and convince us, her readers, of the correctness of her remedies and solutions.

Perhaps the key to her use of humour in the *Book of Foundations* lies at the beginning of the prologue where she stresses the need for humility (*humildad*) in the enterprise. Humility, humour and grounded or ordinary language: all three rotate around each other to produce the necessary effect on the reader. As we read the accounts we realize that she is gently laughing at us too – her readers – with all our pomposities, obsessions with prayers, worldly concerns and judgemental attitudes. Yes, we can laugh at the targets of her humour in the *Foundations*, but we must always remember that her comments are directed equally at us, her readers.

As we have seen Teresa herself is conscious of her style: she calls it 'my rough style rather than that of those more elegant' / '*mi grosero estilo que por otros elegantes*' (CV: 16.9), full of 'imperfection' and 'poverty' (CV: Prologue). As Allison Peers points out in his 1953 essay *Saint Teresa's Style: A Tentative Appraisal* (Allison Peers 1953) the key note in her style is down-to-earthness and naturalness. Here she reveals her debt to Francisco de Osuna and the simple direct style of his *Third Spiritual Alphabet/Tercera Abecedario* that, as we shall see shortly, was to play such an important role in Teresa's development as a spiritual writer. She states, for example, that the manner of writing (like talking) adopted by nuns should be:

Simple, frank and devout, rather like that of hermits and people who live in retirement. They must use none of the newfangled words – affectations, as I think people call them – which are current in a world always eager for new-fangled things. In all circumstances let them give preference to common expressions rather than to unusual ones.

(*Method for the Visitation of Discalced Nuns* in Allison Peers CW: 3.251)

As Allison Peers points out, she avoids learned words (Allison Peers 1953: 84) and her text is notable for the lack of precise theological terms especially concerning 'mystical theology'. Indeed, the somewhat technical word 'mystical theology' is only used a handful of times in the *Life* before it is dropped not to be used again in her work. The humility of ordinary language is close to the humility of humour and central to the effect she wants to produce in her readers.

In his study *The Vernacular Mind of St Teresa* (Rivers 1984), Elias Rivers points out how Teresa's 'vernacularism' was a part of the sixteenth century Spanish humanist movement which deliberately sought to communicate to 'ordinary people' through Castilian rather than Classical Latin. Rivers suggests that in this movement the simple Latin of Augustine's *Confessions*, an influential text on the young Teresa, was clearly an important influence (Rivers 1984: 117):

> Teresa of Jesus knew very little Latin, and she deliberately refused to imitate the new style of classical Spanish prose; in a true patristic spirit, she invented her own vulgar style of substandard written Spanish, a style that is clearly anti-academic and even anti-rational.
>
> (Rivers 1984: 120)

As she wrote in a letter on 19 November 1576 to María de San José: 'God preserve my daughters from priding themselves on their Latin.' Thus, in her prose we find that 'classical' Castilian spellings are twisted and subverted, often using more phonetic spelling than grammatical. Thus she uses *ylesia* and *yglesia* for *iglesia* ('church'), *naide* for *nadie* ('no-one'), *relisión* for *religion* ('religion') as well as a host of diminutives and familiarizations of words: *mariposita* (a little butterfly), *pastorcito* (little shepherd boy), *avecita* (little bird). Peers suggests that she creates words of her own invention 'charging them with emotional content which another language can only approximately express' (Peers 1953: 85): *un disgustillo* (V: 12) 'a little annoyance' / 'a little feeling of frustration'; *estos temorcillos* (V: 31) 'these little fears'; *centellica pequeñita* (V: 15) 'the tiniest of tiny sparks' – this latter being her appropriation of the classical phrase *scintilla* from the medieval mystical theology to describe the point at which the soul meets the divine.

Her conversational and immediate style, Rivers suggests, is deliberate and intentional:

She learned to read Spanish fluently as a young girl and knew that she had an advantage there that she could never have in the official Scholastic language of the Western Church, with its exclusively male priesthood. Her Spanish was not structured, as Louis of Granada's and John de Valdés's was, by a familiarity with written Latin, whether ecclesiastical or neo-classical. When she wrote, she neglected, or perhaps deliberately avoided, the normal spelling and syntax of the Spanish texts that she had voraciously read.

(Rivers 1984: 121)

Teresa in her 'rough speech' is therefore deliberately positioning herself in her writings with her beloved spiritual masters (*espirituales*) such as the saintly Pedro de Alcantara rather than the sophisticated 'learned ones'/*letrados* with their more polished and scholastic Latin rhetoric. As Allison Peers wrote: 'Her vocabulary was that of the people: any word in common use was good enough for her, while any word that was not, apart from a few technical terms, was at once suspect' (Allison Peers 1945: 177).

Changing an Aspect

Teresa's speech, then, may be considered coarse, vulgar or stupid, but she is happy with this as it serves the purpose she wants, to 'change the aspect' of her reader:

Your behaviour and language must be like this: let any who wish to talk to you learn your language; and, if they will not, be careful never to learn theirs: it might lead you to hell. It matters little if you are considered coarse (*groseras*) and still less if you are taken for hypocrites: indeed, you will gain by this, because only those who understand your language will come to see you.

(CV: 20.4–5)

As I have pointed out her texts 'show' as much as they 'say', and they 'show' through her grammatical and linguistic devices in the text. She is using her text as a 'guide to the perplexed' – a way of prodding and prompting us, through hints, sarcasm, humour and ordinary language to see all that lies before us already that our lack of vision had blinded us to. Fray Luis concludes his letter by suggesting that by reading Teresa's texts we enter into a 'school of prayer' and indeed a 'school of Christian life' for, at the end, Teresa is a *practical theologian* who is not so concerned with debating obscure points of faith but in *changing people's lives*. And it is in this spirit, suggests Fray Luis, that we should approach Teresa's works – the spirit with which we will approach them in this book.

2

Heretics, Jews, Conversos *and the Inquisition*

Introduction

Having established that Teresa's writings may not be all that they appear to be, our next question surely must be, 'Why does she need to write in this particular fashion?'

Reflecting on this question in his *St Teresa and the Jewish Question*, Gareth Davies wrote:

> It is always difficult to see a saint clearly through the billowing clouds of incense, but particularly so in the case of St Teresa. It is as though she herself had conspired to reveal as little of herself as possible – a strange remark to make in view of her usual and deserved reputation for frankness and sincerity.
>
> (Davies 1981: 51)

We have a grand paradox here, a woman who is tellingly, often gushingly, open yet a sense that she is holding something back from us. As Davies continues:

> The point is that she is both frank and sincere when she chooses to be so – at other times, she is deliberately vague and prevaricating.
>
> (Davies 1981: 51)

And this is not just something her modern commentators have noticed. Jerónimo Gracián, one of Teresa's closest collaborators and intimates, in a dialogue addressed to Blessed Ana de San Bartolomé, once wrote:

> You have given me an account of your lineage much more readily than the blessed Madre Teresa de Jesús, for when I had enquired in Avila into the lineage of the Ahumadas and Cepedas, from whom she was descended, among the noblest families

in the city, she became very angry with me because of what I was doing, saying that she was content to be a daughter of the Church; and that it grieved her more to have committed a venial sin than if she had been descended from the vilest and lowest peasants (*villanos*) and Jewish converts (*conversos*) in the whole world.

(Gracián 1933: 259)

A careful reading of her writings will reveal an ambiguity regarding origins, class and race – all very dangerous topics in mid-sixteenth century Spain. Thus, if we look at the beginning of her *Life,* she emphasizes that her parents were very 'Christian and virtuous', her father, for example, being a learned man 'fond of reading good books' (V: 1) and averse to accepting slaves. While her mother was 'gentle and very intelligent' suffering a 'truly Christian death' (V: 2). Of her sisters and brothers we are told there are twelve, however no mention is made that two of these are from an earlier marriage. Now I am not suggesting that Teresa is deliberately hiding things from us, but in the opening paragraphs of the *Life,* Teresa wants very much to stress her orthodox Christian credentials and that she is from a God-fearing Catholic Christian family. The famous little story in *The Life* (V: 4) of how she and her brother Rodrigo (who later, like many of her brothers, served as a *conquistador* in South America) set off from their home to seek martyrdom in 'the land of the Moors' only serves to emphasize the militantly Christian virtues of a family striving to establish themselves in the social melting pot of early sixteenth century Spain.[1]

Again, in the *Book of the Foundations,* the sixteenth century Spanish obsessions with lineage (*linaje*) and 'purity of blood' (*limpieza de sangre*) seep out, usually accompanied by Teresa's surprisingly heterodox attitudes towards them. Thus, in the chapter on the foundation at Toledo she describes the merchant Alonso de Ávila (d. 1586) who had been very generous to her sisters but whose family was neither '*ilustres y cavalleros*' / 'illustrious or well-born' (F: 15.15), i.e were very probably from converted Jewish origins (so-called *conversos*). Yet for Teresa this did not matter for she 'esteemed virtue more than lineage' / '*estimado en más la virtud que el linaje*'. Bold words indeed at a time when most well-to-do Spanish society took such matters of racial or religious purity (or at least the outward show of it) very seriously indeed.

---

[1] For more on the origins of Teresa's 'confessional' style in these texts see Slade 1995.

Such hints and suggestions in Teresa's writings have led several scholars to explore the true nature of Teresa's origins which is where we turn next.

Smoke and Rock: Teresa's Lineage

Until the mid-twentieth century most official biographers and commentators on Teresa had accepted the projected Ahumada-Cepeda[2] family picture of an ancient Castilian Christian family always ready to defend the Catholic faith and play a significant role in the 're-Christianization' (*la reconquista*) of Muslim Spain.[3] Although, as mentioned, hints and suggestions find their way into Teresa's writings we had little idea of her actual family lineage itself until comparatively recently. Within a decade of her death in 1582 none of the dispositions for the processes which would lead to her canonization mention any doubt over her 'pure blood' and in fact emphasize her 'noble' lineage or that she was of 'old Christian' blood (see Egido 1980: 135–7).[4] This fiction is repeated for the next four centuries in her ensuing biographies, sadly reinforced by and reinforcing the need to ally religious with political (usually Christian nationalist) sensibilities.

This was to all change dramatically in 1946 when an extraordinary document was found by Alonso Cortés in the municipal archives of Valladolid. What is even more remarkable about this document is that it 'disappeared' from the archives not long after it had been found in 1960 only to mysteriously reappear 26 years later in 1986. At this point it was immediately transcribed by Teófanes Egido and published in his key work *El Linaje Judeoconverso de Santa Teresa* (Egido 1986). The document, a *pleito de hidalguía* or lawsuit of nobility, is reproduced in full in Egido's text and details the attempt by Teresa's father and three brothers to prove their 'noble' blood, largely to avoid the new tax imposed

---

[2] Teresa's family names, literally 'Smoke' and 'Rock'. See, for example, Efrén de la Madre de Dios 1951: 160: 'St Teresa esteemed highly, as did everyone, having been born of noble parents; from her earliest childhood she would hear in her house interminable praise of her noble background.' This statement was corrected in later versions of the work.

[3] For more on the political and social background of *La Reconquista* see my *John of the Cross,* Chapter 1.

[4] 'Old Christian' was a term used to refer to families who had not been 'tainted' by Jewish or Muslim blood during the 'occupation' of Spain by the Muslims. As the sixteenth century proceeded such designations, connected with the so-called 'statutes of pure blood', would become increasingly important in delineating a person's social standing in post-*reconquista* Spain (for more on this see, for example, Elliott 2002).

by the recently crowned King, Carlos I/Charles V, in 1519. The case began that same year and seemed to start off well with good supporting arguments from the four brothers: Alonso (Teresa's father), Pedro and Ruy Sanchez and Francisco Alvares.[5] However as the case proceeds all sorts of counter-witnesses begin to appear from the woodwork. From the testimonies we discover that Teresa's great-grandparents, Teresa and Alonso de Sanchez (presumably 'Teresa' was a popular name in the family) lived in the Saint Olalla or Saint Leocadia district of Toledo. Here their son, Juan Sanchez, the father of the Cepeda brothers, was born, later becoming a cloth and fine silk merchant who would eventually move to the Calle de Andrino in Avila sometime in the 1480s. In Avila the family was known as the *toledanos* (Juan appeared to adopt the name 'Juan de Toledo') and they continued the cloth business in an area known for the many Jews and *conversos* living there. Juan Sanchez, said some of the witnesses, was a man of great importance, having given help to King Henry IV and the Archbishop of Santiago; he also had a considerable fortune. Later, the family would move away from the cloth trade and live the life more fitting to minor nobility or *hidalguía*. The four boys thus had all the qualities for this station in life: they had the good pedigree and were loyal to the crown in the practice of arms.

So far so good, as far as the Cepeda brothers were concerned. However, from spring 1520 contrary voices start to creep into the narrative. On 9 March, for example, Bernardo Platero, a resident of Avila, testifies that Juan Sanchez was 'reconciled' by the Inquisition in Toledo and wore there the '*sanbenitillo*' – the strange garment of humiliation that those tried by the Inquisition had to wear as they processed through the streets for public ridicule (Egido 1986: 167).[6] Juan González de las Piñuelas, another resident of Avila who knew the family well, provided further details on 12 May, testifying that Juan Sanchez 'wore the *sanbenitillo* with its crosses publicly in procession with the other "reconciled ones" and walked in procession from church to church for seven Fridays in succession' (Egido 1986: 170). This was so damning for the brothers' case that it had to be postponed while testimony was sought from the Inquisitorial office in

---

[5] For more on the confusing, often *converso*, practice of switching and adopting multiple surnames see Davies 1981.

[6] We have some later representations of this odd garment. It was like a rough tunic on which was painted the diagonal cross of St Andrew in red ink. Towards the end of the Inquisition, in the eighteenth century, the *sanbenito* would designate all sorts of degrees and types of heresy and apostasy. See Roth 1995.

Toledo. This was duly forthcoming with the final confirmation of Juan Sanchez's 'reconciliation':

> (It is certified by the Holy Office of the Inquisition of the city and archdiocese of Toledo) that on the 22nd day of the month of June, in the year 1485, Johan de Toledo, merchant, son of Alonso Sanchez, inhabitant of Toledo in the district of Santa Leocadia, gave, presented and swore to a confession before the then Lord Inquisitors, in which he said and confessed that he had done and committed many serious crimes and offences of heresy and apostasy against our holy Catholic faith.
>
> (Egido 1986: 189)

However, even more interesting is that one of Teresa's uncles Hernando or Fernando Sanchez did not seem to be reconciled. Egido speculates that this 'mysterious' uncle died early, however we do not as yet know more about him (he appears to have left for Salamanca to study).

Yet despite this damning evidence the Cepedas duly received their noble status in August 1522, suggesting that a certain amount of wealth, liberally disposed, could always have the necessary effect.

The Holy Inquisition and Jewish Spain

So much has been written latterly on the history and persecution of the Jews in Spain that it will not be necessary to repeat the great scholarship available on this area here.[7] However, in order to understand the circumstances of Teresa and her family it is necessary simply to sketch in the historical background that led to the social unease into which Teresa was born and clearly impacted upon her life and work. In many ways these explanations help us get to the heart of the 'open but closed' style of Teresa and why she wrote in the way she did.

Both of the great Castilian cities that Teresa would be associated with – Toledo and Avila – were important cities in the history of Judaism in the Peninsula. Toledo, the 'Jerusalem of the West' had always boasted a vibrant and intellectually active *Judería* and even today the two preserved synagogues of *El Transito* and *Santa María la Blanca* give eloquent testimony to this. Although

---

[7] See, for example, Roth 1995, Alcalá 1987 and Bethencourt 2009.

Avila has not saved its synagogues in a similar way,[8] it too can boast a noble and long tradition of Judaism. Some scholars even describe it as a centre of cabbalistic learning associated with the 'Book of Splendour' – the *Zohar*.[9]

According to Pilar Tello (Tello 1963) the situation of the Jews of Avila was much like that in Toledo and other major Castilian cities at the beginning of the fifteenth century. That is to say, a generally strong and privileged group had been subjected to increasing harassment and pogroms and was beginning to find itself still tolerated but having to live in prescribed areas. In the case of Avila this was situated between the two market squares of Avila – the so-called *Mercado Grande* and *Mercado Chico*, exactly the area that Teresa's grandfather would move to when he left Toledo after 1485. As the century wore on this 'Jewish Zone', or '*Judería*', would become more demarcated with special gates being constructed that would only allow free access at certain times of the day – effectively a curfew on movement.[10] It seems as though the *Judería* of Avila had its entrance near to the now demolished monastery of Saint Scholastica (near the present-day church that marks the traditional birthplace of Saint Teresa), near this spot is one of the few remaining buildings claimed as one of Avila's synagogues. Pilar suggests there is evidence for at least five or six synagogues in Avila in the mid-fifteenth century and she argues that one of these would later become the location of the *beaterio* from which Teresa's convent of the *Encarnación* would arise. We shall return to this in the next chapter.

Before the expulsion of the Jews from Spain in 1492 by the 'Catholic Monarchs', Ferdinand and Isabella, it appears as though Avila may well have been one of the most important centres of Judaism in Castile. Indeed, on the day when Isabella was proclaimed Queen on 18 December 1474 in Avila, the Jews of the city presented the Torah in procession accompanied with trumpets and tambourines (De Foronda y Aguilera 1913) and they were presented with certain privileges on the accession of the monarch. What appears from

---

[8] The remains of at least two have now been identified by the city authorities. One is a hotel and the other a private residence at the time of writing.

[9] In this book I will not be investigating alleged links between St Teresa's writing and the Jewish cabbalistic tradition. This has been done extensively in Green (1989) and Swietlicki (1986). These two academics stretch the arguments for some kind of cabbalistic influence on Teresa as far as it will go until such time as and if more evidence were to come to light.

[10] The *Cortes* of Toledo designated in 1480 that all Jews and Muslims living in the kingdom must live in separate *barrios* to Christians – the origin of the designated *Judería*. This went hand in hand with restrictions on what Jews could wear in public and the prohibition, for example, of them wearing gold or silver jewellery in public. See Roth 1995: 274.

the archives is a rather industrious group who were involved (like Teresa's grandfather) in retail and mercantile activity: cobblers, butchers, carpenters, fishmongers; and millers and tanners down by Avila's River Adaja. Avila's important wool trade was, in particular, very much in their hands (see Pilar 1963: 39).

Yet despite their economic importance to the wealth and life of the Castilian towns, things went from bad to worse for the Jews in Spain in November 1478 when Pope Sixtus IV signed the bull *Exigit sincerae devotionis affectus* responding to requests from the Catholic Monarchs for the establishment of a Holy Inquisition in their Kingdoms. The presenting reason was the need to check covert Jewish beliefs that were spreading among the new converts from Judaism. Yet, as with everything to do with the Inquisition, motives always seem multifaceted (see Llorca 1949). The Bull allowed the monarchs to appoint three inquisitors for every town or diocese in the Kingdoms – members of religious orders, bishops or priests, over the age of 40 and with a Masters or Bachelors degree in theology or Licence in canon law. The first inquisitors, both Dominicans, were appointed in 1480: Juan de San Martín and Miguel de Morillo and the tradition would soon be established of Dominicans occupying many of the key inquisitorial posts. Teresa was always very respectful of their learning. She always gave them their common appellation: *letrados* or 'learned gentlemen', yet, as we shall see shortly, her attitude was always one where she was under no illusion regarding her own ambiguous position vis-à-vis inquisitorial investigation. Although the presenting cause for the establishment of the Inquisition was the perceived 'judaising' among the 'new Christians', their brief detailed that they were there to search for doctrinal breaches in all areas of 'infidelity, heresy and apostasy' (see Bethencourt 2009: 37). A brief, we shall see, that would be put into effect during Teresa's adult life while she was founding her later reformed convents.

As in Seville in 1480, and later in Toledo in 1485, the procedure of their operation became formalized. The inquisitors would arrive and would be welcomed in a public place outside the city walls. Once inside they would set to work and would rely on information given freely by neighbours, or perhaps those wanting to settle scores. Later, lay 'familiars' would be appointed to assist in their work. The Cepeda case above shows just how willing neighbours were to 'snitch' on each other and that in a largely oral culture memories could be long and scores would often need to be settled. Once in action the Inquisitors would be no respecters of rank or title and in Seville hundreds of individuals were imprisoned within the first few weeks of operation, while many more fled the country to Portugal, Italy and North Africa: a pattern that would be repeated throughout the coming decades.

Yet, early on, there was much opposition to the new process and in March 1485 the inquisitor of Zaragoza, Pedro Arbués, was murdered while at prayer in Zaragoza cathedral (see Bethencourt 2009: 40 *et passim*). This however provoked a stronger response against the '*conversos* who have murdered our Inquisitor'. It was in such a climate that the Inquisition visited Toledo in June 1485 under the direction of Vasco Ramírez de Ribera, archdeacon of Talavera and Pedro Díaz de la Costana, a canon of Burgos Cathedral. During their 'edict of grace' which always preceded their work on the population, it is likely that Juan Sanchez would have come forth with his family. Those found guilty in this time would enact the penance prescribed on Juan Sanchez – the wearing of the *sanbenito* and the penitential processions on seven successive Fridays – but not the confiscation of their property. As Juan Sanchez was clearly a man of wealth this would no doubt have coloured his desire to be reconciled at an early stage.

What were the practices that Juan Sanchez would have been guilty of? Commentators suggest that certain activities would have been brought to the attention of the Inquisitors such as lighting lamps on the Friday night before the Sabbath, wearing clean clothes on Saturday or indeed staying at home with the doors closed on that day, or refusing to eat certain foods such as pork. Fernando de Pulgar tells us that the 'reconciled' of Toledo:

> Secretly observed Jewish rites ... but were not circumcized like Jews ... and although they observed the Sabbath and some Jewish fasts, they did not observe all the Sabbaths nor all the fasts, and if they observed one rite they did not observe another, so that they were false to both laws. It happened in some cases that the husband kept certain Jewish ceremonies and the wife was a good Christian, and that one son and daughter would be good Christians, and another hold the Jewish opinion. Thus, in one house there was a diversity of belief, and one would hide from the others.
>
> (Quoted in Roth 1995: 241)

This description of *converso* families living in a strange half-light between Judaism and Christianity seems to fit very comfortably with what we learn about Teresa's family from the Cepeda case discussed above: that is, some family members accepting Christianity in full, some half accepting it (Juan Sanchez himself) and others finally fully rejecting it (the mysterious Fernando/Hernando).

The Expulsion of the Jews: 1492

Thus, on the eve of the expulsion of the Jews from Spain in April 1492, we have a somewhat confusing picture of remnants of Jews living in segregated 'ghettoes' in cities such as Avila and Toledo; groups of 'new Christians' and *conversos* with varying degrees of allegiance to both their old religion and their new one, and groups of 'old Christians' eager to assert their position and their 'pure blood' in an atmosphere charged by inquisitorial processes and a growing social demand for conformity and homogeneity. The decree of 31 March 1492 stressed that earlier 'remedies' such as the separate *Juderías* had failed to stop the 'evils and harm which come to Christians from participating with and conversation with the said Jews' (Roth 1995: 285). The decree, initially declaimed from the palace of Santa Fé in Granada on 30 April, stated that all Jews in the kingdom were given the opportunity to convert to Christianity, in which case they could remain, or to depart within three months, that is by the end of July 1492.

In Avila, some chronicles stated that in 1479 'the majority population of the city is Jewish' (Tello 1963: 42) and right up to the expulsion in 1492 there was clearly a sizeable Jewish population maintaining their property in the traditional Jewish zone, despite there having been the first Inquisitorial *auto de fé* in the main *Plaza del Mercado Grande* the previous year. Tello tells us that there were officially 107 Jewish families registered in the city, which she multiplies by five to give 535 Jews. However, as she points out this official statistic must have been an indication of much larger numbers, and if 'the majority of the population' was Jewish three years earlier we are talking of a much greater number. Of the families that left, most would have headed to Portugal and the more favourable political climate there, perhaps taking boats from there to other parts of the world which would later become the Jewish Sephardic diaspora, a rich and cultured community that continues to the present day despite many vicissitudes and persecutions. Their property would be claimed by those left in Avila. As we have heard, one of the synagogues was handed over to a group of pious Christian women known as *beatas* (literally 'blessed ones'). Later this group would be given a larger plot of land outside the city where they would build the convent that the young Teresa de Ahumada would eventually enter – *La Encarnación*. This land upon which the young Teresa – born of *converso* stock – was destined to live and pray on, was nothing less than the old Jewish cemetery of Avila.

Teresa would spend most of her life literally living over the remains of her ancestors.[11]

A New Spring

Following the political and strategic union of the two crowns of Aragon and Castille under Ferdinand and Isabella and the conquest of the kingdom of Granada in 1492, Spain was striving towards a new identity as a 'reborn' Catholic Christian united state. As we have seen, the expulsion of the Jews in 1492 can be seen as part of this political strategy. However, the period immediately following the end of the fifteenth century was one of great political, artistic and spiritual fervour. Representative of this era is the extraordinary reforming Cardinal, Franciscan friar, crusader and regent, Francisco Ximénes de Cisneros (1436–1517, Archbishop of Toledo 1495–1517).[12] In many ways embodying many of the contradictions of his age, Cisneros would shape the spiritual climate within which the young Teresa grew up. There is no more telling example of this than an incident that she describes at the beginning of the *Book of the Life*.

We have already heard Teresa's description of her ancestry as she presents it to us in the early chapters of the *Book of the Life*. Relying upon the perspectives introduced in the previous chapter we have, I hope, learnt by now to 'listen to her voice' for when we read her writing what is not said is often as important as what is said.

Continuing her story in Chapters 2 and 3 of the *Life* she tells us about her experiences as a young girl growing up in a large, prosperous household. This was an upbringing, however, as narrated in the first paragraphs, without a mother. Her mother, Beatriz de Ahumada, had died in 1528/9 at the age of 33, having borne her husband (this was Alonso Sanchez's second wife) ten children: Hernando (b. 1510), presumably named after the errant uncle – later to become a conquistador in South America; Rodrigo (b. 1511) with whom Teresa set off to the 'Land of the Moors' as described above – he would also become a conquistador dying in battle in Chile in 1557; Teresa herself (b. 1515); Lorenzo (b. 1519), another conquistador who would later return and help finance Teresa's convents; Antonio (b. 1520), a conquistador who would die at the battle of

---

[11] The deeds giving the land to the *beatas* of the Encarnación can still be seen in the convent museum.

[12] For more on his life and times see Rummel (1999) and García Oro (1992).

Iñaquito in Ecuador in 1546 (fighting along with his four brothers); Pedro (b. 1521), another conquistador who would return to Spain in later life and plague Teresa; Jerónimo (b. 1522), again a conquistador, who this time died on his return journey to Spain with his brother Lorenzo; Agustín (b. 1527), yet another conquistador who also returned to Spain; Juana (b. 1528), Teresa's only natural sister (she had one elder half-sister from her father's first marriage – María) and one final child of whom we know nothing (probably deceased in infancy). With the two half-siblings from her father's first marriage to Catalina del Peso y Heñao, María (b. around 1505) and Juan (b. 1507), it was a large and lively household and one where Teresa seems, judging from her *Life*, to have been rather unsupervised – indulging, as she describes, in all the fun and fripperies of a motherless adolescent girl, Teresa being fourteen when her mother died.[13]

Unsurprisingly, ever mindful of family shame and dishonour, Alonso very quickly intervened and arranged for the rather unruly girl to be sent to a nearby Augustinian convent, *Nuestra Señora del Gracia*, presumably to teach her some decorum and calm her down a little (V: 2.6). Even with servants it is hard to imagine this slightly bookish gentleman coping with so many young children as well as grieving the recent death of his second wife with whom he was clearly very much in love.

The Augustinian convent, like many of Avila's convents, performed the role of taking in high-class girls to educate them and prepare them for the future married life that was normally their lot. However, this was not how it was to be with Teresa. According to the *Life* once she had settled into the convent she found the atmosphere not unpleasant: 'My soul began to return to the good habits of early childhood, and I saw the great favour (*merced*) God bestows on anyone in the company of good people' (V: 2.9). The peace and solitude of the convent affected the young girl, but, perhaps unsurprisingly from what we later know of Teresa, it was the company of the sisters that most impressed her: 'Well I began to enjoy (*gustar*) the good and holy conversation of this nun, it pleased me to hear her when she spoke well of God for she was very discreet and saintly' (V: 3.1). But as she later describes in her last book, *The Interior Castle*, a period of illumination, rest and spiritual sensing will often provoke a counter-movement in the soul of disturbance, agitation and unrest. In the case of Teresa, always the most embodied of saints, this often took the form of

---

[13] For complete biographies of all the Cepeda- Ahumada family see Allison Peers (1954) and Efrén de la Madre de Dios and Otto Steggink (1996).

bodily illness. Today, we would probably call this 'psycho-somatic' but there is no doubt that Teresa felt, lived and experienced the spiritual not as an abstract or disembodied phenomenon but as something deeply integrated within her very being – 'in the heart of her entrails' – as she will so memorably describe it towards the end of the *Life* when she is visited by the Golden Cherub (the inspiration of Bernini's famous sculpture at Santa Maria della Vittoria in Rome – we shall return to this in Chapter 6).

Thus, shortly after this blessed period in her life, as will be the case when she finally enters the Carmelite convent of the *Encarnación* in 1535, Teresa finds herself suffering from a mysterious illness ('*una gran enfremedad*' V: 3.3) causing her to leave *Nuestra Señora del Gracia* for a rest and recreation, first at her father's home and then with her half-sister María and her husband in nearby Castellanos de la Cañada. It is on her way there that she visits Don Pedro de Cepeda, the same Cepeda brother whose court case we examined above. It is this man who will have such an impact on the young woman. In this first encounter before she enters the *Encarnación* we learn that 'His exercise (*su ejercicio*) was to read good books in Spanish (*buenos libros de romance*) and to talk usually of God and the vanity of the world. He made me read to him, and although I didn't care much for his books, I acted as though I did' (V: 3.4). Again, if we listen carefully to Teresa's tone here we can discover much that is unspoken. The first thing that appears is the figure of Don Pedro. This son of the *converso* Juan Sanchez, who had been humiliated in Toledo all those years ago, now in old age (and after the death of his wife) spends his time reading *los buenos libros de romance*. What were these books and how had he obtained them?

We discover this in the following chapter of the *Life*. Teresa, having entered the *Encarnación* in 1535,[14] as before experiences a period of great happiness. This happiness she describes in her customary gutsy fashion: '*gran contento, grandísima ternura, deleite, regalo y gozo*' / '*great comfort, the most gentle tenderness, delight, caress and joy*' (V: 4.2).[15] Yet, as before, this moment of opening to the supernatural and its concomitant peace leads to a physical disturbance which she experiences on the most profound level: 'My fainting fits (*desmayos*) began to increase and I had such a great heart trouble (*un mal de corazón tan grandísimo*) that anyone who saw me was frightened' (V: 4.2). She is

---

[14] I shall talk more about this convent and its origins in the following chapter.

[15] We shall return to her 'vocabulary of delight' when we look at the text of *The Book of the Life* in Chapter 4.

sent with her father's insistence to nearby Becedas for treatments which seem if anything to have made her worse. This necessitated another stay at Castellanos de la Cañada and another visit to nearby Hortigosa where Don Pedro lived. Once again the wise uncle seems to have seen that there must have been what we would now call a 'psycho-somatic' dimension to Teresa's disturbance, or at least a 'spirito-somatic' dimension, for again he prescribes his 'good books' this time suggesting one in particular:

> When I was on my way, the uncle of mine I have mentioned who lived along the road gave me a book. It is called *The Third Alphabet* (*Tercer Abecedario*) and treats of the teaching of the prayer of recollection (*oración de recogimiento*) and although during this first year I read good books ... I did not know how to proceed in prayer or how to be recollected (*cómo recogerme*). And so I was delighted with this book and resolved to follow that path with all my strength ... I began to take time out for solitude, to confess frequently, and to follow that path, taking the book for my master (*por maestro*). For during the twenty years after this period of which I am speaking, I did not find a master, I mean a confessor, who understood me, even though I looked for one.
>
> (V: 4.7)

I have quoted this passage in full for this encounter was clearly an essential one for Teresa and one that would affect her life profoundly. This book, its full title being *The Third Spiritual Alphabet* (hereafter 'TA') of the Franciscan, Fray Francisco de Osuna, would have such an effect on the young woman that it would become her guide and *maestro* for the next two decades. Considering the calibre of spiritual guides available in Avila during this time this is saying a lot. It also happened to be one of the books promoted by Cardinal Cisneros in his reform and initiation of new spirituality within the Spanish realms in the early sixteenth century.[16]

Who, then, was Osuna and why was his work so important to Teresa?

---

[16] It was one of a number of works whose translation into the vernacular had been sanctioned by Cisneros, beginning with the Seville edition of the *Obras de Bonaventura* of 1497, followed by the *Incendium Amoris* and *Liber meditationum* from the presses of Montserrat. Subsequently we find editions of Augustine, Bernard and Richard of St Victor rapidly being produced. Others included the *Ejercitatorio de la Vida Espiritual* of García de Cisneros of 1500 (which was to have such an impact on the young Ignatius Loyola), Gómez García (*Carro de dos Vidas,* 1500), Alonso de Madrid (*Arte de Servir Dios,* 1521), Bernabé de Palma (*Via Spiritus,* 1531) and Bernardino de Laredo (*Subida de Monte Sion/Ascent of Mount Sion,* 1535) and the *Viae Lugent Sion* of Hugh of Balma published in Toledo as the *Sol de Contemplativos* (1514). The *Third Spiritual Alphabet* itself appeared in Toledo in 1527.

Fray Francisco De Osuna (c. 1492–c.1540/1)

What little we know of Osuna's life and background is largely due to the pains-taking researchs of Père Fidèle de Ros at the beginning of the twentieth century (see Ros 1936) and what little information we can glean from the 'spiritual alphabets' and other texts he wrote.[17] The *Third Alphabet* being one of a series of six *Spiritual Alphabets* published between 1527 and 1554 (after his death), the 'spiritual alphabet' being a characteristic pedagogical spiritual tool during this period. Osuna would, for example, have certainly been familiar with the *Alphabetum divini amoris* attributed to Jean Gerson or the *Suma de los ejemplos por ABC* by Clemente Sánchez de Vercial (d. 1426) and *Parvum alphabetum monachi in scola Dei* of Thomas á Kempis.[18]

It seems that he was born around 1492 in Osuna in Andalusia where his family had been in service to the counts of Ureña. We know two facts about his childhood from his own references in the *Abecedarios*: that he was present at the capture of Tripoli by Navarro in 1510 and that he undertook the pilgrimage to Santiago de Compostella sometime between 1510 and 1513. Andrés (1982) speculates about whether he belonged to a *converso* family but Santidrián (1998) thinks the family were probably 'old Christians'. Comparing his life as a Franciscan at Salamanca with that of his contemporaries, Ros speculates that he may have entered the Friars Minor of the Regular Observance around 1513 and then have studied for a minimum of eight years humanities, philosophy and theology, the latter at Cisneros' newly founded Renaissance University of Alcalá.

After studies it appears that Osuna lived at the hermitage of La Salceda, outside Madrid and associated with Cardinal Cisneros. Here Osuna would have undoubtably first encountered the style of prayer which his name is forever associated with and which seemed to be so important for St. Teresa (it is mentioned twice in the key passage quoted above). That is, the prayer of *Recollection* or *Recogimiento* (literally: 'gathering together'). As this is the ostensive subject of Osuna's *Third Spiritual Alphabet* which was to so influence

---

[17] I will draw here on the following sources: Andrés Martín (1976, 1982), López Santidrián (1998), Ros (1936), Peers (1930) and Giles (1981).

[18] Apart from the *Spiritual Alphabets*, other significant works by Osuna include: *Gracioso Convite* (1530), *Norte de los estados* (1531), and two collections of Latin sermons: *Sanctuarium Biblicum* (1533) and *Pars Meridionalis* (1533) as well as the Latin works: *Missus Est* (1535), *Pars Orientalis* (1535), *Pars Occidentalis* (1536) *and Trilogium evangelicum* (1536).

the young Teresa it is worth spending a moment just explaining what is meant by this term.

Recogimiento and Alumbradismo

As a term, *recogimiento* is one of the most used phrases in all of Teresa's works. It is found consistently in each of her major works as well as in her correspondence with colleagues and family alike. Yet, again, following the principles of our narrative, if we look and see what is there and what is not there we notice that the other term that is closely associated with it – *dejamiento* or 'abandonment' – is hardly mentioned at all, in fact only once (in the *Interior Castle* as we shall see in Chapter 6), and there in a negative context. As with so much of Teresa's vocabulary and usage she is making a clear, and even political, decision to adopt a phrase that had found favour with the Spanish Christian establishment, especially the Inquisition.

The history of the term is intimately connected with another which never appears in Teresa's writings but will also shape them: *alumbradismo* – literally 'illumination' – a name given by the Inquisition to a group of religious charismatics in the 1520s.

Contemporary scholarship differs as to the role, nature and scope of the *alumbrados* (see especially Márquez 1980), the term *alumbrado* (literally: 'enlightened', 'illumined') seems to have originally been one of mockery and abuse used to denote 'excessive piety and to suggest hysteria and hypocrisy and fraudulence' (Hamilton 1992: 28). At the beginning of the sixteenth century it began to be associated in Spain with a loose-knit group who were condemned at various times by the Church and State. The propositions for which they were condemned were first collected together in the Edict of Faith issued by the Inquisitor General, Alonso Manrique (Archbishop of Seville) on 23 September 1525. The edict contained forty-eight propositions directed against '*alumbrados, dexados e perfectos*' (literally: 'the enlightened, abandoned and perfect' see Bataillon 1982: 166) which comprised a collection of questionable and heretical statements held by and attributed to the group. As well as certain apocalyptic statements they included propositions such as 'prayer must be mental and not vocal'; the denial of the necessity of any sacramental intermediary between God and humans – thus rejecting the efficacy of external works as well as the authority of the church to interpret scripture; contempt for the cult of the saints, the worship of images, bulls, indulgences, fasting and abstinence. Although the Edict condemned what appeared to be a homogenous and coherent group scholars such as Bataillon and Márquez have concluded that the 'group' was a fragmentary grouping of various collections of people with differing motives, ideas and spiritualities.

From the point of view of our study here and Teresa it is important to note that the groups of *alumbrados* were often associated with *conversos* and new Christians. Some commentators go so far as to see the Christian heresy as a way for these groups, both ex-Jewish and ex-Muslim, to practise aspects of their former faith within the Christian fold. This, however, is not a view accepted by most scholars and one that still needs more justification.

Contemporary commentators have been divided over whether the group were a 'movement' of interior Christianity akin to Erasmianism (Bataillon 1982) or a native, heretical protestant sect with justification by faith as their basic doctrine (Márquez 1980). Hamilton, following Márquez, suggests their emphasis on the working of the Spirit in the individual, their pessimism about human nature, their interest in St Paul and their quest for greater simplicity in religion ally them to the movement of Catholic reform at the time of the Northern European Reformation, known as *evangelism*. It is clear, as Bataillon points out (1982: 166) that in the minds of the Inquisition, *alumbradismo* had to have somewhere a connection with the wider religious reforms of Northern Europe, even if, as appears likely, little such connection existed in reality.

It was the emphasis within these groups on the importance of personal prayer that caused the most problems for Teresa as one of the main thrusts of her own life and work was the restitution of personal and private prayer as central to the life of the average Christian.

A key phrase used in the condemnations of the *alumbrados* was *dejamiento* / 'abandonment' which was used to describe the type of prayer advocated by the *alumbrados*. It is unclear what exactly was meant by the term however it seems to have arisen as a variant of the prayer of *recogimiento* popularized and taught by reforming Spanish Franciscan friars at the beginning of the sixteenth century. This, of course, is what will later be described in Francisco de Osuna's 'Third Spiritual Alphabet'. In my earlier book, *The Return to the Mystical*, I suggested that the importance of this work for Teresa lay precisely in the fact that Osuna gave Teresa a vocabulary with which she could articulate the call for private prayer in her nearly founded convents precisely in a fashion which would mean that she would not fall foul of the Inquisition. A lesson, as we shall see, that Teresa learnt early on and never forgot.

The teaching of *recogimiento,* as Andrés Martín (1975) points out, placed an emphasis on the importance of withdrawing from activity once or twice a day, usually to a dark room, for quiet contemplation with lowered or closed eyes. The teaching of *dejamiento,* often ascribed to Isabel de la Cruz, suggested that such a withdrawal was unnecessary and the contemplation could continue in all states and places – even allowing evil thoughts and temptations to arise.

When does the term *recogimiento* first make its appearance in the spiritual literature? According to Andrés Martín we cannot be sure about the exact date of its origins. We can say with certainty that a form of prayer entitled *recogimiento* was being practised by groups of Franciscans at the beginning of the sixteenth century. When Osuna and Laredo talk of the prayer in 1527 and 1529 they say that it has been practised for between twenty and fifty years (TA: 21.4). This would mean that the prayer had been practised from at least 1480. Andrés Martín preferences the Franciscan hermitages of La Salceda (and possibly earlier in San Pedro de Arlanza) associated in particular with the reforms of Villacreces (d. 1422) as its place of origin.[19] Both Cardinals Cisneros (1527) and Francisco de Quiñones (1523 – later Minister General of the Franciscan Order) would be custodians of the shrine of La Salceda, signifying its importance for the possible spread of *recogimiento.* Whatever its origins, it was in these Franciscan *conventos* and hermitages that it became widely practised at the turn of the fifteenth and sixteenth centuries. Eventually the practitioners of *recogimiento* would 'form a circle at the heart of Spain' (Andrés Martín 1975: 46): La Salceda, El Castañar, Cifuentes, Torrelaguna, Escalona, Alcalá, Ocaña, Toledo, Oropesa and the *Descalzas Reales* of Madrid, as well as circles of *recogimiento* in Andalusia, Extremadura and Catalonia/Valencia.

As to the first occurrence of the term in a published work, Andrés Martín cites García de Cisneros's 1500 *Ejercitatorio* as possibly the first occurrence:

> Recollect (*recógate*) often from low things to high, from temporal to eternal, from exterior to interior, from vain things to those that endure.
>
> (Andrés Martín 1975: 39)[20]

---

[19] See also the Prologue of de Osuna *Sanctuarium Biblicum,* 1533. On Salceda and its connections to the *alumbrados* see Márquez 1972: 109.

[20] *Recógate muchas veces de las cosas bajas a las altas; de las temporales a las eternales, de las exteriores a las interiors; de las vanas a las que siempre han de duran.*

Although Andrés Martín would like to see a clear distinction between the prayer of the *recogidos* and that of the *alumbrados* it is unlikely that such a clear distinction existed. According to him the separation proper between *recogidos* and *alumbrados* begins in 1523 in Pastrana between Francisco de Ortiz (*recogido*) and Pedro Ruiz de Alcaraz (*alumbrado*). Whether such a clear distinction existed between the two forms of prayer remains a moot point.

The Condemnation of *Alumbradismo*

After the Edict of 1525 an inquisitorial process was initiated against Pedro Ruiz de Alcaraz and Isabel de la Cruz of Toledo (see Márquez 1980: 244–57) who were both found guilty of the practices condemned. In 1529 they were flogged, their property confiscated and condemned to 'perpetual reclusion and habit'. From this time any groups of laypeople, women and those associated with the Franciscan *recogitorios* were suspect of the heresy.[21] Thus, over the next thirty years, effectively culminating with the Index of Forbidden Books by the Inquisitor General Juan Valdés in 1559, four separate movements within Spanish society began to be conflated by the Inquisition:

a) The '*alumbrados*'.
b) Erasmianism
c) Lutheranism/Protestantism
d) Remaining non-Christian elements, especially the threat of Jewish influence through *conversos*.

The condemnation of the *alumbrados* by the Edict of Seville in 1525 marked in many ways the beginning of the end of the wave of openness and 'renaissance' within the spiritual tradition in Spain begun by Cardinal Cisneros at the beginning of the century (see Bataillon 1982: 699–737).

Following years of tension between the 'Erasmians' and the Inquisition, events in Spain came to a head in 1559 when many works of the 'Cisnerosian

---

[21] For a full list of the condemned propositions see Marquez 1980: 250. A similar situation happened to the young Ignatius Loyola who at about the same time was exploring simple forms of devotional lay religious life. Although questioned by the Inquisition several times as described in his 'Autobiography' he was able to convince them he did not follow *alumbrado* teaching.

Spring' of the early sixteenth century (including Erasmus and Luther) were condemned in the Valdés Index. Valid only for Spain, it contained many of the writings of the people who had already fallen foul of Valdés and the Inquisition: Cardinal Carranza, Luis de Granada, Juan de Avila and the works of Erasmus in Castilian and Latin. It also incorporated many of the writers and works who had contributed to the Cisnerosian revolution at the beginning of the century: as well as Francisco de Osuna's *Tercer Abecedario* (but not the other *Abecedarios*), it included Herp's *Theologia mystica* and de Balma's *Via Spiritus* (Martínez de Bujanda 1984: 303–592). Thus, Teresa of Avila, born in 1515, was able to have access to many great spiritual texts such as the *Third Spiritual Alphabet* which would be unavailable to lay people, especially women, after 1559. As Hamilton puts it:

> By forbidding so many books published with the approval of Cisneros, the Index could also be regarded as the first official statement condemning his spirituality, the coronation of the trials which had started in the 1520s and of which the *alumbrados* had been the first victims.
>
> (Hamilton 1992: 111)

Some works remained uncensored such as those of Alonso de Madrid and Bernardino de Laredo. In total it listed some 253 titles including fourteen editions of the Bible. In addition to the mentioned titles it also created a wider sense of alarm and caution on a whole range of areas.[22] In Ahlgren's words:

> In summary, the Valdés Index of Prohibited Books was not merely a list of books prohibited to the public; it was an edict intended to limit the scope of religious speculation and to define religious faith and practice very narrowly as the province of an educated elite whose task was not speculation but transmission of dogma.
>
> (Ahlgren 1996: 17)

For Andrés Martín, the Valdés Index 'tried to banish affective spirituality in its various manifestations, encouraging the traditional spirituality of the practice

---

[22] Other entries included books by known heretics, partial or whole translations of the Bible, books in Arabic or Hebrew or that tell of Muslim or Jewish practices, books regarding witchcraft and superstition and manuscripts that mention biblical tradition or the sacraments of the church. See Ahlgren 1996: 17

of virtues and the destruction of vices over other ways of spirituality considered mystical' (Andrés Martín 1976: 1.362).

Commentators such as Ahlgren have noted the paradox that the period after 1559 while being one of repression also encouraged a great flowering of 'mystical literature' (Ahlgren 1996: 30). In this context we once again return to Teresa's 'hiding-revealing' strategies that she needed to adapt to survive in the new climate and that we discussed in the previous chapter. Ahlgren suggests that Teresa employed four strategies to survive in the post Valdés climate:

a) She was careful about the literary and theological sources she cited.[23]
b) She employed a series of rhetorical devices to justify her right to write as an 'unlettered woman'.[24]
c) She practised a form of self censorship in the spirit of Valdés: 'her allusions to controversial subjects, such as her *converso* origins, permitted contemporary readers (especially those who knew her) to understand the subtext, but she never spoke openly enough to attract attention'.
d) Finally, in exact language she explained 'mystical phenomena as thoroughly and accurately as possible', her overall aim being to show how 'charismatic experience did not have to be viewed as a potential danger to the institutional church but could instead be an important source of Roman Catholic identity'.

As she notes:

> As the new mystical pathways opened in the first half of the century narrowed to a dogmatic and disciplined orthodoxy, so did the range of subjects appropriate for theological debate ... If the works were to survive intact, certain topics had to be handled with extreme care, and authors used language to hide rather than reveal their intent.
>
> (Ahlgren 1996: 19)

---

[23] Even today commentators cite Teresa's partial or unformed biblical quotes as evidence of her lack of sophistication. It may be, as Ahlgren and others suggest, that this was a deliberate ploy to avoid the restrictions of the Valdés Index.

[24] We surveyed many of these in the previous chapter.

As Ahlgren points out this particularly applied to laypeople and especially women.[25] As most women did not read Latin, the Valdés prohibition of spiritual books in the vernacular posed a particular problem. However, as these ideological concerns impacted upon her, Teresa was able to respond, largely I would argue because of the 'training' and 'education' she had received from 'her master' Fray Francisco de Osuna and his exposition of spiritual theology in the *Third Spiritual Alphabet*. In this respect her schooling in the mystical strategies of the *theologia mystica* from the *Third Spiritual Alphabet* were an ideal preparation for the challenges of the environment within which her mature work was to be written.

What Teresa learnt from the *Third Spiritual Alphabet*

From the account above we can begin to see why the *recogimiento* movement which places the heart and the *oración afectiva/affective prayer* at the centre of its concerns (as taught in the *Third Spiritual Alphabet*), would have appealed so strongly to the young Teresa. This is nowhere better expressed than in the First Letter of the *Alphabet,* A:

> Always walking together – the Person and the Spirit... The meaning of our letter is that wherever you go carry your thought (*pensamiento*) along with you, for no one should go divided in themselves. Do not allow the body to travel one path and the heart another.
>
> (TA: 1.1–2)[26]

Recogmiento then, according to Andrés Martín, is primarily a way of '*contemplativa afectiva*' centred on love: '*sin pensar nada*' / 'Without thinking of anything', without any necessary prevenient or concomitant understanding.

Central to Osuna's affective theology in *The Third Spiritual Alphabet* is the notion of 'taste' of God rather than knowledge. In many passages he plays on the word *saber* ('know') and *sabor* ('taste') much as we will later see Teresa does.

---

[25] She notes that between 1550 and 1600 no books by female authors were printed from Alcalá.

[26] *Anden siempre juntamente la Person y Espíritu: El sentido de nuestra letra sera que doquiera que vayas lleves tu pensamiento contigo y no ande cada uno por su parte divididos; así que el cuerpo ande en una parte y el corazón e otra.*

In Osuna's words, the 'mystical theology'[27] is a *sabroso saber* – literally, a 'tasty knowledge':

> They also call this type of prayer 'wisdom' because, as you can see, it is a tasty knowledge (*sabroso saber*); such knowledge, according to Saint Paul, is only found amongst the perfect, for the imperfect are not given such tasty morsels or such high doctrine (*tan buen manjar*). And it is called 'wisdom' for through it people will know how to taste God (*saben los hombres a qué sabe Dios*); of which taste the Wise Man says when he speaks of God: He gave wisdom to those who worked mercifully.
>
> (TA: 6.2)[28]

Another theme Osuna develops in the text is his notion of the spiritual *gustos*, or 'taste/delight' of God, a key term later taken up by Teresa as we shall see. For example, Chapter 12 of the *Alphabet* is entitled: '*No entiendo, mas gustando, penses alcanzar reposo*' / 'Not by thinking, but more by tasting, think to attain rest.' Early on in the treatise he had spoken of the importance of desire in the search for God (TA: 4.3, 11.5) and in Chapter 12 he explicitly emphasizes the role that the *gustos/delights* play in this.[29]

Thus, knowledge of God, for Osuna, is derived not from 'knowing' (*saber*) but from 'tasting' (*sabor*), in particular tasting the delights of the *gustos espir-ituales*, the spiritual delights. This *gusto espiritual* is 'so excellent that it is almost impossible for a person who has experienced it not to praise it … We should

---

[27] Again, I refer the reader to *The Return to the Mystical* for a fuller exposition of the medieval tradition of 'mystical theology'. I shall come back to it in a later chapter. For now, suffice it to say I use it in the late medieval sense of a method or way of engaging in affective theology.

[28] '*Llámese también esta manera de oración sabiduría, que, según viste, es sabroso saber; la cual sabiduría dice San Pablo que hablaba entre los perfectos solamente, porque a los imperfectos no les daba tan buen manjar ni tan alta doctrina. Y dícese sabiduría porque mediante ella saben los hombres a qué sabe Dios; donde de aquésta dice el Sabio hablando de Dios: A los que piadosamente obran dio la sabiduría.*' Mary Giles writes in her translation of this passage (1981: 164): 'Osuna's play on the word 'saber' which means both 'to know' and 'to taste' defies translation.'

[29] See, for example, TA: 12.6 'The Excellence of Spiritual *Gusto*': 'Spiritual *gusto* is so excellent that I think it is almost impossible for one not to praise it who has had it; and he knows that to have this *gusto* is a quite contrary condition to having the tasty morsels of this world; for the one who eats the morsels of this world in quantity we judge will have no hunger; but the more we enjoy the things of God it is the reverse; for the one who tastes this hungers to know and enjoy more, and opens more the eyes of the soul to see, and the heart to receive; and sharpens the understanding to know, and the more water they discover, so they want to plunge into the sea.'

realise that he who tastes spiritual food hungers to taste and enjoy more' (TA: 12.6).

Osuna continues by justifying the use of pleasure as a marker of spiritual progress, dismissing those who object for 'not differentiating among the types of pleasure' and classing them all together. He calls on Jean Gerson to justify his approach which is the emphasis on the importance of experience over understanding. At this point Osuna employs a quote from Proverbs 8.31 which we shall see later is of fundamental importance to Teresa. The original verse from Proverbs reads:

> The Lord created me at the beginning of his work
> The first of his acts of long ago.
> Ages ago I was established,
> At the first, before the beginning of the earth ...
> When he established the heavens,
> I was there,
> When he drew a circle on the face of the deep ...
> When he marked out the foundations of the earth.
> There I was beside him, like a master worker.
> And I was daily his delight
> Rejoicing before him always.
> Rejoicing in his inhabited world
> And delighting in the human race. (Proverbs 8.31)

De Osuna transcribes this thus:

> Our souls would delight in an increase of consolation, and, as we delighted in God, he would grant the petitions of our hearts, for it is said that his delights are to dwell in the sons of man so they will cause them to delight in him.
>
> (TA: 12.4)[30]

As already mentioned Osuna, following the medieval tradition, named this type of theology the 'mystical theology' as opposed to what the medievals would call the 'speculative theology' – which corresponds more or less to what is

---

[30] As well as Proverbs 8.31, Osuna also makes reference here to Psalm 103.27 and Proverbs 5.19.

taught in most universities today within the Theology Faculty. For Osuna, and later Teresa, the 'mystical theology' is thus a way of 'tasty knowing', a way of 'unknowing' and even, as we have seen, a way of speaking:

> (Theology) has two forms: one is called 'speculative' or 'investigative', which is the same thing, the other is called 'hidden', which is treated of here and which gives the title to this Third Alphabet. I do not presume to teach it here, as no mortal can, for Christ alone reserves this teaching only for himself, in secret and in the hearts in which this hidden theology dwells as divine science and something much more excellent than the other theology of which I spoke first ... This theology (the mystical theology) is said to be more perfect and better than the first, so says Gerson, as the first serves as an introduction leading to the second.
>
> (TA: 6.2)[31]

Thus by combining his exposition of the ancient Jewish texts with the medieval tradition of mystical theology inherited through Jean Gerson and the Victorines, Osuna would have provided Teresa with a primer in over a thousand years of Christian spiritual writing. No wonder she referred to him as her '*maestro*'. Not only that, by navigating a safe passage between the tricky shores of *recogimiento* and *dejamiento* Osuna was able to equip Teresa in her later battles with the Inquisition as she tried to establish a form of contemplative Christian life that was open to all – lay and clergy, men and women. This battle would constitute the reform of the Order which she conceived in her mid-fifties after 20 years of living in the convent of the *Encarnación*. To examine this reform we need to explore something of the Carmelite context within which Teresa found herself at the *Encarnación* and how she envisaged her role as a reforming contemplative. We will turn to this in the next chapter.

---

[31] *La cual aún es en dos maneras: una se llama especulativa o escudriñadora, que es el mismo, y otra escondida, que es la que se trata o a la que se intitula este tercero alfabeto; no que en él presuma yo enseñarla, pues ninguno de los mortales la enseñó, porque Christo guardó para sí este oficio de enseñar en secreto a los corazones en que viviese aquesta teología escondida como ciencia divina y mucho más excelente que la otra teología de que hablamos primer ... Esta teología se dice más perfecta o mejor que la primera, según dice Gersón, porque de la primera como de un principio se servir.*

3

Hermits, Friars and Reformers

The School of the Prophets

As we have heard (V: 4.1), Teresa entered the Carmelite Convent of the *Encarnación* of Avila on 2 November 1535 taking the Carmelite habit a year later on 2 November 1536 aged 21. This early and brave move (she describes how heart-wrenching it was to leave her beloved father and family) was to have far-reaching consequences not just for Teresa but for the whole Carmelite Order itself. What was the order she was entering and how had it established itself at Avila? In answering these questions we will also examine why Teresa felt, like so many of her age, that her vocation was to be a reformer of religious life.

The Carmelite order traces its origins to the Jewish 'School of the Prophets' traditionally established by Elijah on the sides of Mount Carmel near Haifa in present-day Israel. Varied etymologies are suggested for the origins of the word including that from the words *krm* and *l* suggesting 'a vineyard', others include 'a scrubby area'. Today it remains a green verdant place that dominates the Mediterranean landscape for miles around. As well as its Jewish and Christian associations, for the Muslims it is associated with *Khidr* – 'The Green One' or 'Verdant One', another name given to Elijah in this tradition. Thus the cave of Elijah, situated adjacent to the present day Carmelite Priory of 'Stella Maris', and currently a synagogue, has during its 2,500 year existence been a church, a mosque, a synagogue and possibly a Roman shrine (See: Giordano 1995 and Florencio del Niño Jesús 1924[1]).

Carmel is frequently mentioned in the Jewish scriptures, perhaps most famously in the Song of Songs 7.5: 'Your head crowns you like Carmel and your

---

[1] P. Florencio's book written before the troubles in the Holy Land in the middle of the twentieth century gives some fascinating details about the mutual respect between the 'dervish and sufi' communities of the Holy Mountain and the Carmelite Order.

flowing locks are like purple.' It is the place where Elijah performs some of the most important acts of his ministry, in particular the fight with the prophets of Baal (1 Kings 18.20–40), the prophecy from the cloud in the sea and his final taking up in the fiery chariot watched by Elisha (2 Kings 2).This last is said to have inspired the original habits of the Carmelite order which were streaked to represent the cinders from the chariot scorching their robes.

Thus, the mystical mountain maintained and maintains a pull and a power for Christian, Jewish and Muslim people alike and throughout the history of the Carmelite order the metaphors and tropes of Elijah and his mountain continue to recur: the ascent of the mountain, the chariot, the raven, the fire, the cloud from the sea, the desert and the vineyard.

Historically the origins of the order are cloudy. The eleventh and twelfth centuries had seen the first significant medieval encounter between Islam and Christianity known as 'The Crusades' begun with the First Crusade preached by Pope Urban II in 1095 at Clermont-Ferrand in France and continuing throughout the twelfth century. By the early thirteenth century we begin to hear reports of groups of former Crusaders settling on the 'Holy Mountain' near the Wadi 'ain es-Siah associated with Elijah. Thus we find Jacques de Vitry, Bishop of nearly Acre, writing around 1216:

> Others after the example and in imitation of the holy solitary Elijah, the Prophet, lived as hermits in the beehives of small cells on Mount Carmel … near the spring which is called the Spring of Elijah … Where in little comb-like cells these bees of the Lord laid up sweet spiritual honey.
>
> (Smet 1988: 1.4)

It was this disparate group, of whom we know so little, who approached Albert of Vercelli, Patriarch of Jerusalem, for a Rule sometime between 1206 and 1214. This Rule, the original form of which is not known[2], was finally promulgated by Pope Innocent IV in his 1247 Bull *Quae honorem conditoris*.[3] After 1214

---

[2] Bernard Oller in the late fourteenth century wrote that 'good faith and prescription were sufficient for them' (Smet 1988: 1.18). A manuscript that comes closest to the form of the original is that preserved in the collection of Carmelite writings edited by the Catalan provincial, Philip Ribot (d.1391). Although many scholars dismiss the reliability of Ribot, Waaijman, whose account of the *Rule* I draw heavily on here, is happy that this manuscript gives us a close perspective on the original rule (Waaijman 1999: 18ff.).

[3] Just to complicate scholarship, the original text of this Bull is also lost. A copy of the original is however still in the Vatican (see Waaijman 1999: 19).

the fortunes of the young order underwent another twist as increasing Muslim incursions into the Christian lands around Acre had made it necessary for the group of hermits to leave the Holy Land in 1238. Arriving in Europe new communities of the Order were first established at Cyprus, Messina (Sicily) and Aylesford and Hulne in England. On this early expansion Smet comments:

> It is interesting to note, with regard to the expansion of the Order in Europe, how often early foundations are made in seaports. The Carmelites were truly a sea-going nation; the topography of the Order expands outward from the coasts of Europe. It is obvious that Carmelites are not an indigenous product, but arrived from 'parts beyond the sea'.
>
> (Smet 1988: 1.31)

It is not for nothing that the nascent Order very quickly adopted the Marian devotion to *Stella Maris* – 'Star of the Sea' – as particularly apt for their charism. Teresa, like her sea-faring *conquistador* brothers, had also chosen a expansionary, adventurous enterprise to join.

Once established in England, a General Chapter of the Order in Aylesford, Kent in 1247 eventually produced *Quae honorem conditoris*. Thus this final version of the Rule holds all the contradictions and tensions that the fledgling order had experienced up to this point. In it we find echoes of the free-range hermits of the Holy Land, the small group who wanted to live as a community on the Sacred Mountain and the final manifestation of the order as a European mendicant order akin to the well established Franciscans and Dominicans. It is these tensions and contradictions that make the *Rule* such a fascinating and potentially controversial document. As Kees Waaijman puts it:

> The Rule of Carmel embodies three religious concepts: the eremitic way of life, the cenobitic form of life and life as a mendicant brother. The combination of these three concepts is not the product of careful thought but of life lived within a single century: from hermit to cenobite, from cenobite to mendicant. The tensions between these three types of religious life have internally led to conflicts, down to this day. But they have also forced the Carmelites to go below the surface, to a deeper level, to look for the mystical space of contemplation, a level from the perspective of which all forms and concepts are relative.
>
> (Waaijman 1999: 9)

The simplicity and openness of the *Rule* contains a *nostalgie* for the fresh vistas and solitariness of the Holy Mountain of Carmel and it is to this *nostalgie* that later reformers such as Teresa of Avila and John of the Cross would respond in their sixteenth century 're-formation' of the Order. The 'mitigations' of 1247 included stipulations that brought the order closer to the mendicant life as then envisaged in Europe. Thus, foundations no longer needed to be made in desert places, meals were to be taken in common, the canonical office was recited, abstinence was mitigated and silence restricted to between the canonical offices of Compline and Prime. In the words of Joachim Smet: 'The Carmelite Rule of 1247 brought solitude to the town when life in the desert was no longer feasible ... and all reforms in Carmel have always been to their contemplative origins' (Smet 1997: 47). For McGreal 'the essence of the Rule (of 1247) is the desire to live a life of allegiance to Jesus Christ, serving him faithfully with a pure heart and a clear conscience' (McGreal 1999: 26). This service of Christ, through prayer and service to one's neighbour, is at the heart of all subsequent Carmelite spirituality. The life is lived through seeing the face of Christ in the people around us and in service of the world. Thus, the early Carmelites were part of the struggle to regain the Holy Land from Muslim control, but they saw that struggle not in armed terms but in the terms of a peaceful and God-centred prayerful ushering in of the Kingdom. Thus, solitude, silence, prayer and reconciliation are central to this task. Chapter 7 of the Rule, which is taken by many Carmelites to be the heart of the Rule, states 'Let each remain in his cell or near it, meditating night and day on the Word of the Lord and keeping vigil in prayer, unless he is occupied with other lawful activities' (Waaijman 1999: 31). As well as an emphasis on finding silence and solitude the Mitigated Rule exhorted its friars to find God in the midst of the world and active engagement in, for example, preaching and works of mercy: 'The following of Christ, the great project of the Rule, is achieved by becoming a community of disciples who are everything to Christ' (McGreal 1999: 30). It was a vision of community inspired by that described in the Acts of the Apostles, Chapters 2 and 4, the original vision of the early Carmelites. However, the Order had subtly changed from one concentrated on holy community and life in 'desert places' to one that was more active and engaged with the newly emerging medieval towns. It would be this tension introduced into the Order that would be harnessed by Teresa in her later reform, or perhaps 'return' of the Order to what she perceived to be its original charism.

This new form of life, the prototype of all later orders in the church, was ratified at the Second Council of Lyon of 1274, with the Rules of Life of the three other great mendicant orders of the Western church: the Franciscans, the

Augustinians and the Dominicans. From hereon, the wildness of the original denizens of Mount Carmel would be tamed as they became assimilated into mainstream religious life in medieval Western Europe. Vincent de Beauvais gives 1238 as the traditional date for the move of the order from the Holy Land to Europe, however this is probably just an approximation. What we do know is that by the middle of the thirteenth century communities with the name 'Carmelite', and a connection to the Crusader states of the Middle East, were appearing throughout Europe. The origin of the Carmelites in England was largely typical of how the order spread throughout Europe. The original invitation to come to Aylesford in Kent was given by Sir Richard Grey of Codnor in 1242, who had earlier gone on Crusade with Sir Richard of Cornwall, having landed in Acre in the Holy Land in October 1240. There he would no doubt have met the order, been impressed by their presence and later been happy to offer them sanctuary on his own lands when they needed it. Similar foundations were quickly followed in Kent (Lossenham) and Norfolk (Bradmer).

As has been said, in this transition from the semi-eremetical life of Palestine to the cold Northern European lifestyle many changes had to be adapted in the mitigation of the order of 1247 and by 1291 the Carmelites had had to abandon their beloved Mount Carmel altogether. It would be five hundred years before they were allowed to return to their spiritual home.

In the meantime, the order spread with some success throughout Western Europe, so that by the end of the thirteenth century in England, for example, the order had 30 houses under four 'distinctions': London, Norwich, Oxford and York as well as new houses in Scotland and Ireland. Around this time (1281 at a General Chapter in London) the order began to assert its origins among the 'school of prophets' of Elijah and Elisha around the 'fountain of Elijah' at Carmel. Marian devotion was also enshrined at the heart of the order and in particular to Our Lady of Mount Carmel.[4] John Baconthorpe ('doctor resolutus', d. 1348) was instrumental in reinterpreting the story from 1 Kings 18.44 about the small cloud that arises from the Mediterranean Sea which will eventually float over the land and form a downpour to refresh the land. He interpreted the cloud as representing the Virgin Mary – the pure essence of water condensed from the saline of humanity – from whom would eventually come the saving cloudburst of Christ, refreshing and bringing the Water of Life to humanity.

---

[4] Found in the so-called *Rubrica Prima* at the beginning of the new Constitutions of the Order.

At this time the order also took to itself the special titles accorded to Mary such as 'Stella Maris' and 'Rosa Mystica'. The replacement of the original sizzled striped mantle of the order in 1287 with a white one resembling the more conventional habits of the Franciscans and Dominicans and Pope John XXII's Bull of 1326 *Super Cathedram*, which extended to the order all the rights and exemptions as existed for these older established orders, meant that by the middle of the fourteenth century the order was firmly established at the heart of Western medieval theocracy.

The Call of the Desert

Despite this phenomenal growth, however, the Order still retained its slight unease with the new urban settings within which it found itself and had not forgotten the 'smell of the Desert' – the whistling of the love-stirring Mediterranean breezes of Carmel. Long before Teresa of Avila and John of the Cross called the Order back to the solitudes and vastnesses of the desert the Prior General of the Order, Nicholas of France (Prior General 1266–71) summoned the Order back to its desert origins in a stirring tract: *Ignea Sagitta* / 'The Flaming Arrow', written in 1270 towards the end of his Generalship.[5] As he stresses in this work:

> Those who have left the desert for the city are not the true sons of Carmel, but stepsons only … the citadel of Carmel is not the walled town but the open desert.
>
> (*Ignea Sagitta*: 5)

In terms that will reflect those used later by John and Teresa, Nicholas sings of the beauties of the desert and how here alone can the soul find its true rest in God:

> All the creatures which we see and hear in the desert bring us refreshment and comfort as our companions. Yea, though silent, they preach in wondrous wise words and excite our inner soul to the promise of the Creator.
>
> (*Ignea Sagitta*: 11)

---

[5] Reproduced in *Carmelus* IX and *Aylesford Review* 1.

However, the tension remained at the heart of the Order so that by the beginning of the fifteenth century there were more calls for 'mitigation' of the original *Rule*. This was achieved in February 1432 following Pope Eugene IV's Bull *Romani Pontificis*. The new mitigations clarified two ambiguous points in particular, the obligation of the Original Rule to remain continually in the cell and the need to abstain perpetually from meat. When Teresa and John would later talk of renouncing 'mitigations' of the Rule it is these later ones of the early fifteenth century that they meant, not the thirteenth century ones that followed the Order's move to Europe. Thus the new mitigations of 1432 allowed the friars to eat meat for three days a week and deemed it suitable for the friars to walk about in their 'churches, cloisters and periphery' (Smet 1988: 1.85). As the later Prior General, the Englishman Bl. John Soreth (1395–1471, Prior General 1451–71) wrote:

> Foods must be used that be more easily or cheaply obtained – in many cases meat of this kind – lest on account of abstinence one be found to seek after food of a more expensive kind and difficult to obtain.
>
> (Smet 1988: 1.86)

Which sounds to me like a good case of English pragmatism! As well as being something of a pragmatist, Soreth was able to take the Order in a new direction that would directly impact upon Teresa's life. In May 1452, after the chapter of Cologne, he received into the Order its first women – a group of pious women, known as Beguines, from Ten Elsen in Guelders. This was shortly before the Order received the Bull *Cum Nulla* from Pope Nicholas V in October 1452 allowing the Prior General and Provincials of the Order to receive admission of 'religious virgins, widows, beguines and *beatas*' (Smet 1988: 1.92). This move is noteworthy, as the Carmelite practice of receiving into its ordinances already pre-established groups of pious lay people, usually but not always women, would be one that Teresa herself would emulate when she came to found her convents in sixteenth century Spain; a practice encouraged by the Council of Trent which urged religious people without a formal canonical attachment to join an already canonically established order. In such a fashion the female wing of the Order rapidly established itself in France, Belgium, Italy and Spain throughout the fifteenth century. Which is how a group of 'holy women', or *beatas,* in Avila found themselves seeking refuge within this holy and ancient Order.

Sixteenth Century Reform

I think it would be a mistake to regard Teresa as a stand-alone reformer against a sea of obscurantist reaction. As will be already clear from this brief overview of the origins and medieval history of the Carmelite Order, the order from the earliest inceptions of its *Rule* appeared to enshrine a struggle between its three founding elements: the eremetical 'children of the desert'; those living in community; and the travelling, restless preachers, missioners and mendicants. Teresa's Spanish reform in the mid-sixteenth century can be seen in historical perspective as the latest turning of the Carmelite page. Just as Bl. John Soreth (like Nicholas of France before him) had been a strong voice for reform in the Order, so their sixteenth century successor, Giovanni Battista Rossi (1507–78), was to play an equally important role in the drama which would have Teresa of Avila at its centre.[6] Like Teresa he was young enough to have been born into that early spring air at the beginning of the sixteenth century which preceded the turmoil and ructions of the mid-century Reformation. He was elected Vicar General of the Order in May 1562 and General in May 1564, these being the crucial years when Teresa decided to leave the *Encarnación* and establish her own reformed convent in Avila of *San José*. Thus, we can see these two contemporaries as having a like-minded desire for the reform of what had surely become a somewhat moribund order (especially in Spain) in need of a little pruning.

From early on after his election it was clear that Rossi would be a new broom in the Order. For example, after the final Night Prayer of the day he insisted:

> Let (the brethren) devote themselves to some interest such as letters, meditation or prayer or manual labour ... and not succumb to idleness and sluggishness ... for idleness and the Carmelite profession are completely and mutually irreconcilable.
>
> (Smet 1988: 2.3)

The words could have been Teresa's own. Thus, with a reforming brief in hand, Rossi left Rome in April 1566 arriving in Spain a month later where he proceeded immediately to Madrid for an audience with King Philip II, Emperor Carlos' heir and successor and a gentleman also very keen to initiate reform of

---

[6] Teresa and the Spaniards would always hispanize his name to 'Juan Bautista Rubeo'.

religious life within his realm. The accounts of Rossi's visitation to Spain are instructive for they give us a clear, sometimes bald, picture of the state of the Carmelite order in Spain in the middle of the sixteenth century, as well as the nature of the sometimes larger-than-life personalities with whom Teresa had to deal in her reforming work. As Rossi visited the communities the shape of his visitations would take a similar form. Like the Inquisitors, he would be met in solemn procession before taking up residence in each Carmel. Once there, after a period of rest he would begin the process of interviewing each religious separately to see how far their lifestyle was conforming to the Carmelite ideal.

Meanwhile, his assistants would go through the community's accounts, business matters and legal documents to see if there were any irregularities – which sadly was often the case. In his interviews with the brethren he was particularly keen to discover their positions regarding private ownership (did they have private possessions?); their attendance at the choral offices of the Carmel, as stipulated in the Rule; their own prayer life, silence and 'recollection'; how they related to their fellow community members – were they, for instance, the cause of dissent or disturbance; their pastoral work, for example how far did they care for the sick; fasting; the conduct of their superiors and the education of novices and students (Smet 1988: 2.9).

Once the enquiries were over the General and his assistants would set to work in putting right some of the abuses they had discovered. Musical instruments and arms were confiscated (lutes and pistols being particularly favoured). Collars and cuffs of wool and other fine materials were cut off. For the severest infringements of the Rule, the General had the power to impose harsh penalties including expulsion from the Order and even a sentence on His Majesty's galleys as an oarsman.

As the General made his way through Andalusia he encountered all sorts of abuses.[7] Certain people in particular would incur the wrath of the General, an ominous sign as some of them would later rally to John and Teresa's flag in the so-called 'Discalced' reform.[8] Three brothers in particular would prove thorns

---

[7] Despite being under one crown, that of Philip II, the regions of Spain at this time were still utterly distinct (as in many ways they remain to this day). Teresa had a lifelong disdain for Andalusia and its people only visiting it once: 'I don't get along with the people of Andalusia' she said (Letter to Diego Ortiz, 26 December, 1575), they are a 'strange people (*una gente estraña*)' (Letter to Rossi, 18 June 1575).

[8] The association of being shoeless (*Descalzo*) with spiritual reform pre-dated John and Teresa. Teresa of Avila's great mentor, Pedro de Alcántara was one of the most famous 'shoeless' Franciscans who were to shape so much of Spanish sixteenth century spirituality. The possession of shoes was associated with wealth,

first in Rossi's side and later in Teresa's: Caspar, Baltasar and Melchor Nieto, of whom Smet says in one of his rare unkind asides: 'whose only resemblance to the holy Magi was their names' (Smet 1988: 2.11). These three gentlemen stand out in Rossi's visitation for the depth of their naughtiness and disobedience. The most disruptive of the three was Melchor whom Fray Cristobal de Vargas describes as 'a lost man, a destroyer of convents' (Smet 1988: 2.12) while the Prioress of Ecija, Doña María Ponce de León called him simply '*un loco*'.

He was removed from office as prior of Ecija in August 1565 having attacked the General's visitor Mazzapica in a punch-up. Caspar had him put in irons and sent to Seville. On the way Baltasar got into his cell, provided him with a sword and helped him to escape. Caspar, on the other hand, was said to 'keep himself in power by treating his fellow friars like captives or slaves while living comfortably himself'. While in other friaries each friar was so undisciplined that he brought his own wine to the refectory at meal times and students were regularly physically punished.

In the Chapter of Andalusia convened by Rossi in 1566, Baltasar was sentenced to three years exile in Castille or Portugal for aiding the misde-meanors of his brother Melchor. Caspar was moved to the insignificant house of Castro del Rio while Melchor, the worst malefactor, was sentenced to three years at King Philip's pleasure in service as an oarsman on one of his galleys. Other sentences handed out included that to Juan de la Magdalena who was found guilty of living with a prostitute: he was also condemned to the galleys.

This same Baltasar would later transfer to the Discalced friars in Pastrana in 1569. When we look at the subsequent turbulent history of the Discalced reform (including John of the Cross's imprisonment by the Mitigated fathers, see Tyler 2010) it is perhaps not surprising that these events would come to a messy end considering the past records of some of the characters involved in

---

akin to the English phrase for well-off people – 'well heeled'. A number of commentators (e.g. Crisógono) refer to the un-Discalced Carmelites as 'Calced' Carmelites. Conversations with un-Discalced Carmelites suggest that this term is not considered appropriate. Thus, throughout this book when I refer to the un-Discalced Carmelites I shall call them the Carmelites of the Ancient Observance, Mitigated Carmelites or simply Carmelites. Teresa uses the term *Descalza* for her own reformed nuns and *Calza/Calzado* or *Del paño* (literally: 'of the cloth') for the Mitigated Carmelites. In her letters to Gracián she adopts even more interesting terms – referring to her own nuns as 'doves' or 'butterflies' and the Mitigated as 'ravens' or 'crows'!

the Reform. Both John and Teresa had a hard job 'making straight with crooked lines' in their efforts at reform.[9]

Having begun the task of cleaning the Augean stables of Andalusia, Rossi turned his attention to Castile in February 1567.[10] Here things were little better and among the cases he had to deal with were Doña Aldonza de Valderrabano at Avila, who asked permission to retain her 'black slave girl', as well as other nuns of the *Encarnación* who were engaged in buying and selling convent cells, keeping their own rents and incomes, as well as having their own maids and slaves like Doña Aldonza.

Thus when Rossi finally met Teresa in April 1567 the meeting must have seemed like a breath of fresh air to both reformers.

Teresa as Reformer

From all accounts the Carmel of the *Encarnación* that Teresa entered in 1535 was far from the ascetic desert envisaged by the first Carmelite fathers and later reformers. Yet, despite all the descriptions of its somewhat chaotic disordered state there is no doubt that it could provide a place of spiritual growth not only for Teresa but many other sisters as well. Having over one hundred nuns,[11] it was clearly one of the favourite places for the daughters of Avila's upper echelons. Its origins, as already suggested, were somewhat heterodox. It was originally founded as a *beaterio* – a house for the pious single ladies or *beatas* mentioned in the previous chapter – by Doña Elvira González de Medina, one time concubine of a Canon of Avila Cathedral, Don Nuño González del Aguila, from whom she bore four children. Originally her house, established in 1479, housed a community of some fourteen women living under the Carmelite Rule. Later, as we have heard, after the expulsion of the Jews from Avila, the young community was given the deeds to the Jewish cemetery of Avila in 1495. The house was officially opened as a Carmelite convent in 1515, the year of Teresa's

---

[9] For more on Baltasar and his antics, including his later defamation of Jerónimo Gracián, see Kavanaugh 2001: 612–13.

[10] The abuses of the Andalusian province continued well into the era of the Discalced reform in Andalusia. When Gracián visited the Convent of the *Encarnación* in Seville in 1576 he discovered a room of the convent was used for holding dances, feasts and masques 'such as is on in the streets' (Smet 1988: 1.73).

[11] María Pinel suggests that the number reached 180 nuns. See BMC 2: 140, *Noticias del S. Convento de la Encarnación de Avila*.

birth (see Bilinkoff 1989: 41 and González y González 1976). In this somewhat unorthodox institution, the daughters of wealthy families (such as Teresa) lived in a suite of rooms, often entertaining visitors and making frequent trips outside the enclosure, and even, in some cases as we have seen, having 'slaves'. Teresa's own apartment at the *Encarnación* had two sets of rooms with a connecting staircase and facilities for cooking and eating.[12] The daughters of less well-off families would sleep in a dormitory and effectively act as servants to their better-off sisters. As opposed to most monasteries today, rank in the *Encarnación* was not dependent on date of entry or profession but effectively reflected the social circumstances the nuns had held before they entered. Thus, the daughters of nobility (as Teresa would have been classed) would automatically hold more esteemed places in choir. This was a practice that Teresa herself had to fight hard against later on in her reformed convents, perhaps most notoriously when the widowed Princess of Éboli entered the newly founded convent of Pastrana with her retinue and insisted on retaining all her former privileges (see F: 17).

The death of her father Alonso in 1543 when Teresa was 28 (V: 7.14), with whom she was clearly very close, affected her badly, and she began to review the state of life she was living at the *Encarnación*. The language she uses here, as always in the *Book of the Life*, is quite precise and one we shall turn to in the next chapter. Thus, in Chapter 7 of the *Life*, she describes the state of her soul at this time of one of losing the 'taste (*gusto*) and caress (*regalo*) in matters of virtue' (V: 7.1). Induced, she suspects, by the emphasis within the convent upon continual 'vocal prayer' (*vocalmente*) rather than what we would nowadays call 'contemplative prayer' or 'mindfulness' (Teresa uses the term 'mental prayer', *oración mental* throughout).[13] This desire to promote 'mindfulness' or spiritual insight, Teresa suggests from the later vantage point of the *Book of the Life*, lay behind all that was going wrong in her life as then lived at the *Encarnación*.

It is at this point in the *Life* that Teresa makes one of her most striking statements for modern ears, the enunciation of a principle which, along with her call for greater mindfulness in religious life, is one that would guide the rest

---

[12] Still preserved in the convent to this day.

[13] Teresa's insistence on promoting silent interior prayer at the expense of outward vocal prayer, especially for the souls of the dead, is for Jodi Bilinkoff (1989) another reason why she was so vehemently opposed by certain sections of Avilan society. For more on mindfulness and contemplation in Teresa's writing see Chapter 8 below.

of her foundations. In paradoxical terms she states that the freedom of lack of enclosure 'did me great harm' (*me hizo harto daño*) (V: 7.3). These more open convents, she says, are places where 'much wickedness can be hidden.' 'Poor souls' / '*pobrecitas*' (V: 7.4) in such a convent are not to be blamed but this is rather what they 'pick up' from those around them: 'Youth, sensuality and the devil invite and incite them to follow those very things of the world which are said to be "alright" as it were' / '*la mocedad y sensualidad y demonio las convida y enclina a siguir algunas cosas que son de el mesmo mundo.*'

Following Rossi's accounts above he would no doubt agree with Teresa's 'cry from the heart' in V: 7.5: '*Oh grandísimo mal, grandísimo mal de relisiosos – no digo ahora más mujeres que hombres – adonde no se guarda relisión!*' / 'O most terrible, terrible evil of religious – and I speak here as much about women as men – where they do not practice religion!' In each religious house, she tells us, there are two possibilities, to follow religion and virtue and the lack of it. No doubt, she has in mind here not just the abuses she saw around her in the convents and monasteries of Spain at the eve of the Reformation, but also her own lack of virtue that she had lived in the *Encarnación*. Yet, the compassion with which she talks about the 'poor ones' who have succumbed to this, suggests she realizes that the atmosphere and ambience of a community must be carefully maintained if the individual is to respond on a 'path of religion'.

Bold, as ever, in her condemnation of the abuses of religion, Teresa is as finely attuned to the capacity for self-deception that lies at the centre of the human heart, and especially at the centre of those who seek God, religion and spirituality. For Teresa recognizes as perhaps few have, that the place of religion is a most dangerous place where deception and lies can lead to the most appalling atrocities in its name. As we saw in the previous chapter, she did not have to look far to see this happening all around her in the Spain of her era.

Perhaps today, in the time of a 'rebirth of religion' where those committed to or following religious life have to give an account of themselves to the wider world in a way perhaps unknown for many centuries, Teresa's penetrating socio-critical analysis of the self-deception of religion resonates again. Her prescription for 'spiritual freedom' is as much freedom from self deception as any external pressure to conform or renounce any particular religious life style. Religion for Teresa, in these perceptive passages in the *Book of the Life*, is a question of changing a state of life and point of view as much (or in fact more) than following a particular guide book or set of rules. Her religion is inspired by the fresh wind that blows from the top of Carmel, not the foetid smell of the convent-prison of those who deceive themselves as to their righteousness against the wickedness of the world.

A New Dawn

As Teresa prayed and thought through the implications for her view of religious life as described in the *The Book of the Life*[14] it seems that the breeze from Mount Carmel, the stir of *nostalgie* from the Holy Mountain, filled her nostrils. Like others of the order such as the future John of the Cross, she briefly contemplated (V: 31.13) leaving the *Encarnación* for another Carmel or order but ultimately she felt that the more recollected life she desired, emulating her ideals Francisco de Osuna and Pedro de Alcántara (1499–1562),[15] could be found by reforming the Carmel and order within which she found herself.[16] This reformed Carmelite life, like all the other reforms of the Order we have discussed in this chapter, would take her back to what she conceived as the original inspiration and desires of the early denizens of the Holy Mountain.

As time went on she began to articulate the malaise as being the fact that the Rule was not kept in its 'primal rigour' / '*su primer rigor*' (F: 2.3). At this time it seems that Teresa was at the centre of a group who gathered at the *Encarnación* to discuss these notions of living a simpler religious life. According to Ribera (1908: 153) these were largely friends and relatives of Teresa including Beatriz de Jésus (Cepeda y Ocampo, d. 1607), Leonor de Cepeda (d. 1572), María de Cepeda (d. 1614), Isabel de San Pablo (Cepeda y Ocampo, d. 1582), Inés de Jésus (Tapia, d. 1601), Ana de la Encarnación (Tapia, d. 1601), Juana

---

[14] We shall explore the *The Book of the Life* in more depth in the next chapter as a spiritual document of 'saying and showing'. For now we shall concentrate on the historical circumstances of Teresa's life and reform before we return shortly to the *Vida* as a spiritual document in its own right.

[15] Famously described by Teresa as 'appearing to be made of nothing but tree roots' (V: 27.18), this austere Franciscan friar was one of the initiators of the 'Discalced' reform of the Franciscan Order in Spain which was to prove so influential on Teresa's own 'Discalced' reform. An austere figure, he had total confidence in Teresa and her project and it was largely through his influence that the Bishop of Avila felt able to take her reform under his wing. He died shortly after the reform commenced but, Teresa tells us in the *Life*, he returned to her several times after his death 'in his glorious body' to counsel her as to the direction the reform should take (V: 36.20).

[16] Various suggestions have been given for the convent Teresa wanted to join. Federico de San Antonio in his *Vitta della Santa Madre Teresa di Gesú* (Book 1, Chapter 22) suggests a convent in Flanders or Brittany. Other possible destinations suggested include Valencia and Nantes (see Allison Peers CW 1.209).

Suárez and María Bautista (Cepeda y Ocampo, d. 1603). Most of this small nucleus of Teresa's followers would form the prioresses and sub-prioresses of the future reform houses. Interestingly, many too were also descendents of the Cepeda brothers we discussed in the last chapter who were reconciled with the Inquisition in Toledo.[17] According to María de San José it was María Bautista who first suggested in conversation that the group should form a group of 'shoeless' – *Descalza* – sisters modelled on those founded in Madrid from the inspiration of Pedro de Alcántara:

> One day the Saint together with María de Ocampo and other nuns from the *Encarnación* began to discuss the saints of the desert. At this time some of them said that since they couldn't go to the desert, they should found a little monastery with few nuns and that there they could join together to do penance. And the said Madre Teresa de Jésus said that they might resolve to reform themselves and keep the primitive Rule (*la Regla primitiva*).
>
> (Alvarez OC: 305)

According to this account the sisters were then joined by the wealthy Avilan widow and lay collaborator of Teresa, Doña Guiomar de Ulloa (b. c. 1527) who offered, as so many times in the past, to provide financial assistance for the project (V: 32.10). Thus was born Teresa's 'great project' of reform based on the lives of the 'holy fathers of old'. Yet, as we have already seen, the notion that arose among the sisters was based on a misapprehension. Teresa and her followers felt that she was returning to the original Carmelite Rule 'as it began' / *como se principió* (CE: 3.5). In fact, as we have seen, the 'mitigation' Teresa was referring to was the later one of 1432 enacted by Pope Eugene IV in *Romani Pontificis* in response to the efforts of Bl. John Soreth. She was therefore returning to Innocent IV's mitigated Rule of 1247 written, as we have seen, on the migration of the Carmelites from the Middle East to Europe (even though Teresa gives it the wrong date of 1248 in Chapter 36 of the *Life*).

The little house of St Joseph's – *San José* – was formally opened by Teresa in Avila on 24 August 1562. The timing is significant. As she writes in the *Life*: 'I experience (deep distress) because of the great number of souls who are bringing damnation upon themselves – especially of those Lutherans, for they

---

[17] For the full biographies of these sisters and their family relations see Allison Peers 1954.

were made members of the Church through baptism' (V: 32.6). As Calvinist influence grew in France and the ensuing persecution of the Huguenots developed, Spain had seen, as we have seen, the imposition of the Valdés Index in 1559 and the consequent arrest on suspicion of heresy of leading Spanish clergy including Bartolomé Carranza, the Archbishop of Toledo. King Philip himself had asked the religious, in words not unlike Teresa's above, to be careful to live up to their calling in order not to bring the church into disrepute. Teresa's little group of nuns who founded *San José* were all part of what Bilinkoff calls the 'reform party' of Avila: Antonia del Espíritu Santo (Heñao, b. 1535), recommended by Pedro de Alcántara; Ursula de los Santos (Revilla, 1521-74), recommended by Teresa's confessor Gaspar Daza; María de la Cruz (de la Paz, d. 1588), a former servant of Doña Guiomar de Ulloa and María de San José (de Ávila, b. 1525), sister of Julián de Ávila. With Teresa came two other sisters from the *Encarnación* and members of the 'spiritual conversation' on the Rule two years earlier: Inés de Jésus (Tapia) and Ana de la Encarnación (Tapia), both of whom were her cousins.

In following what she saw as the ideals of the first desert Carmelites, Teresa had insisted that the house be founded with no endowment and in complete poverty (only Antonia del Espíritu Santo brought some money as 'dowry'). Although very much in accord with the 'primitive' Carmelite ideal it meant that the foundation was immediately resisted by the elders and municipal officials of the city (see Bilinkoff 1989: 137). The presenting legal issues such as the problems the house caused with the public water supply (obstructing the melting of snow and a public fountain) were probably, most commentators agree, excuses for the threat of having to provide for another convent in a city already overflowing with religious of all kinds. Despite initial enthusiasm from the Carmelite Provincial, Ángel de Salazar (c. 1519-1600), he later withdrew his consent so the foundation had to be made in secret. Teresa's Jesuit confessor Baltasar Álvarez wavered but eventually supported her.

It was at this point that her good friend Doña Guiomar de Ulloa and the Dominican Pedro Ibáñez wrote directly to Rome for permission to found the convent. This crucial document arrived in Avila in July 1562 just before the foundation of *San José*. Addressed to Doña Guiomar and her mother Doña Aldonza de Guzmán, it gave them permission to found the monastery under the jurisdiction of the Bishop of Avila, at this time Alvaro de Mendoza (d.1586), a fervent supporter of the reform who would eventually be buried in San José (see Efrén 1996: 161–5).

Although Teresa's Prioress at the *Encarnación*, Doña Maria Cimbron, was persuaded by Teresa as to the good intentions of the convent, the Castilian Carmelite provincial Ángel de Salazar initially rebuked her but he too was eventually persuaded by Teresa to support the foundation (V: 36.12).

Thus, when Rossi finally arrived in Avila, Teresa was understandably nervous. On the one hand she suspected that Rossi, like herself, recognized the need for Carmelite reform that would restore the original fervour of the eremetical-cenobitical life while not destroying the unique charism and spirit of Carmel established over nearly 500 years. However, as she tells us in the *Book of the Foundations* (F: 2.1) she realized that her house was in a canonical grey area and in theory the General could have ordered her to return to the *Encarnación*.

Unsurprisingly, from what we have seen above of his character and mission, he was on the contrary delighted with what Teresa had achieved. After his experiences in the rest of Spain it must, after all, have come as something of a pleasant surprise:

> He was delighted to see our manner of life and with it a picture – no matter how imperfect – of the beginnings of our Order, and how the primitive rule was observed in all its rigour, for in the whole of the Order it wasn't observed – only in mitigation.
>
> (F 2.3)[18]

The result of the visitation was perhaps greater than Teresa could have hoped for. He granted her extensive patent letters 'so that more monasteries could be founded along with censures to prevent any provincial from restraining me' (F: 2.3).[19] The first letter allowed the foundation of new houses of no more than 25 nuns each under the jurisdiction of the order while the second limited the foundations to New and Old Castile. This latter stipulation, as we shall see, would later cause Teresa many problems as the order spread throughout Spain and she encountered her 'difficult' Andalusians. The nuns would follow the 'first rule' of the original Carmel and would wear coarse habits of grey *xerga*. Later, as

---

[18] Contrary to Teresa's statement there were in fact at least two communities observing the 'Primitive Rule' at the time: in Monte Oliveto in Genova, Italy and Onda near Castellón de Plana. Julián de Ávila suggests that Rossi was unhappy with Bishop Mendoza's jurisdiction over *San José*, however he seems to be the only source that suggests Rossi criticized Teresa on this point.

[19] The patent letters (27 April and 16 May 1567) can be found reproduced in the *Monumenta Historica Carmeli Teresiani*, ed. Institutum Historicum Teresianum (Rome: Teresianum 1973–present) 1: 67–71. Hereafter MHCT.

she tells us in the *Foundations*, Rossi would write to her urging her to found as many convents as there were 'hairs on her head' (F: 27.20). The final act of Rossi before he left Spain was to give a letter patent for the foundation of two priories of Discalced friars (given at Barcelona in August 1567).[20]

Thus, with the letters patent of Rossi, the story of the Order comes full circle. From the vastnesses of Carmel to the move to Europe and its various mitigations, Teresa's 'little doves' once again wished to breath the fresh air of the desert as she built her little 'nests' where her doves could experience the 'spiritual freedom' she had striven for in her own life. It is my argument in this book that this project of 'spiritual freedom' lay at the heart of Teresa's life and work and it is to her formulation of a unique 'Language of Spirit' in her struggle to articulate this aim in her writings that we shall turn to in Part Two of this book, beginning with an examination of the *Book of the Life*.

---

[20] For more on the history of the male reform see my *John of the Cross* 2010, Chapter 1.

PART TWO

The Writings

4

'The Language of Spirit': The Book of the Life

Approaching *The Life*

> So then, when I say 'they shouldn't rise unless God raises them', it is the language of spirit; those who have had this experience will understand me, for I don't know how to say it here nor how it will be understood.
>
> (V: 12.5)[1]

The strange babbling of Teresa's *Book of the Life* will be familiar to anyone who has ever attempted to articulate the action of spirit in their lives. As we have seen, the book, her first major writing, arises from particular social and ecclesiological pressures, not least the need to justify her actions as a reformer and also as someone who was clearly moving into the suspect territories of *alumbradismo, recogimiento* and *dejamiento*. As we listen to her voice we must also remind ourselves that this is the voice of a woman of *converso* origins – with its own particular resonance and timbre.

She tells us in the preface to the book that it was written in response to requests from her confessors, in particular the Dominican García de Toledo. However, as she gets into her stride we hear the 'tumbling, half formed' sentences of someone trying to articulate what is frankly unsayable. In this respect the closest I can find to her style is the half-opened/half-closed writing of the Austrian philosopher Ludwig Wittgenstein (1889–1951) who 'shows' in his writing by 'not saying' and 'says' by 'not showing'.[2] Thus, in Teresa's *Life*, in passages such as that above, we hear a strange choreography of saying and not-saying as she comes close to the boundary of what is and isn't expressible.

---

[1] *Pues lo que digo 'no se suban sin que Dios los suba,' es lenguaje de espíritu; entenderme ha quien tuviere alguna esperiencia, que yo no lo sé de decir si por aquí no se entiende.*

[2] See *The Return to the Mystical* (Tyler 2011).

At such moments (and there are several in this important work) the whole structure of her grammar and language begins to break down – for here we find ourselves on the very boundaries of language itself.[3]

Therefore, as we approach the *Book of the Life*, especially in English translation, we must do so knowing that, as much as the later *Interior Castle*, we are entering a multi-dimensional language-world within which we must be prepared to be challenged and our perceptions re-aligned. Her task in writing the *Life*, I would suggest, is not so much as an *Apología de sua Vida* (although this was clearly what motivated its origins) as the desire to change the point of view, or indeed, perspective, of her reader. With the advent of modernism the desire has always been to concretize or 'pin down' Teresa's gossamer-light prose so that it fits into the dominating categories of whichever interpreter she happens to find herself in the hands of – whether they be psychological, sociological or literary. Such brutal concretization will always, I suggest, end in failure, as her gentle contradictions reflect the spiritual life – forever just beyond categorization. Teresa's realm is the realm of 'spiritual freedom' – as vital today as it was 500 years ago.

La Teresa Inglesa

Part of the problem with understanding Teresa for English-speaking readers lies in the difficulty of translating such a delicate web of prose. We have already heard in Chapter 1 the groans of her twentieth century translators – Kieran Kavanaugh and Edgar Allison Peers. As we heard, these two experts spent most of their lives working on their translations of Teresa and even they felt that they had somehow failed to capture something of the living essence of her work, so easily detectable to her Spanish-speaking readers. This is nothing new. Unlike her compatriot John of the Cross, Teresa's reception in English was relatively rapid and welcoming.[4] The first translation in English appears in 1611, over a decade before her official canonization by Pope Gregory XV in 1622. It bears

---

[3] *Alles Vergängliche ist nur ein Gleichnis; das Unzulängliche, hier wird's Ereignis; das Unbeschreibliche, hier ist es getan; das Ewigweibliche zieht uns hinan/* 'Everything passing is only an image; the unattainable is here achieved; the undescribable is here done; the eternal-feminine draws us above.' Goethe *Faust* Part Two, concluding chorus. For Kristeva (2008) this will be the unspeakable semiotic breaking into the symbolic web of language, see also Kristeva (1984).

[4] For the reception of John in English see my *John of the Cross* (Tyler 2010).

the title: *The Lyf of the mother Teresa of Iesus, foundresse of the monasteries of the discalced or bare-footed Carmelite nunnes and fryers, of the first rule. Written by herself, at the commmaundement of her ghostly father by W.M. of the Society of Jesus.* Although this translation by the Jesuit William Malone (1586–1656) was the first to appear, the translation itself suffers from many defects.[5] Her next translator, Sir Tobias or Tobie Matthew or Mathews (1577–1655), produced his translation the year after Teresa's canonization in 1623 where he criticized William Malone in that 'he had lost a little of the puritie of his English Toung and on the other, not to have acquired enough of the Spanish' (Matthew 1623: Preface). But, concedes Matthew, 'such a book, as was so sublimely conceived, by such a Hart, and so vehemently posted-out, by such a Penn, could never be exactly translated' (Matthew 1623: Preface). Whereas Malone's translation seems somewhat hurried, and perhaps appearing to come from a French translation of Teresa rather than the Spanish original, Matthew's work is of a different order.[6] He recognizes the problems and difficulties in encountering her style, exactly in the fashion of his twentieth century successors Kavanaugh and Allison Peers. For Matthew this is partly because of the perennial complaint of her use of elliptical sentences and colloquialisms:

> Through her forbearing to use those Particles, in the begining of the said Sentences; as namelie, For, But, Yet, Therefore and the like ... without which it is not alwayes so easie to discerne, whether the Discourse be either continued, or interrupted or ended.
>
> (Matthew 1623: Preface)

And partly because of the subject matter of her writings:

> The strangeness of her experiences but so also are there infinit other Particulars, the Ecclesiasticall Historie, concerning other Saints, which, howsoever they seem, are strange yea and much more strange than these, yet are they generally, and most iustly admitted, to the degree of Morall belief.
>
> (Matthew 1623: Preface)

---

[5] Malone himself was a Jesuit and Catholic apologist, born in Dublin in 1586. Studying in Rome and Portugal he returned to Ireland as part of the Irish Jesuit mission where he engaged in lively polemics with the Protestant ascendancy. He died in Seville, where he had been made Superior, in 1656, having been expelled from Ireland (see Cunningham 2004).

[6] The full title of Matthew's translation is: *The Flaming Hart, or, the life of the gloriovs S. Teresa foundresse of the reformation of the order of the all-immaculate Virgin-Mother, our B. Lady, of Mount Carmel.*

Sir Tobie himself could not have better placed to undergo the work of producing one of the first definitive translations of Teresa's *Life* into English. The eldest son of Tobie Matthew, Dean of Christchurch, Oxford (who would later become the Archbishop of York), he was born in Salisbury in 1577. With all the privilege due to his rank he entered parliament 'when very young' in 1601 as MP for Newport in Cornwall in the last Elizabethan parliament. However in 1605 we have reports of him visiting The Hague, France, and later Italy.[7] It is here, in Florence, that he was received into the Catholic Church by the Jesuit Lelio Ptolomei in 1607, for which he was imprisoned in the Fleet Prison in London for six months on his return to England. He was then exiled from England for nine years which he spent on mainland Europe, including an extensive period in Spain whither he travelled in 1609. At this time he would no doubt have met people still alive who knew Teresa and would certainly have first read her works in Spanish. In 1617 we find him back in England where he engaged in controversial Catholic apology which led to his exile again in 1619. However this second period of exile in the Low Countries led to his translation of Teresa's *Life* in 1623 as well as other works such as the first full English translation of Augustine's *Confessions*.[8] In 1621 we find him back in England where King James I was persuaded of his value for diplomatic negotiations with Catholic Europe, including a mission to Madrid in 1623 to help arrange the marriage of the future Charles I to the Infanta of Spain. For this service he was knighted in 1623, the year of the publication of his translation of *The Life*. The years leading to the Civil War were not kind to him and, with the Protestant ascendancy, he was inevitably forced to leave England for a third time in 1641 on threat of imprisonment. He ended his days in Ghent where he died in the companionship of the Jesuits on 13 October 1655. Of all the pre-twentieth century translations of Teresa, Sir Tobie's is the most interesting and I will draw on some of the stylistic points he makes in the rest of this book.

Before we turn to that, however, mention must be made of the three other pre-twentieth century English translations of Teresa. The late seventeenth century Restoration period saw the publication of Abraham Woodhead's

---

[7] Most of this account is from Dalton (1851), Loomie (2004) and from Sir Tobie's own biographical writing, especially the 'True Historical Relation' (1904).

[8] Loomie in the DNB suggests that the translation of the *Life* appeared in 1642 in Antwerp. This was the second revised edition, the first having appeared in London in 1623. Matthew no doubt worked on the text in the ensuing years, including some considerable time in Spain.

(1609–1678) translation in 1671: *The Life of the Holy Mother St Teresa, Foundress of the Reformation of the Discalceate Carmelites, according to the Primitive Rule.* This would quickly supersede Matthew's work and run into several eighteenth century editions (not least because Woodhead translated other key works such as *The Interior Castle* and *The Way of Perfection*). Woodhead was the first author to translate all of Teresa's works then available beginning with *The Life* and *The Foundations*. More distant from the origins of the text than Matthew, Woodhead presents a text that is more akin to those we are used to seeing today, however he still retains some 'Matthewisms' as we shall see shortly.

John Dalton's (c. 1814–74) *Life of Saint Teresa written by herself and Translated from the Spanish* appeared just after the restoration of the English and Welsh Catholic Hierarchy in 1851 and is dedicated to 'Nicholas, Cardinal of the Most Holy Roman Church, Archbishop of Westminster etc.' As well as being a Catholic priest, largely for the Diocese of Northampton, he also spent time at the English St Alban's College in Valladolid where he would no doubt have encountered Teresa's works and visited her foundations. As well as his work on translating Teresa he was one of the first English writers to present John of the Cross's work in translation. Today his translation is probably chiefly known through its influence on George Eliot who references it in the Preface to her *Middlemarch*.

The final translation to mention is David Lewis' (1814–95) *The Life of Teresa of Avila by Herself*, published in 1870. With its preface by Zimmerman added in 1904 (who himself would have a leading role in propagating Teresa's work through the 'translations by the nuns of Stanbrook') this would be the definite version of Teresa's works before Allison Peers' emerged in the 1930s based on the more up-to-date and critically refined Spanish edition of P. Silverio de Santa Teresa.

In the account that follows of *The Life* I shall draw on all of these translations to clarify my own stylistic approach to Teresa's work.

Teresa's Language

Gustos, gozos, regalos, deleites and *sabors* pepper Teresa's works and especially the *Life*. On the one hand, as Allison Peers argues (Peers 1944: xxi), they can be seen as manifestations of her 'rough hewn style' ('*grosería*' V: 6.4), the homely style of ascetics and hermits that we analysed in Chapter 1. That is, a desire to avoid the hifalutin terms of a spiritual elite (the *letrados*) for more simple homely words which her audience will respond to. The words themselves are ambiguous and Teresa's use of them opens up a whole new 'epistemology of delight' for her exploration of the supernatural and mystical. In her use of the erotic and spiritual, the blending of *eros* and *agape*, the human and divine, the key style and tone, as we may have become accustomed to by now, is *ambiguity*. Before we analyse her use of the terms in the *Life* it is useful to review them.

Gusto is a favourite word of Teresa's. Despite attempts to 'tidy up' her prose both Allison Peers and Kavanaugh and Rodriguez convey something of the ambiguity in their translations. In all the word appears one hundred and eighty-five times in her works: fifty-two in the *The Life*, twenty in the *Book of Foundations,* nineteen and twenty-two in the *Way of Perfection* – Valladolid and Escorial codices respectively, thirty-two in the *Interior Castle* and thirty-three in the *Meditations on the Song of Songs.*

Kavanaugh's favourite word to translate *gusto* is 'delight' (V: 8.8/9, 9.9, 11.13, 15.4 *et passim*) however at other times he chooses 'enjoyment' (V: 14.5), 'favour' (V: 8.5), 'spiritual delight' (V: 30.1), 'joy' (V: 30.1), 'consolation' (V: 11.12, 16.1, 23.17) and 'spiritual consolation' (V: 12.4). Allison Peers, on the other hand, preferences 'consolation' (V: 11.12/13, 8.5/8/9, 9.9, 23.17 *et passim*) while occasionally preferring 'pleasure' (V: 15.4, 16.1, 25.11), 'delight' (V: 14.2) and 'taste' (V: 11.11). John Michael Cohen (1903–89) in his 1957 translation largely follows Allison Peers in preferencing 'consolation' and 'delight' however he occasionally gives us 'taste pleasures' (V: 12.4, 25.11) and 'savour' (V: 14.2). The obvious sensual ambiguity of the Spanish *gusto* is somewhat weakened by some of these translations. The ambiguity in the use of the word in the Spanish original is something even her Spanish editors have to explain. Thus Tomás Alvarez in his notes to one of its first appearances in Chapter 11 of the *Life* emphasizes that we must understand that the saint is using it 'en acepción mística' – 'in its mystical sense' (Alvarez OC: 90). This, I would suggest, is really a back reading of nineteenth century categories on to a sixteenth century author.[9] The term '*mística teología*'/'mystical theology' is one, we shall see, that Teresa was never really comfortable with and after using it a few times at the beginning of the *Life* drops it never to use it again in her works (not even the highly 'mystical' *Interior Castle* – see Chapter 6 below). From a study of her

---

[9] For more on my reasons for making this claim see *The Return to the Mystical* (Tyler 2011).

style I would suggest this is a deliberate action on her part. She has no desire to bamboozle her readers with 'hifalutin' spiritual terms – something her academic commentators and editors may have occasionally slipped into in the five hundred years since her death.

In fact, *gusto* makes its first appearance in *The Life* (and in the whole of Teresa's writings) in Chapter 3 where Teresa contrasts her new (enforced) life in the Augustinian convent of *Santa María de Gracia* with her previous life of sensuality: 'I looked more to the *gusto* of sensuality and vanity than to what was good for my soul' (V: 3.2).[10] Thus at its earliest appearance *gusto* is associated with the dubious sensual pleasures she has described in the previous two chapters:

> I began to dress in finery and to desire to please and look pretty, taking great care of my hands and hair and about perfumes and all empty things in which one can indulge, and which were many, for I was very vain.
>
> (V: 2.2)

This struggle between the 'things of God' and the '*contentos y gustos y pasatiempos sensuales*' (V: 7.17) continues throughout the early stages of the young girl's journey to discover herself. Teresa herself was clearly a lady of some sensuality and she found in prayer a difficulty to reconcile the two 'so inimical to each other'. At this stage in the *Life*, and in her writing about these experiences, Teresa contrasts the *gustos* and *contentos* with the *mercedes*, the greater 'favours' that the Lord will give her in prayer (V: 7.17). Yet already by Chapter 8 she talks of the *gustos* 'bestowed by God'; one of her first uses of the term as a description of that which occurs in prayer rather than that which is connected purely with the sensual appetites. Of these *gustos* ('delights' [Kavanaugh and Rodriguez V: 8.9], 'consolations' [Allison Peers V: 8]), as she now begins to call them, she will tell us more later. But she makes clear, and this will be a constant theme throughout her writing, one of the purposes of prayer is *gusto* – delight, sensuality, sensuousness – and 'The Lord' will indeed 'take delight' (*regalarla*) by entering the soul. This new description of prayer in terms of sensuality and delight climaxes towards the end of *The Life* in passages such as the famous description of the soul caressed by the Golden Cherub in V: 29.13.

---

[10] *Mirava más el gusto de mi sensualidad y vanidad quo lo bien que me estava a mi alma.*

It is no surprise, then, that her editors and translators have had such problems with this term. Of her early translators, Matthew turns to an original and perhaps surprising solution which at a stroke solves the problem of the word. He preferences the word 'gust' for *gusto* and is reasonably consistent in this translation (unlike most of her other translators, including Allison Peers and Kavanaugh who switch translations many times). Thus we get in Matthew 'gusts' (V: 8.5, 8.9), 'hours of gust' (V: 11.11), 'spiritual gusts' (V: 11.13), and 'he gives them so much gust' (V: 8.8). Here is a typical example:

> With one of these howers of gust of himself, which he hath given me heer, afterwards I esteem all those sad afflictions to have been very well rewarded.
>
> (V: 11.11)

The word may seem odd and a little surprising but when we look at its sixteenth century Oxford English Dictionary definitions it is perhaps not so surprising:

> 'gust' (from Latin *gustus*) = 1. The sense or faculty of taste 2. Individual taste or liking 3. Aesthetic or artistic taste 4. Keen relish, appreciation or enjoyment 5. Pleasing taste or gratifying flavour, relish.
>   'gust' (from the Old Norse *gust-r*) = 1. A sudden violent rush or blast of wind (windstorm, whirlwind) 2. A burst, outbreak, outburst.
>
> (OED)

This combination of taste, relish, suddenness and force seems peculiarly apt to what Teresa is trying to describe in her map of the spiritual life.

Although surprising and disconcerting at times, Matthew's work does return some of the earthiness to this key Teresian term that the rather insipid 'consolation' or 'delight' lose. That is, in Teresa's words, the understanding of *gusto* as '*una recreación suave, fuerte, impresa, deleitosa, quita*' / 'a sweet, strong, well-imprinted, quiet, delightfull kind of pleasure and joy' (V: 25.11, Matthew's translation). As I feel *gusto* is ill-served by most of its English translations, and that Matthew's 'gust' is probably now too removed from our ordinary everyday usage to warrant its use, I will continue to leave it untranslated when discussing Teresa's work.

Teresa's ambiguous use of *gusto* is often accompanied by *regalo*. Of the two terms it is perhaps the more ambiguous. Allison Peers translates it as 'joy' (V: 15.4, 24.1), 'favour' (V: 8.5, 9.9, 11.14, 10.2), 'happiness' (V: 8.7, 27.2), 'delight'

(V: 8.9, 14.10, 13.22), 'pleasure' (V: 10.2) and 'grace' (V: 24.1, 24.3) whereas Kavanaugh prefers 'mercy' (V: 8.5), 'delight' (V: 8.7, 30.11, 13.22, 15.4, thus confusing it with his translation of *gusto*), 'favor' (V: 8.9, 25.3, 27.2, 9.9, 10.2), 'comfort' (V: 10.2), 'gift' (V: 24.1, 7.19, 24.3, 11.14) and 'joy' (V: 14.10).[11] But of her recent translators Allison Peers comes nearest to acknowledging the ambiguous difficulty of the word:

> The real meaning of this ubiquitous word here is 'show signs of affection for'; and 'pet', 'caress', 'fondle' though hardly seemly in the context, would not, as far as the actual sense is concerned, be too strong.
>
> (Peers CW: 3:27)

In this instance Peers was reflecting upon this passage from the *Book of Foundations*:

> I would like to know how to explain myself here and it is so difficult that I do not know if I shall be able to do so … I am quite sure, however that souls who are deceived in this way will understand if only they will believe me. I know some, souls of great virtue, who have been in such a state for seven or eight hours and everything appeared to them to be rapture (*arrobamiento*), and every virtuous exercise affected them in such a way that they immediately relinquished control of themselves, because they thought that it was not right to resist the Lord; and little by little they might die or become fools if a remedy is not procured. What I understand to be the case here is that when the Lord begins to caress (*regalar*) the soul, our nature, being so fond of pleasure/delight (*deleite*), abandons itself completely to this pleasure (*gusto*) such that it would not move, or lose what it has gained, for anything in the world. For, in truth, it is much more pleasurable than anything of the world.
>
> (F: 6.2)

Peers is not the only one to feel unease with her sensual and ambiguous language here, a strategy that she will employ in those other two mature works, the *Interior Castle* and the *Meditations on the Song of Songs*. Further on in this passage Teresa describes how love will cause the novice 'sense pleasure' (*gusto en el sentido*). Jerónimo Gracián, one of the first of her reader-editors,

---

[11] Cohen, again, largely follows Allison Peers with *gift, joy, delight, favour* and *comfort*.

substituted this with *sensible en el sentido* which perhaps is less ambiguously sensual than *gusto en el sentido*. However, her later editor Domingo Báñez restored the original. Such problems arise throughout her manuscripts and suggest the difficulties her first readers had with her sensual language (see Peers 1944: 27, De la Madre de Dios and Steggink 1997: 693–5). Even Alvarez warns us in his notes to the *Life* that, as with *gusto*, *regalo* should be understood in '*la acepción de gracias místicas*' / 'in the sense of "mystical graces"' (Alvarez OC: 90). Despite, or perhaps because of this, this ambiguous *regalo* remains one of her favourite words for describing things of God and occurs frequently in her works, starting with the *Life*.

As with *gusto*, her early translators did not share some of the squeamishness of their later successors. Even Dalton in 1851 is happy to go with 'caress' for *regalo* in Chapter 8 of the *Life* (Allison Peers has 'consolation' and Kavanaugh 'favor'). Matthew, unsurprisingly, comes up with his own unique solution (remember, that of all Teresa's English translators he was probably the closest to the *Madre's* daughters and her late sixteenth century Spanish usage). He prefers *regale*, or even at times leaving it simply as *regalo*.[12] Which suggests to me that he too recognized that *La Santa* was using this word in a unique fashion that would be spoilt by weaker English terms such as 'favor' or 'grace'. Once again his translation comes nearest, I would suggest, to the pungent savour of Teresa's original. For example, when Teresa describes her first encounter with Osuna's *Third Spiritual Alphabet*, Matthew translates the passage as: 'Our Lord began to regale me so much'[13] (V: 4.7, Allison Peers: 'the Lord began to be gracious to me,' Kavanaugh 'the Lord began to favor me,' see also V: 7.19, 8.5, 9.9, 11.14). The appropriateness of the translation is reinforced by Woodhead who keeps it in 1671, e.g. 'If in these reflections, the party be possessed and seized with any love of God, the Soul is all regaled' (V: 10). The fact that these seventeenth century translators keep a particular translation of *regalar* and *regalo* that seems closer to the original medieval Spanish 'flatter or pamper' seems to bear out Allison Peers' intuition that the word has a stronger flavour than 'console' or 'favor'.

Teresa's savoury and pungent language of the spirit recurs in other key terms in her vocabulary. Like *regalos* and *gustos*, *deleites*, *gozos* and *sabor* again occur with abundance throughout her works. *Deleites* appears one hundred and eight

---

[12] OED 'Regale' = 'To please or delight with some agreeable event or activity. An entertainment, a festivity; later, a sumptuous meal, a banquet, a feast. From Spanish *regalar* – to spoil, to pamper.'

[13] *Comenzó el Señor a regalarme tanto por este camino.*

times, almost as many as *gustos,* and *gozos* eighty-two times. Together with *sabor* Teresa frequently uses them to convey the right mixture of the sensual and spiritual that she hopes to achieve. By these means, I would suggest, she is able to initiate the necessary *transformation of affect* so central to her 'mystical strategy'.

Deleite (Kavanaugh 'delight', Allison Peers 'delight'), as we have seen, is the word she always associates with her favourite passage from Proverbs: 'I delighted to be with the sons of men' and it occurs with regular occurrence throughout her work (see V: 14.10).

Gozo (Kavanaugh and Allison Peers 'joy' but also 'delight' [Kavanaugh V: 12.1] and 'contentment', [Allison Peers V: 14.2]) is likewise employed frequently by Teresa to convey the necessary reaction that the Lord's presence evokes in us and will often come beside the weaker *Mercedes* ('favours/favors', Allison Peers, Kavanaugh and Matthew e.g. V: 7.19, 9.9), *Consuelos* ('consolation' or 'spiritual consolation' Allison Peers and Kavanaugh) and *Consolaciones* ('spiritual comforts' Allison Peers). See, for example, V: 11.6: 'in the other degrees of prayer, the most important thing is enjoyment.'[14]

Finally, presumably following her 'master' Osuna in his descriptions of prayer as the 'tasty knowledge' / '*sabrosa saber*' (see Chapter 2 above), Teresa is fond of *Sabor* and *Sabrosa* to spice up her tasty prayer dishes:

> The sorrow and teares which grow from thence is a very savourie, and delightfull kind of thing ... (it) moves us to ioy, which is neither wholly Spirituall, nor wholly Sensuall, but this is a vertuous kind of ioy
>
> (V: 12.1, Matthew)[15]

Also, see V: 29.8 where we experience '*un muerte tan saborosa*' / 'a sauvorie kind of death' (Matthew, 'delightful' Kavanaugh, 'delectable' Allison Peers, Cohen) and V: 25.17 'How delicately, and how smoothly, yeah and how savourily also, dost thou know how to treat such Soules' (Matthew) / '*¡Qué delicada y pulida y sabrosamente los sabéis tartar!*' (*sabrosamente*: Kavanaugh 'delightfully', Allison Peers 'delectably', Cohen 'sweetly')

---

14 *Que en los otros grados de oración lo más es gozar.*
15 '*Muévenos a compassion, y es sabrosa esta pena y las lágrimas que proceden de aquí ... muévenos a gozo, que ni es del todo espiritual, ni sensual, sino gozo virtuoso y la pena muy meritoria.*' Kavanaugh omits 'sabrosa', Allison Peers gives 'sweet', 'sweet' is also used by Dalton and Lewis.

Whether we feel *sabrosa* should be delightful, sweet or savoury, there is no doubt that the translator's job should be to preserve the surprising, homely and often frankly down-to-earth pull of Teresa's language. Although some of my translations that follow may not feel so polished I hope that they will convey some of the raw pungent quality of Teresa's original prose, a quality I feel has faded a little over the 500 years of exposure to the hard light of critical and academic scrutiny. Teresa's 'language of the spirit' does indeed occupy a unique space: neither wholly spiritual nor wholly sensual its very ambiguity invites us into a liminal space where we must drop all pretence and subservience to the ego. Teresa's vocabulary, I would suggest, creates a deliberate aura of studied imprecision as it challenges our most fundamental understandings of our Self and our relationship to the Divine – notions we shall return to later in this book.

Teresa's Map of the Soul

Having assembled the tools by which Teresa performs her difficult task in the *Life* we now turn to that spiritual narrative itself. Teresa's discourse on the 'language of spirit' is concentrated into the twelve extra chapters she added to the original manuscript once García de Toledo had seen it and asked for more explanation of her experiences of prayer.[16] The resulting Chapters 11 to 22 inclusive form a distinct 'treatise within a treatise' presenting Teresa's view of the nature of prayer in a surprisingly masterful fashion. The over-arching narrative structure is her justly celebrated analogy of the 'four waters'. However, as we would expect by now, Teresa never sticks smoothly to the narrative but employs all the *gustos, regalos, deleites* and *gozos* at her disposal to present her savoury picture of the growth of the soul in God's hands. She begins her treatise in customary fashion:

> So then, let us speak now about those who are beginning to be servants of love (for this doesn't appear to me to be anything other than following the path of the one who loved us so much), when I think of this I am strangely caressed by a great dignity (*que*

---

[16] The original draft of the *Life* is lost.

me regalo estrañamente), for servile fear vanishes at once if at this first stage we proceed as we have to.

(V: 11.1)[17]

From the beginning she introduces us to her 'way of love' which is full of caresses, joys and delights:

> We are so miserly and slow in giving ourselves entirely to God that since His Majesty does not desire that we enjoy something as precious as this without paying a high price, we do not fully prepare ourselves.

(V: 11.1)

This path, of great dignity and freedom, is foremost one to be *enjoyed*. Without this joy in the 'path of love' we shall never be able to get started. This path, though, is as much a path of non-attachment as anything. First and foremost non-attachment to that old demon '*honra*' – honour and status – as she tells us in the second chapter of the *Life*. That poison that infected the whole Spanish society of her time and at whose hands her family had suffered so much. As with John of the Cross she believes that 'if one perseveres, God does not deny himself to anyone' (V: 11.4). Verging sometimes on the Pelagian, both of them are convinced that right effort in meditation and prayer will be met 'half way' by God who cannot resist entering the soul, as John says, like light streaming into a cloudless sky (see LF: 3.46). Perhaps this explains the appeal of Teresa and John in our own age of self-help manuals and self-improvement programmes. Neither can be described as quietist in any sense (even though both were, as we shall see, accused of variations of quietism). If anything there is an activist spirituality here which exhorts the individual to bestir oneself if we desire to let God enter our lives. Much as St Benedict urges us at the beginning of his *Rule* 'to run if we desire to see good days' so Teresa is offering us at the start of our journey 'good things'. But we too must work for them, they will not simply drop into our laps. However, in a careful balancing act, this path is pursued and

---

[17] *Pues hablando ahora de los que comienzan a ser siervos de el amor (que no me parece otra cosa determinarnos a seguir por este camino de oración al que tanto nos amó), es una dignidad tan grande, que me regalo estrañamente en pensar en ella; porgue el temor servil luego va fuera, si en este primer estado vamos como hemos de ir.*

initiated by the grace of God who plants in us the 'little spark' (*centilla*) of love which we must gently fan into the roaring flames of consummation (see V: 15).

Yet as the stirrings of love arise in one's heart, the intellect, or as she usually refers to it, the *pensamiento*, will also stir to suggest ways we should be wary of the spiritual path and resist its pull (V: 11.4): 'so many dangers and difficulties are put before (the seeker) that no little courage, but much, is needed if they are not to turn back, and much favour from God.' In her last work, *The Interior Castle*, she brilliantly describes such thoughts:

> We shall always be glancing around and saying: 'Are people looking at me or not?' 'If I take a certain path shall I come to any harm?' 'Dare I begin such and such a task?' 'Is it pride that is impelling me to do this?' 'Can anyone as wretched as I engage in so lofty an exercise as prayer?' 'Will people think better of me if I refrain from following the crowd?' 'For extremes are not good' they say, 'even in virtue; and I am such a sinner that if I were to fail I should only have farther to fall; perhaps I shall make no progress and in that case I shall only be doing good people harm; anyway, a person like myself has no need to make herself singular!'
>
> (M: 1.2.10)[18]

This, as we shall see later, is the 'monkey mind'[19] of the Buddhists – that which contemporary practices of mindfulness, for example, seek to bring into stability by means such as awareness exercises (see Chapter 8 below). From the very beginning of her writing career Teresa is aware of this internal conflict between stabilized awareness of 'the heart' and the need to work with distracting *pensamientos*. In this respect I am not persuaded, as some commentators are, that the *Life* is an inferior work or somehow a preparation for the *Interior Castle*. The *Castle* is, as we shall see, a brilliant work, but in many ways the *Life* is even more innovative and radical. At this stage Teresa had not put into place so many 'self-censoring' mechanisms which she later discovered were necessary if her work was to survive in the tough spiritual climate of late sixteenth century Spain.

At this stage, she emphasizes, the most important thing is not so much to worry about the 'work' being done in prayer, but 'the most important thing is

---

[18] I have used Allison Peers' translation here as he brings out perfectly Teresa's sense of an 'inner dialogue' which proceeds in the mind of one starting out on a path of prayer or contemplation.

[19] Or as Teresa calls it poetically in V: 15. 6 'the grinding mill of the intellect'– *moledor/entendimiento*. In the same passage she also refers to 'restless bees' that 'gad about' (Matthew's translation).

to enjoy it' / *lo más es gozar* (V: 11.5) while the Lord 'grants the increase'. The path of the saints, she believes, is impossible for us to follow, with all its trials and difficulties. However if we have what John of the Cross called the '*otra inflamación major*' – the greater enkindling flame of God – then we will be able to proceed on the path. This is the love we should feel and enjoy on these first faltering steps.

At this point she makes one of her handful of references to the 'mystical theology' / '*teulogía mística*' which we shall return to in a later chapter when we discuss her debt to this tradition.[20] Suffice it to say at this point that for Teresa this, as we would expect, will be no exposition of the 'mystical theology' in a medieval sense (such as we find in John of the Cross, the prize student of Salamanca University). But rather, she will introduce her own mystical theology by means of one of her most important pedagogical tools – the symbol. Again, we shall return to the use of symbology by Teresa at a later stage in the book. For now it is worth remembering the phrase from Hugh of St Victor: 'A symbol is a juxtaposition, that is a gathering together of visible forms in order to demonstrate invisible things' ('On the Celestial Hierarchy' iii in PL CLXXV 960D).

Having made her usual declamations of her own 'stupidity' *torpeza* (V: 11.6)[21] she launches immediately into her classic description of what has since become known as the 'Four Waters of Prayer':

> (The seeker) begins by having a plot in very infertile land (*un huerto en tierra muy infructuosa*) in which grow many weeds (*malas hierbas*) which will be for the delight (*deleite*) of the Lord. His Majesty digs up the weeds and plants good plants instead. Well then, let's imagine that this has already been done – that a soul has resolved to practise prayer and has already begun to do so and with the help of God we, like good gardeners, have to make these plants grow and make sure they are well watered and will not die, for from them will come flowers which shall send forth great fragrance to give refreshment to this Lord of ours so that He may often come into the garden to take His pleasure (*se deleite*) and delight himself (*holgarse*) among these virtues.
>
> (V: 11.6)

As with the start of *The Interior Castle*, Teresa presents her programme, or rather her theology of the self, at the beginning of her task. As with the book of

---

[20] Teresa alters the spelling of 'teología mística' with each reference. We shall return to this in Chapter 6.
[21] 'Since I have a bad memory I don't know where or for what reason it was used' (V: 11.6).

Genesis (which, as we shall see, she will make explicit reference to in the *Castle*) we begin our journey in a garden.[22] However, this is no garden of Eden – it will become so with God's help and our own efforts – but at this point it is the garden of the Fall – or rather – a patch of dead earth covered in weeds. Yet, by the resolution to begin prayer we have already received the favour of having the weeds cleared by the great gardener Himself. The 'good plants' of the spiritual life have been planted and now it is our job to cultivate them. Yet, the plants are not cultivated for their own sake but are there to produce the flowers (*flores*) which will give such pleasure to God who will take delight in them. As with the garden symbol, so the one of 'the flowers' as representations of the virtues, or as she often calls them, *las obras*, the 'good works', is a surprisingly consistent one for Teresa and one that she will return to in her later works – perhaps to most effect in the hybrid manuscript between *The Way of Perfection* and *The Interior Castle* – *The Meditations on the Song of Songs*.

In *The Meditations*: 7, written perhaps just two years before the *Interior Castle*, she comments on the 'flowers' mentioned in Chapter 2 of the Song of Songs with these words:

> I understand by these words that the soul is asking to perform great works (*grandes obras*) in the service of our Lord and of its neighbour. For this purpose it is happy to lose that delight and satisfaction (*deleite y contento*)… For in the active – and seemingly exterior – work the soul is working interiorly… So I say that much good is done by those who, after speaking with His Majesty for several years, when receiving His gifts and delights, want to serve in laborious ways even though these delights and consolations are thereby hindered. I say that the fragrance of these flowers and works produced and flowing from the tree of such fervent love lasts much longer.
>
> (C: 7.7)

For Teresa's spiritual search of love must always lead to the 'good works' and 'virtues' of selfless action in the world. The very same service which will be described in *The Way of Perfection* and *Book of Foundation* that we shall consider in the following chapter.

The structure of the rest of her treatise is provided by the conceit of the watering of the garden of the virtues by four methods:

---

[22] See also V: 14.9 where again explicit reference is made to the Lord walking through the gardens of paradise in Genesis 3.8.

It seems to me (*paréceme a mí*) that it can be watered in four ways: by taking the water from a well, which is a lot of work; or by a water wheel and aqueducts, when the water is drawn by a windlass (I have sometimes drawn it in this way; it is less laborious than the other and gives more water); or by a stream or a brook, which waters the ground much better, for it saturates it more thoroughly and there is less need to water it often, so that the gardener has less work to do; or by heavy rain, when the Lord waters it with no labour of ours, a way incomparably better than any of those which have been described.

(V: 11.7)

Again, this fundamental model of the spiritual life as one of decreasing effort on our behalf with a concomitant increase on God's behalf will remain her essential spiritual anthropology for the rest of her life. With minor modifications, it will survive up to her last work, the *Interior Castle*. As with John of the Cross' spiritual anthropology, it is a dynamic view of the self where as we seek God, so 'God is seeking us even more'. In John this had been almost a divine love-game of hide and seek where we 'go out unseen' 'seeking our Beloved'. For Teresa there are no love chases but rather something more solid, dare I say it, more practical. Her love chase is one that builds up a castle or a garden in which we will entice our Lord to enter with streams, flowers, rain and love. Once He is there we shall embark on John's 'fiestas of the Holy Spirit' with singing, dancing and games, however before that happens we must build up the arena with work, love and devotion. As with John, though, Teresa is at pains to use her whole battery of *gustos, regalos, gozos* and *deleites* to convey the experience of the 'whistling of love stirring breezes' that refresh these mansions of the soul. For, finally, her God is not a God of the intellect or *pensamientos* but an embodied God who will be 'tasted' through prayer (V: 11.11). Yet although the *gustos* and *deleites* are necessary for the beginning of the journey, Teresa stresses throughout that service and *obras* in the world are the goal of the journey:

Yes, for the love of God does not consist in having tears or in *gustos* or tenderness, which for the greater part we desire and find consolation in, but in serving with justice and fortitude of soul and humility. Without such service it seems to me we would be receiving everything and giving nothing.

(V: 11.14)

Thus, although the language of *gustos* and *deleites* will play a large part in the beginning of the Story of the Waters, as the self moves more into its God-self this language will feature less. Teresa will employ the terms less as she moves through the waters in her Treatise.

The Path of Spiritual Freedom: The Language of the Waters

The First Water

By employing an ambiguous language of sensuality and spirituality Teresa is deliberately encouraging her reader to leave any 'safe zone' to move into a highly precarious libidinal/spiritual space. This, as we have seen, is uncomfortable for many of her commentators who would rather spiritualize her ambiguity to a rarefied transcendence, or reduce her spiritual aspirations to simple physical, or indeed neurotic, struggles. What I am suggesting here, in line with the general thrust of my Teresian interpretation, is a middle way between these extremes which, I argue, comes closer to the pungent ambiguity of Teresa's prose. Teresa herself makes the same point in Chapter 12 of her exposition of the First Water:

> For in thinking about and carefully examining what the Lord suffered for us, we are moved to compassion, and the sorrow and tears that come from this are savoury, and in thinking about the glory we hope for, the love the Lord bore us, and His resurrection, we are moved to a joy that is neither wholly spiritual nor wholly sensual, but a virtuous type of joy and a meritorious pain.
>
> (V: 12.1)[23]

By following this way, says Teresa, that is by contemplating prayerfully upon the life, death and resurrection of Christ, we shall be led to an 'inflammation of love' (*enamorarse* V: 12.2) that proceeds from our contemplation of Christ's 'sacred humanity':

> This method of bringing Christ close to us is beneficial at all stages and is a very sure means of making much progress in the first degree of prayer, and arriving quickly at the second degree and, for the final degrees, of walking secure against the dangers the devil can present.
>
> (V: 12.3)

---

[23] '*Que ni es del todo espiritual, ni sensual, sino gozo virtuoso y la pena muy meritoria.*' Matthew gives: 'neither wholy Spirituall, nor wholy Sensuall; but this a vertuous kind of ioy.'

All the time, this engagement with the sacred humanity of Christ is one that will be bound up with the feeling of *gusto* (V: 12.4 Allison Peers 'consolation', Kavanaugh 'spiritual consolation', Cohen 'taste pleasure', Matthew 'gust'). Teresa emphasizes here that this is not a path based on thinking (*el pensamiento a pensar cosas altas* V: 12.4) and on the 'high things of God and heaven' but rather it is by means of the 'language of spirit' (V: 12.5 *lenguaje de espíritu*) with which we began this chapter. The strange, half-stuttering, Teresian language punctuated with *gustos, regalos* and *deleites*:

> Returning then to those who reason a lot (*los que discurren*),[24] I suggest that they don't spend all their time doing so, because although it is very meritorious, for it appears to them to be a very tasty prayer (*oración sabrosa*), they should have a kind of Sunday, when they do not work (to them it appears a waste of time, however I believe they will gain a great deal from this); as I have said, they should represent themselves before Christ and without tiring the understanding (*entendimiento*), speak with and caress Him (*hablando y regalando con El*)[25] and not wear themselves out in composing Discourses, but present their needs before him, contemplating why he does not allow us into his presence.
>
> (V: 13.11)[26]

As I will argue throughout this book, it is this very 'otherness' in Teresa's language which I believe makes it accessible once again to our generation. Children of Freud and Jung, we have now, perhaps more than at any time since the late medieval period, an appreciation of the libidinization of thought and the necessary link between intellect and affect. Teresa, living with her late medieval heritage, was able to construct her unique 'language of spirit' which, with very little adjustment, is entirely accessible to us today. For Kristeva, Teresa's approach is not through 'thought' or 'illumination' but is rather what she calls a 'Freudian intuition' (Kristeva 2008: 36). In this respect, her use of 'water' is itself a fluid metaphor: 'under the pen of Teresa, the referent of "water" is not an "object"... for her, language is not an instrument, but the terrain itself of the

---

[24] Matthew has the rather charming 'those able to serve themselves of Discourse.'

[25] This is a difficult passage to translate. Kavanaugh has 'speak and delight in Him', Allison Peers, 'in converse with Him and delighting in Him'. Matthew has 'regale themselves with Him'.

[26] See also V: 15.7: 'The soul will lose a great deal if it isn't careful in this matter, especially if the intellect is sharp. For when the soul begins to create discourses and search for ideas, though insignificant, it will think it is doing something if they seem clever.'

act called "mystical" (*mystique*)' (Kristeva 2008: 117). Teresa, she suggests, is inviting us to an entirely subversive (in her terms 'semiotic') moment where spiritual and sensuality are merged.

However, as always in Teresa, there is a perceptive eye as to the dangers or extremes of any position. For despite her passions and 'gusts' she is a very wise-assured woman with her 'feet on the ground'. As we shall see in the following chapter, to found her convents she learnt very quickly that the spiritual life is not just about the 'seraphs and exstasies' of the transcendent, but, as she so aptly put it in *The Way of Perfection* – 'God walks among the pots and pans'.

Thus, in Chapter 13 she outlines the traps and subtle self-delusion that a person who follows this path may fall into.

> Another temptation is then very common: as they begin to taste the tranquillity (*sosiego*)[27] and gain which they have then they desire that everyone should be very spiritual. This is not wrong. However striving to bring it about could have unhappy results if there is not a lot of discretion and dissimulation (*discreción y disimulación*)[28] and in doing so in such a way that one does not appear to be teaching.
>
> (V: 13.8)

Once again Teresa shows herself to be a master and trained observer of the foibles and conceits of those who follow the spiritual path. In our own era of bogus 'New Age' gurus and shamans her words are as powerfully relevant as ever. For, as she recognizes, the pedagogy of the spirit is most unlike any other form of pedagogy and one that requires a subtle insight into the state of one's own motivations and manners. In this respect she emphasizes here (V: 13.14) a theme which we will look at more in a later chapter – the necessity for the spiritual seeker to have a guide or spiritual director who can offer good counsel along the way:

> The one who commences needs advice in order to see what is best for them. For this a master (*maestro*) is very necessary providing he has experience. If he doesn't he can be greatly mistaken and lead a soul without either understanding it or allowing it to understand itself. For since (the soul) sees that there is great merit in being subject to a master, it doesn't dare depart from what he commands it. I have come across souls so

---

[27] Another key Teresian word, as we shall see shortly.

[28] Rodriguez chooses 'simulation' here for *disimulación*. Allison Peers preferences 'dissimulation'.

constrained and afflicted because of the inexperience of their director that I have felt great pity. And there are some (guides) who don't know what to do with themselves because, not understanding the spirit, such guides afflict the soul and body, obstructing progress. One of these (souls) who spoke to me told me about a master who held her bound for eight years and wouldn't let her go beyond self knowledge; even though the Lord had already given her the prayer of quiet and so she suffered much tribulation.

(V: 13.14)

I have quoted this passage in full for Teresa is surely here referring to her own trying experiences with spiritual directors, something we shall return to later. Like John of the Cross (Prologue to the *Ascent of Mount Carmel*) she understood that a misguided director or 'guru' can do significant harm in a person's spiritual development, often misdirecting or even in some cases abusing their freedom. Throughout, her watchword is 'self-knowledge' (*propio conocimiento*) and what she is advocating is a 'path of self-knowledge' (V: 13.15), something surely at the heart of her enterprise and closely bound up to her promise of achieving 'spiritual freedom' by following this path. For such a path a master with prudence, experience and learning is necessary (V: 13.15). Her guides were not to be university professors but wise guides tempered in the practical experience of guiding souls:

Learning is a great thing because learned men teach and enlighten us who know little, and when brought before the truths of Sacred Scripture, we do what we ought. May God deliver us from foolish devotions.

(V: 13.16)

For within her approach, although she recognizes the dangers of over-intellectualization of the spiritual path, she equally recognizes that faith without learning can also be very debilitating to the soul.

The Second Water

This then is the 'libidinal labour' of the early stages of the spiritual journey. It requires, suggests Teresa, humility, vigilance and self-knowledge. Only with these three can we acquire the openness of spirit necessary to carry us forward. 'The water', of course, 'is for the flowers' and the end point of this great life-journey are the flowers of 'good works', not some navel-gazing, self-indulgence that simply serves to reinforce the ego, however subtly and covertly.

As Teresa's emphasis shifts in Chapter 14 to the 'second water' so, as we would expect, does her vocabulary and spiritual terminology. The *gustos* are as strong as ever, but now we find her using more frequently the Osunan terminology of 'recollection' / *recogimiento* (V: 14.1–3 *et passim*) as well as the very Teresian phrase 'Prayer of Quiet' / *Oración de Quietud*. Of course, considering her situation in the middle of the *alumbrado/dejado* controversy we would expect this. However, despite her best efforts, as we shall see in the next chapter, she still managed to fall foul of the Inquisition later in her life. For having told us in V: 14.2 that 'this is a recollection of the powers of the soul within itself so that (the soul) may enjoy this experience with much *gusto* (*con más gusto*)', she is immediately at pains to emphasize that these same powers 'are not lost or sleep' in this state – if that had been the case this would have been perilously close to the descriptions of *dejamiento* then circulating among the Inquisitors (see also V: 15.1 where this is reiterated). '*Gusto*', however, still remains a strong sign of God's action at this point in the journey and she emphasizes the increasing power of the *gusto* here:

> In arriving here it begins soon to lose its craving for earthly things – and little wonder! It sees clearly that one moment of this *gusto*[29] is not possible here below, neither can riches, seniorities, honours nor delights (*deleites*) provide this contentment even for the blink of an eye (*a dar un cierra ojo y abre*), for this is true joy and the soul realizes that this gives genuine satisfaction.
>
> (V: 14.5)

It is indeed a 'tasty knowledge' and we can contrast it, perhaps, with John of the Cross' severe 'Ascent of Mount Carmel' that although fuelled by the 'more intense enkindling love' of the Holy Spirit is somehow more severe and lacking the voluptuousness of Teresa's account, at least in these early stages of the path (see Tyler 2010). God alone can give this *gusto*, and without it, all the spiritual life, its penances and hardships, would literally be impossible. Without the *gusto* we cannot proceed:

---

[29] Kavanaugh switches his translation of *gusto* to 'enjoyment of glory' at this point, Allison Peers stays with 'joy', Matthew with 'gust'.

Because if one crushes oneself under penances and prayer and all these sort of things, if the Lord does not give (the *gusto*), then it will be to little advantage.

(V: 14.5)

Teresa's embodied epistemology is always necessarily accompanied by a concomitant 'unknowing' or *apophasis*. This she would have acquired from her twenty-year study of Osuna who gleaned it from the medieval apophatic tradition of *theologia mystica* of such masters as Dionysius, the Victorines and Jean Gerson.[30] Accordingly, Teresa at this point emphasizes that the embodied experience of *gusto* at this stage must be accompanied by unknowing:

> This satisfaction is in the most intimate (part of the soul),[31] and it doesn't know where it comes from or how, nor does it often know what to do, nor what it wants, nor what to ask for. It seems to find everything and doesn't know what it has found, nor do I know how to explain this for these are difficult things requiring much learning.

(V: 14.6)

The other key innovation of her account of the Second Water is, as we have said, her concern with the *oración de quietud*. Here, as we have seen, she needs to be particularly careful because of inquisitorial pressure.[32] Here she uses her vocabulary very carefully and introduces new words that will become increasingly important from hereon: *sosiego* – quiet, calm, tranquillity;[33] *paz* – peace and *suavidad* – softness, subtlety[34] (V: 15 onwards). She seems to suggest that with time the passion of the *gustos* is increasingly accompanied by a concomitant

---

[30] We shall return to this 'spiritual genealogy' later, see also Tyler 2011.

[31] '*Es en lo muy intimo de ella esta satisfaction*.' Kavanaugh gives the spatially skewed 'in its very intimate depths,' Allison Peers 'the most intimate part of the soul,' Matthew 'is in the most intimate part thereof.' See Chapter 8 below on the spatiality and non-spatiality of Teresa's concept of self. There I will argue that she chooses her descriptions of 'the centre of the self' very carefully.

[32] As we have heard, largely due to the malign influence of the Princess of Éboli, the *Book of the Life* was placed in the hands of the Inquisition shortly after it was written. Teresa herself had access to a copy, but not the original manuscript, for the rest of her life. Only after her death could Ana de Jésus get it returned for Luis de León's first edition of her works. The autograph now lies in Philip II's Escorial to whom it was presented.

[33] Perhaps the most beautiful use of this term is found in John of the Cross's Spiritual Canticle, CB 14: '*La noche sosegada en par de los levantes del aurora...*' See the following chapter.

[34] Matthew gives the rather quaint 'suavitie' for this term. Other translators choose 'sweetness' e.g. Dalton, Allison Peers. I am indebted to Terence O'Reilly for pointing out the similarities with Francis de Sales' use of *suavité* in his works here.

peace and calm – surely a reflection of her own life of prayer over twenty years, from turbulent and often violent beginnings to the peace and serenity which she seemed to possess from her mid-forties onwards and that she seems never to have lost despite the great trials that beset her later:

> What the soul must do during these times of quiet amounts to no more than being gentle and without noise.[35]

>   (V: 15.6)

The Third Water

With the third water we see a gradual increase of both trends described in the second water: that is the *gustos* and *deleites* 'are incomparably greater' (V: 16.1) while the underlying *sosiego* continues to take hold. As these two forces interact so the soul is marked with greater paradox, and often incomprehension (and apophasis):

> Such a soul can no longer move forward; nor does it know how; nor can it move backwards... the prayer is a glorious folly (*un glorioso desatino*),[36] a heavenly madness (*un celestino locuro*) where the true wisdom is learnt and it is a most delightful manner of enjoyment for the soul.

>   (V: 16.1)

As the libidinal meets the spiritual the paradox deepens (V: 16.3 *un desasosiego sabroso* – a dissatisfied tastiness; V: 16.4 *un sabrosa pena* – a tasty pain; *santa locura* – holy madness). As we shall see, when she comes to write the *Interior Castle* she will dedicate the longest part of the book, the Sixth Mansions, to this phase. It is the realm of the strange and extraordinary phenomena that tormented her during her twenties and thirties and these descriptions remain, to this day, one of the chief things she is remembered for. As we shall see, in the later book she concludes by relativising the importance of these phenomena. At this stage in her writing she presents them as best she can by means of paradoxical statements. Considering the ecclesiological climate within which

---

[35] Matthew: 'with suauitie and without noyse.'
[36] Matthew: 'A glorious kind of Frensie.'

the *Life* would be received this was probably a very wise move. Throughout these passages she addresses her remarks more pointedly to 'her reverence' García de Toledo (sometimes even '*mi hijo*', my son) as though to emphasize that this section of the manuscript must be the most open to inquisitorial scrutiny. And surely she is right. For if there was a reason why the *Life* had been written then it was for the examination of these 'crazy phenomena' that she had become notorious for. She herself calls it 'a kind of madness' (*locura*) as we part company with the normal rules of rational discourse and follow our 'mad' God:

> I beg your Reverence that we may all be mad for love of Him who for love of us was called mad.
>
> (V: 16.6)

Yet she is also very careful to emphasize the other side of the Third Water: the blooming of the flowers we met at the beginning – the good works and deeds which for Teresa will always remain the hallmark of true spiritual encounter:

> The virtues are now stronger than in the previous prayer of quiet. The soul can't ignore them... it begins to perform great deeds (*a obrar grandes cosas*) by means of the fragrance the flowers give.
>
> (V: 17.3)

We have moved from the 'holy leisure' (*ocio santo*) of the Second Water to more active movement to practical matters – 'business affairs and works of charity' as she calls them (V: 17.4). Here she uses one of her favourite similes which will recur in the *Interior Castle* and will be familiar from the medieval tradition – the union of Martha and Mary. This all helps to build up the picture that Teresa wants to convey of a 'practical mystic' who as well as enjoying God's favour can engage in business matters, run a household, and where necessary marshall her forces to found convents. As we shall see in the *Foundations* she approaches her task of founding her convents in Spain in the same way as her brothers fight their military campaigns in far off South America. There the enemy is the Inca and Aztec peoples, in Spain it will be duplicitous landlords, unreliable and superstitious nuns and wavering clergy, all commanded by their great general – the devil himself.

The Fourth Water

In her description of the Third Water, Teresa had mentioned three types of union (V: 17.5); however it is to the final Water that she affixes her attempts at presenting the 'union of the soul with God.' It is, of course, an impossible task that pushes, as we have seen, linguistic capability to breakdown and one she will attempt again at the end of her life in the *Interior Castle*. She herself realizes the challenges of the task and begins this section of the *Life* with an evocation that will occur many times in the later *Castle*, especially as she approaches these 'interior mansions': 'May the Lord teach me the words so that I will be able to say something about the fourth water' (V: 18.1), for this state is the ultimate paradox:

> If this prayer is the union of all the faculties, the soul is unable to communicate its joy even though it may desire to do so – I mean while being in the prayer. And if it were able, then it wouldn't be union.
>
> (V: 18.2)

We are once again in Wittgenstein's realm of 'saying and showing'. She recognizes that what can be said cannot be shown and what can be shown cannot be said. In the passages that follows she will have to show as much as say. Indeed, she prefaces her comments with words God spoke to her after communion:

> 'It is no longer the soul that lives but I.' Since it cannot comprehend what it understands, there is an understanding by not understanding.
>
> (V: 18.14)

To which she adds 'The intellect, if it understands, doesn't understand how it understands. It doesn't seem to me that it understands, because, as I say, it doesn't understand – I really can't understand this!' (V: 18.14) Which is really how she leaves it. She is not concerned, as some commentators suggest, to give us a phenomenological description of union. She knows such a task is impossible.[37] As we shall see later she accepts the restrictions of applying essentially

---

[37] Despite this numerous commentators seek to establish a definitive topographical Teresian 'map of the soul'. One of the aims of this book is to decry this as an illusory task and one Teresa herself deliberately did not engage in.

spatio-temporal language to what is ungraspable by such language. Thus, she will concentrate on the manifestations of union (*los flores*) rather than the union itself.[38] As well as the benefits to neighbours (V: 19.3) there will be another attempt at explaining the 'charismatic phenomena' to which she will return in the Sixth Mansions of the *Interior Castle*; the 'words' (*palabras*) she heard from God (of which 'she was very frightened' V: 19.9), rapture – *arroba-miento*, levitation or flight – *elevamiento u vuelo*, transport – *arrebatamiento* and ecstasy – *éstasi* (V: 20.1). From this point onwards (as she will later do in the *Castle*) Teresa drops the earlier '*gustos*' and refers instead to these 'charismatic phenomena'. However, where they will differ from the earlier *gustos* is that they will all have external manifestations as part of their nature – they are indeed *flores* producing a fragrance. The *gustos* had the sense of a '*muy muy interior*' nature, these others have a more extrovert quality appropriate for their nature as manifestations of the fragrance of the flowers.

In Freudian or Jungian language, the self is completely decentred. The ego has no control and one is operating from a completely different energetic centre. An aspect of Teresa's spiritual anthropology we shall return to in Chapter 8:

> There is a manifestation of the tremendous power of the Lord and of how we are incapable, when His Majesty desires it, of holding back the body any more than the soul, nor are we its master... there is one who is superior, that these favours are given by Him and that of ourselves we can do absolutely nothing; deep humility is impressed on the soul.
>
> (V: 20.7)

I would like to suggest that psychologically these passages of the *Life* are best approached in this spirit of 'decentred self' rather than with an empirical reaching after psycho-spiritual phenomena fuelled by the empirical research question: 'Did it really happen?' The question, I would suggest, is largely irrel-evant to Teresa's project –which is to present a path of the Christian spiritual journey, not to analyse psycho-pathological phenomena. As we read Teresa's and her sisters' accounts of levitations we are left in no doubt that they claimed to witness these phenomena (see V: 20.4). In my earlier *Way of Ecstasy* (Tyler 1997) I suggested that one explanation for this phenomenon could be found

---

[38] We shall return to this theme in Chapter 8 as we consider the 'non-centre' at the centre of Teresa's self.

in Indian notions of the opening up of energy centres or *chakras* in the body (Tyler: 1997: 112–14) which still seems to me as good an explanation as any for the fascinating descriptions of the libidinal force of Teresa's experiences at this point.[39] They are intense, loving and painful and reach a crescendo in the *Life* with the famous descriptions of the libidinal encounter with the cherub in Chapter 29. Teresa's 'I' at this point, suggests Kristeva, is as much 'I' as 'not-I': 'Her *castle* is not "interior", rather, it is a condition of being infiltrated by the "exterior" Other' (Kristeva 2008: 36). Self has been entirely destabilized in a quite radical way that we shall return to later in Chapter 8.

What cannot be denied about these chapters of the *Life*, however, is the impact they will have on the future of mystical theology. Before Teresa the practice of mystical theology had largely portrayed it as an affective manifestation of 'speculative theology'.[40] Thus, Jean Gerson, writing for the students of the University of Paris around 1400, understands that if he is to present a course of speculative theology there must be a concomitant course of affective mystical theology accompanying it. From Teresa onwards 'mysticism' and 'the mystical' will increasingly concentrate on the 'mystical phenomena' such as the ones she describes in these chapters in such minute precision.

Teresa, as she will reiterate in the *Castle*, despite her precise explanations, senses that these raptures, levitations and ecstasies are only important if they lead us to God, manifest in good works (see V: 21.8). In themselves they are unimportant. From this 'decentred perspective' the self can 'laugh at its former self' (V: 20.26) even to the point of seeing the stupidity of Spain's sixteenth century obsession, honour, 'that greatest lie' as she refers to it now (V: 20.26):

---

[39] A lengthy description of this phenomenon would probably require another book to be written. For now I quote a typical example of this phenomenon, known as the 'Kundalini' as described by Sri Gopi Krishna which came upon him while meditating in Jammu, Kashmir in winter 1937: 'Entirely unprepared for such a development, I was completely taken by surprise; but regaining self-control instantaneously, I remained sitting in the same posture, keeping my mind on the point of concentration. The illumination grew brighter and brighter, the roaring louder, I experienced a rocking sensation and then felt myself slipping out of my body, entirely enveloped in a halo of light. It is impossible to describe the experience accurately. I felt the point of consciousness that was myself growing wider, surrounded by waves of light. It grew wider and wider spreading outward while the body, normally the immediate object of its perception, appeared to have receded into the distance until I became entirely unconscious of it ... I was no longer myself, to be more accurate, no longer as I knew myself to be ... but was a vast circle of consciousness in which the body was but a point, bathed in light and in a state of exaltation and happiness impossible to describe.' G. Krishna (1971) *Kundalini: the Evolutionary Energy in Man*, London: Robinson and Watkins.

[40] See Chapter 2 above and Chapter 6 below.

The soul laughs to itself over the time when it esteemed money and coveted it ... the soul sees such great blindness in pleasures and how with them one buys trouble.

(V: 20.27–8)

The seeker, through work on themselves following the spiritual path she has outlined, has been completely decentred, indeed they have experienced 'ecstasy' in its literal sense – they have been thrown out of themselves. The world has been turned upside down and now they see it aright. For Teresa, this will be placing Christ at the centre of one's life (V: 22.1). It is as though the individual ego has now been replaced by the *persona Christi*, a theme she reinforces by reiterating her devotion to the humanity of Christ. This absorption, she tells us, is the end goal of the journey which began with mindfulness and *gustos*. Indeed, as the *persona Christi* grows in the self then the need for such *gustos* diminishes – this, for her, is true 'freedom of spirit' (V: 22 5). In this respect, as a Catholic nun of the sixteenth century, this bodily presence of Christ will be most particularly pronounced in the reception of the Blessed Sacrament at mass, a devotion to which Teresa was attached all of her life. This removal of '*gustos*' at the later stages of prayer is to be replaced, as it were, by the pure presence of Christ (see V: 22.6).

This is perhaps the nearest Teresa comes to the way of purification of St John of the Cross. We know that the two saints shared many opinions and ideas of the spiritual life, yet, in a way, their works tend to complement each other rather than merge. It is, as it were, a question of emphasis. Teresa, the passionate ecstastic will always preference the need for *gustos* and *deleites* in the journey to God. John, the withdrawing ascetic, felt more comfortable with the '*nada*' of the Ascent of Mount Carmel. Yet, just as John will stress the need for the *inflamación major*, so Teresa too recognizes that the *gustos* must come to an end at a place, as it appears to her, where the boundaries of ego are completely dissolved, which she terms the place of 'poverty of spirit' – *pobreza de espíritu*. At this point she passes from what we might term the language of phenomenological psychology to that of theology – which especially for her will be expressed in the symbolic theology she studied as a young nun in her late medieval texts and to which we will return in a later chapter.

Summary

Of all Teresa's works *The Book of the Life* would perhaps become the most influential and famous. This is not surprising. Although it lacks something of the polish of its older brothers and sisters – *The Way of Perfection, The Book of Foundations* and *The Interior Castle* – it has a raw, sometimes earthy and pungent tone that becomes quieter and more refined in the later works. A lot of this *tinta* is, I have suggested in this chapter, due to her unique fruity-salty language which she employs with masterly precision. Numerous sisters recounted after her death that when she wrote she seemed to be possessed in ecstasy. Examining her writings with care cannot help but reinforce this impression. Throughout the *Life* Teresa tells us how important books had been to her and her family – her uncle Pedro, her father and then herself. Osuna had saved her 'as her master' and Augustine, Jerome and Bernardino de Laredo had initiated her into the spiritual language of the Catholic Church. After the *Life* finally saw the light of day it was time for her work to join this pantheon of Christian classics. I have alluded to its long history of translation into English and it has been since translated into most of the world's languages.[41] Teresa had written a book that could change people's lives. I have suggested here that this was due in no small part to her style and vocabulary: that wonderful half-open/half-closed Teresian style that gushes – or indeed gusts – at us with the full force of a woman inebriated by the Spirit. We shall turn now to the force of that Spirit as it proceeded from Avila to found convents first in Spain and ultimately throughout the whole world.

---

[41] It would be one of these translations, into German, that would change the life of a young atheist German philosopher at the beginning of the twentieth century – Edith Stein – later killed at Auschwitz as Saint Teresa Benedicta of the Cross. See Tyler and Woods 2012.

5

'The Lord Walks Among the Pots and Pans': The Book of Foundations *and* The Way of Perfection

Introduction

We left our historical account of Teresa's life with the young foundress clutching her letters of permission from General Rossi allowing her to found as many convents as she wanted in the kingdoms of New and Old Castile (roughly Castilla-León and Castilla-La Mancha of present-day Spain). We also heard about the complicated process of reform by which the Carmelite order was implementing the recommendations of the recently concluded Council of Trent under the guidance of Rossi, the great reforming General.

Teresa, as we have heard in her own words in the previous chapter, had undergone a life-changing experience that began with her initiation into the mindful prayer of recollection. After the mindfulness had come the ecstasies and raptures so lovingly described in the *Life*. But, Teresa realized too, to use a phrase of Jack Kornfield, 'after the ecstasy comes the laundry'. She was so excited by what had happened to her, how her life had been completely turned upside down by the love of God, that she wanted to share that with everyone she encountered. Not only that, she appreciated that in the Spain of her day there was a hunger for this sort of experience and that she had the unique gifts to enable this to happen. While she was founding the convent of *San José*, as described in the *Life*, she did not seem to identify herself as a mother foundress. Rather, as we have seen, the idea arose from conversations with a group of like-minded people, religious and lay, where Teresa acted as *prima inter pares* – the spokeswoman or chair, as it were, of a reforming committee. Yet, as we read *The Book of Foundations* and *The Way of Perfection*, we share with Teresa her growing realization of her own vocation as someone who must bring the opportunity for quiet contemplative prayer to the turbulent Spain of her time.

Her 'crusade' took place against the wider backdrop of a Europe 'in flames' (CE: 1.5) as the conflicts of the Reformation boiled to a head in Northern Europe. Teresa herself seems to have had little idea of the main points upon which the manifesto of the Reformation was proceeding. What she did under-stand, however, was the need for reform in a church sadly weakened over the past century. As with her writing, Teresa was a true original who offered a path for her contemporaries between the Scylla of fundamentalist iconoclasm and the Charybdis of inquisitorial reaction. In the *Book of Foundations* and the *Way of Perfection* we hear the voice of a sometimes lonely woman trying to walk that precarious path of liberation on behalf of her sisters and brothers in Christ. For Teresa, central to this reform was the belief that each baptized Christian should be able to have access to the contemplative life which she saw as the natural home of all the faithful.[1] In this respect she was of course simply returning to the original foundational charism of Carmel that we explored in Chapter 3. As she says later in the *Interior Castle*:

> All of us who wear this sacred habit of Carmel are called to prayer and contemplation (*a la oración y contemplación*) – because that was our origin, that is, we are descended from those Holy Fathers of ours of Mount Carmel who in such great solitude and with such contempt of the world sought this treasure, this precious pearl of which we speak.
>
> (M: 5.1.1)

The aim of her reform, then, was to recreate, or perhaps better, create the condi-tions where, at first, 'her daughters', and later, 'her sons', could cultivate that special pearl of great price. The description of this would be the task of all her works after *The Life*. That book, as we have seen, really acts as a template for all her later books. Of the two books under consideration in this chapter, the first, *The Way of Perfection*, reads like a manual for community life and prayer and in this respect mirrors the *Constitutions* which she wrote at the same time while living quietly at *San José*. The *Foundations*, on the other hand, is a more historical document, or better still a testimony, that announces the progress of the reform on an external level. The final part of her great tetralogy, *The Interior*

---

[1] While, as I have said, Teresa was rather uncomplimentary about what she referred to as 'the Lutherans', her daughters, when they moved into Northern Europe, saw their reform as allowing all Christians, including those at this point separated from Rome, to have access to the contemplative life. For more on this see Wilson (2006).

Castle, to which we will return in the next chapter, continues the 'mystical themes' of *The Life* and develops them into a final mystical theology. All three elements – the chronicle, the guidebook and the treatise of mystical theology – had been mixed up together in *The Life*. After that book, however, she perhaps wisely decided to separate the different strands to create three separate books.[2]

Nevertheless, the three strands will continue to intertwine and we find elements of all three in each of these three later works. Thus, all three books can be seen as different aspects of that one great cause she held in her heart after the initial success of *San José* – the creation of 'safe havens' for prayer and contemplation (what she refers to as her 'dovecots') amidst a 'world in flames' (CE: 1.5).

She addresses herself initially to this new task in the Prologue and early chapters of the *The Way of Perfection*.

The Genesis of *The Way of Perfection*

As with most of Teresa's texts the history of the origins and reception of *The Way of Perfection* is not at all straightforward. What we do know, from testimonials and references in her own work, is that having finished the manuscript of the *Life* at about the end of 1565 she embarked almost immediately on this second text. The *Life* was by now in the hands of her confessors, and ultimately the Inquisition.

The Valdés Index of 1559 meant, as we have seen, that the spiritual books that had nurtured Teresa as a young woman were no longer available to the new sisters of *San José*. So, as the young community settled down to the business of living the new reform it became clear that instruction had to come to them from somewhere. Teresa, we imagine, felt herself equal to the task and thus embarked upon her second literary work – *The Way of Perfection* / *El Camino de Perfección*. If she had begun to develop her special style in *The Life*, by the time she came to write *The Way* her pen was in full flow, using all the skills and techniques she had acquired in the earlier work to full effect.

The genesis of the *Way* is thus intimately connected with Teresa's extrinsic circumstances around 1566 when she appears to have done most of the work on

---

[2] I have already made reference to the 'minor works' such as the *Meditations on the Song of Songs*. However I shall weave reference to these into the discussion of the four main books. See also Tyler 2010a.

the first redaction. Thus, as well as her mystical musings it contains reflections on how to live together as a community, how to deal with fractious and difficult people, the purpose and origins of religious life, and the nature and form of vocal prayer and liturgy. The title could well be the epigram she uses later in *The Book of Foundations*: 'The Lord walks among the pots and pans' (F: 5.8).[3]

However all this, as we have seen, takes place against the backdrop of the Valdés Index and its consequences. As Ahlgren points out, Teresa criticizes the Valdés Index in no less than four places in *The Way*, albeit indirectly (Ahlgren 1996: 89). She famously remarks, for example, that 'even they (The Inquisition) cannot take the Our Father and the Hail Mary away from (the sisters)' (CE: 21.8). Upon which García de Toledo remarks 'she seems to be reproving the Inquisitors for prohibiting books on prayer'.[4]

Once written, the text, like its older sister *The Life*, had to be put into the censoring hands of García de Toledo. This manuscript, with his notes and corrections is preserved today in the royal library of the Escorial. This is usually referred to as the Escorial Codex (CE here) and is divided by Teresa into 72 chapters. Of the various versions it is clearly the one that is closest to Teresa's original inspiration and preserves the magic of her distinctive style in its rawest form.

The second redaction, preserved today in the Discalced Convent at Valladolid (and thus known as the Vallodolid Codex, here CV), marks an important stage in the development of Teresa's style as she responds to García de Toledo's critique and realizes that the document will be read by a wider circle than just her nuns. She is more cautious, and explains in greater depth the controversial areas of prayer of quiet and recollection.

The final version of the *Way*, known as the Toledo Codex after the Discalced convent of that city where it is kept (here CT), represents the culmination of this slow process of redaction and opening of *The Way* to 'the general public' (Efrén de la Madre de Dios and Steggink 1962: 181). For this codex represents her desire to have the book published openly, a new direction for her and one that gives the lie to the idea that Teresa only intended her books to be read by her nuns in enclosed seclusion. She clearly understood that the teachings contained here would be of interest to a wider audience, as *The Life* had been,

---

[3] *Entre los pucheros anda el Señor.*

[4] '*Haced bien, hijas, que no os quitarán el Pater nóster y el Avemaría.*' '*Parece que reprehende a los Inquisidores que prohiben libros de oración.*' See also the discussion in her *Vejamen.*

and wanted to facilitate this process as much as her limited resources would allow. Unfortunately her unknown editor, like so many of her editors, was unhappy with her style and tried to tidy it up. As will be clear by now, this would have been disastrous to what Teresa was trying to achieve.[5] The Toledo codex preserves this bowdlerized manuscript with Teresa's corrections attached. One of its most significant omissions (understandable in view of the climate then holding in Spain) is the removal of Chapter 31 of the Valladolid codex – on the Prayer of Quiet. Fray Luis de León was clearly unhappy with this codex when he came to edit the first complete edition of her works and chose the corrected Valladolid version for his publication, inserting passages from Escorial and from other versions corrected in Teresa's hand: an editorial decision which was subsequently followed by many of his successors, thus leading to a proliferation of variants on the text.

Woodhead (1675) and Dalton (1852) both used Fray Luis' text as the basis of their translations (Matthew did not attempt a translation). Allison Peers used P. Silverio de Santa Teresa's text as the basis of his translation which adopts the Valladolid codex with the Escorial variants and an appended full text of Escorial and Toledo. When Allison Peers decided what to include in this first English translation of the Silverio de Santa Teresa edition he would ask himself at each point: 'Would St. Teresa have included or omitted this if she had been making a fresh revision for a world-wide public over a period of centuries?' (Allison Peers CW: 2.xxii). It was an editorial decision fortunately backed up by extensive footnotes and explanations for each amended passage.

Kavanaugh and Rodriguez in their 1980 translation chose the Valladolid manuscript (like Fray Luis) but inserted the original unedited passages from the Escorial text where there was a significant difference.

Thus, of all her works, as Weber puts it: 'The revisions of the *Way of Perfection* allow us to observe, with particular clarity, not only the degree to which Teresa's stylistic decisions were deliberate but also the extent to which style was, for Teresa, a pragmatic issue' (Weber 1990: 80).

---

[5] Has the style of a spiritual writer ever been so bound up with their message as is the case with Teresa of Avila?

The Book of Foundations

Unlike the *Way of Perfection*, written rapidly after the *Life*, the *Foundations* was (by necessity) longer in its gestation and, in fact, was left uncompleted as *la Madre* lay dying in October 1582. From the foundation of *San José* to her death, Teresa's life had been absorbed with the task of creating a network of Discalced Convents dedicated to promoting and protecting the contemplative life that she had discovered in Avila and now sought to share with the world. This task was completed after her death when her foundations spread across the whole globe.

Beginning with Medina del Campo in 1567, the foundations Teresa made in her lifetime were as follows: Malagón (1568), Valladolid (1568), Toledo (1569), Pastrana (1569), Salamanca (1570), Alba de Tormes (1571), Segovia (1574), Beas de Segura (1575), Seville (1575), Caravaca (1576), Villanueva de la Jara (1580), Palencia (1580), Soria (1581), Granada (1582, although Teresa did not personally visit this one) and Burgos in 1582, after which she died at Alba de Tormes in October 1582. Considering the state of transport and communication in Spain at the time,[6] the rapidity with which Teresa made these foundations is a quite remarkable testament in itself.

According to the Prologue to the *Foundations* (F: Prol. 3) she began the work in Salamanca in August 1573, eleven years after *The Life* was written. This was after the suggestion of her Jesuit confessor, Jerónimo Ripalda, who had been so edified after reading *The Life*. However, according to a testimony written by Teresa in Malagón around 1570, the origin of *The Book of the Foundations* had a divine mandate. Having seen a vision of the wounded Christ after communion, so the Saint relates in her *Spiritual Testimonies,* and shown concern for his sufferings, Christ turned to her and said:

> That I shouldn't grieve over those wounds, but over the many that were now being inflicted upon Him. I asked Him what I could do as a remedy for this because I was determined to do everything I could. He told me that now was not the time for rest, but that I should hurry to establish these houses and that He would find rest with the souls that would live there; and that I must take all the houses that might be given to me because there were many souls who could not serve Him because they had no place in which they could do so; that the houses I founded in small towns should be just

---

[6] See F: 18.4 and Kavanaugh and Rodriguez CW 3.48–52 for good descriptions of this.

like this one ... and that I should write about the foundation of these houses. *Spiritual Testimonies*: 5

(Hereafter CC)[7]

Teresa, according to the testimony, felt unable to write, but rather than being a hindrance, the Lord felt this 'place of unknowing' was exactly what he wanted as a starting point for her narrative:

I thought of how with regard to the house at Medina I never understood anything of how I could write of this foundation. He told me that that was all the more reason to write of it since He wanted it to be seen that the Medina foundation had been miraculous ... and as a result I determined to undertake this work (of writing about the foundations).

(CC: 6)

Thus, the *Foundations* was begun from a specified position of 'unknowing'. The Lord would reveal the purpose of the text as it appeared.

Consequently, work on the text would proceed in a stuttering fashion as and when she found time in her busy schedule of founding the new convents. From what we can derive from the internal textual evidence, Chapters 1–9 were written while at Segovia and Salamanca between 1573 and 1574; Chapters 10–19 were begun in Valladolid and written variously up to 1576 (Chapter 13, for instance, was written in 1575). Chapters 20–27 were written in Toledo and the final chapters 28–33 were left uncompleted at her death in Alba in 1582. Thus, along with *The Interior Castle*, *The Foundations* contains some of Teresa's most mature writing. Yet, as I indicated earlier, her task in this book is, as it were, to extract the narrative part of the *Life* and present it without the 'mystical context' of, say, *The Interior Castle*. But, Teresa being Teresa, this is not quite

---

[7] The English title of this collection of memorials is from Kavanaugh and Rodriguez. Allison Peers, following the tradition of other English translations, calls them the 'Spiritual Relations' and 'Favours of God'. Her two Spanish twentieth century editors again give different titles: Alvarez gives *Las Relaciones* and Efren de la Madre de Dios and Steggink give *Cuentas de Conciencia* (literally 'Accounts of Conscience'). The texts are interesting 'X Rays into Teresa's soul', as Kavanaugh and Rodriguez call them, and consist of accounts of varying lengths, some for herself and others for inquisitors and confessors. I shall give them Kavanaugh's English title but stay with the ordering of Efren de la Madre de Dios and Steggink's *Cuentas de Conciencia*. As most of the *Cuentas* are not in Teresa's hand we must be aware that the essential Teresian *estilo* is sometimes missing. The copyists seem to have polished up her work or at times altered it to fit into their own theological categories. For a good account of their textual history see Allison Peers CW: 1.301–5.

possible. She cannot forget the divine mandate of her actions as we shall see shortly. The book itself is her answer to the question, 'How does God act in the world?' The answer is simple – Look around you! Look at His workings in bringing these convents into the world! This then is the subtext of the book.

In contrast to her other later works, *The Way of Perfection* and *The Interior Castle*, the *Book of Foundations* had another inbuilt problem. She tells us in the Prologue that 'the account will be given in all truthfulness ... in conformity with what has taken place' (F: Prol.3) yet many of the people and incidents, some as difficult and controversial as anything so far in her life, had to be dealt with no little tact and diplomacy, not least because many of the characters involved were still alive at the time of writing. Although *la Santa* never utters any 'untruthfulness' we sometimes have to 'read between the lines' to see her true view on situations. We discussed a good example of this in Chapter 2 earlier regarding her discussion of the *converso* lineage of Alonso Alvarez in connection with her Toledo foundation (F: 15.15).

Despite her best efforts the work was not included in Fray Luis' first edition and the first printed edition appeared in Brussels in 1610 under the supervision of her two co-workers Ana de Jésus and Jerónimo Gracián. However, as both were now regarded with some suspicion by the Order in Spain they were not given access to the original autograph (by this time deposited at the Escorial) and this edition was not perfect, also containing much editing and omissions. The situation with regard to the text was only clarified in the late nineteenth century when P. Silverio used the autograph to present an authentic text. This text formed the basis of Allison Peers' English translation and most subsequent English translations.

Reading *The Foundations* and *The Way of Perfection* as our guides it is, then, possible to trace the shape of the reform of the Carmelite Order in Spain as Teresa led it through her final two decades.

The Shape of the Reform

The new houses that Teresa was creating were a far cry from the chaotic and often disturbed world of the Order she had been formed in. By restricting her foundations to an apostolic thirteen the immediate result was the promotion of a close community character and family atmosphere.[8] Much of her writing

---

[8] However Fernández in his decrees of 1571 allowed houses with incomes to have 20 sisters, see below.

from now on would consequently emphasize the nature of community life and the importance of respecting each other within its confines. As in the earliest Carmelite rules, the cenobitic spirit where God was discovered by service to one's fellow community members, would be rediscovered and emphasized. The canker of honour and social prestige was removed and, at least in the early foundations, there were no lay sisters. All sisters now shared in the household chores of the convent, Teresa, it seems, particularly relishing this aspect of her life. As María de San Jerónimo later recalled:

> In those early days there were no lay sisters and we each took a week at a time in the kitchen. Despite all her numerous occupations, the Holy Mother would take her week like the other sisters; and it gave us no small happiness to see her (Teresa) in the kitchen, for she worked very gaily and took great care to look after us all.
>
> (Allison Peers CW: 3.338)

Unlike in the *Encarnación*, strict enclosure was the norm and sisters were encouraged to stay 'near their cells' when not engaged in liturgical offices, work or recreation just as the 'primitive rule' had specified. Having no endowments the convents (in the larger cities at least) had to rely on gifts and donations so that a spirit of austere poverty prevailed – something which seems to have delighted *la Madre* especially.

Her second foundation after Avila, Medina del Campo, saw the next signif-icant moment in her campaign of reform: her meeting with Fray Juan de San Matía, who would later become better known under his Discalced name – Juan de la Cruz/John of the Cross (1542–91). Along with Fray Antonio Heredia (1510–1601), she felt that she had found men of similar disposition to her own who could start the male reform of the order.[9] They immediately had a strong spiritual rapport and Teresa took John with him to Valladolid where she was embarking upon her next foundation so that he could experience something of the reformed Carmelite life as she envisaged it.

Calling him 'my novice' she persuaded John to begin the first male house of the reform at Duruelo, near Avila, with Fray Antonio and two others, the house having been given to Teresa by Don Rafael Mejia of Avila. Thus, on 28 November 1568 the Carmelite Father Provincial heard the four friars renounce

---

[9] For more on the history of the male reform see Tyler 2010.

the Mitigated Rule of the Carmelites and embrace the Primitive Rule of Our Lady of Mount Carmel. John also now took the name for which he has become universally known – John of the Cross.

Duruelo has been described by Ruiz as 'an unknown, out-of-the-way place. Rather than a town, it amounted to an insignificant group of farmhouses' (Ruiz 2000: 96). Even today it is still a remote place and virtually nothing remains of the original foundation. Although primitive and poor in the extreme the little hermitage of Duruelo gave John and the first companions exactly what they were looking for. Julián de Ávila, a frequent visitor, wrote:

> This little house, and the other friars who began to take the habit, so stirred one's devotion that I, along with a very religious priest, named Gonzalo de Aranda, felt devoutly moved to go there on a pilgrimage by foot; and we stayed there I don't know how many days, for it seemed we were in paradise.
>
> (Ruiz 2000: 106)

The primitive community at Duruelo would always stay close to John's heart even if, as we learn from accounts of his death bed, he vowed never to speak of it. Teresa gives a touching description in *The Foundations*:

> The choir was in the garret. The centre part was sufficiently lofty to enable them to say the Hours, but they had to stoop a great deal to get in far enough to hear Mass. In the two corners nearest the church they had two small hermitages (full of hay – for the place was very cold), in which there was only room for them to lie prostrate or be seated, for the roof was almost on their heads ... I knew that from the end of Matins until Prime they did not retire to their cells but remained there in prayer – for their prayer was so deep that it sometimes happened to them to go to Prime with a consid-erable quantity of snow on their habits and not to feel it.
>
> (F: 14.7)

In spring 1569 the Father Provincial raised the status of the foundation to that of a Priory with permission to receive novices and in June 1570 the community moved to Mancera de Abajo as they had become too numerous for the old farmhouse.

Teresa, meantime, had gone on to start the foundations at Toledo and Pastrana (1569), the latter involving the tempestuous Princess of Éboli whom we have already met in connection with *The Book of the Life*. For the description of this foundation Teresa has to employ all her tact and wit, as the troublesome Princess was still alive when she wrote the *Foundations*.

Having founded the convents of Salamanca and Alba de Tormes in 1570 and 1571 respectively, Teresa's reform was abruptly interrupted in October 1571 when the Dominican Visitor to the Castilian Carmelites, Pedro Fernández (d. 1580), unexpectedly appointed her Prioress of the *Encarnación* in Avila.[10] The appointment seems doubly surprising as she had only just formally renounced the 'mitigated' Rule in July 1571 in favour of the 'primitive' Rule at a ceremony in Avila.[11] Before proceeding it might be worth summarising the increasingly complicated circumstances under which Teresa was attempting her task of reform of the Carmelite order in Spain.

As we have seen, initially Teresa's reform had met with great support from Rossi, who, for example, wrote in 1569, after the foundation of the house at Medina del Campo:

> (Teresa) profits the Order more than all the friars in Spain. I admonish all to obey the above-mentioned Teresa as a true superior and a jewel to be much valued as precious and a friend of God.
>
> (McGreal 1999: 59)

However, as the need for reform following the Council of Trent and the Northern Protestant Reformation was being felt across the continent (see MacCulloch 2003) King Philip II in Spain also felt the need to be involved in the reform of the three orders left untouched by previous reforms initiated by Ferdinand and Isabella and Cardinal Cisneros, that is, the Mercedarians, Trinitarians and the Carmelites. After much argument with Rome, Philip agreed in July 1564 to promulgate the Tridentine decrees allowing the orders to reform themselves. However, as Rossi set out to oversee the reform, Philip obtained from the new Pope Pius V what he had wanted, the right to oversee the reform through the appointment of ordinaries ultimately responsible to himself.

---

[10] Silverio (*Historia, III, 442*) and Efrén (*Tiempo y Vida* 438) both accept the account of Maria Pinel, the seventeenth century chronicler of the history of the *Encarnación*, that the appointment was a trick of the Carmelite provincial who was motivated by the fact that the nuns of the *Encarnación* had not accepted his own candidate as prioress and his desire to prevent Teresa founding any new convents.

[11] She was to remain prioress of Avila until 1574.

The complications continued until Philip proposed dissolving the whole Carmelite Order in Spain and handing over its houses to more compliant Orders. In 1571 the two newly appointed Papal apostolic visitors, the Dominicans Pedro Fernández (for Castile) and Francisco de Vargas (for Andalusia), had taken up their posts and were undergoing visitations. The Carmelite Provincial Chapter of September 1571 was told that each Mitigated house was to have a small cluster of Discalced to act as seed germs for reform. Nuns were allowed to join the reformed house without having renounced the Mitigated Rule, however only those who had may be appointed superiors in these houses. This is what prompted Fernández's desire that Teresa should act as a Discalced head of a Mitigated house at the *Encarnación*. This same scenario would be imposed on the male Carmelite house in Avila to which John of the Cross was sent in 1572 to take up his new appointment as confessor to the sisters of the *Encarnación*. He was shortly joined thereafter by a Discalced Prior, Sub-Prior, Porter and Sacristan to act as further 'leaven of Reform' to the Mitigated house (see Letter from Teresa of Avila to Gaspar de Salazar, February 1573).[12]

Of the two Dominican visitors appointed by Pius V, Fernández appears to have been much more subtle in his approach. In Andalusia the excesses and extreme personalities we mentioned in Chapter 3 still held sway, making Vargas' task less than straightforward.[13] In response to the circumstances Vargas seem to have adopted a less tactful approach which included handing over to the Discalced a Mitigated Priory (Huelva in 1572). This, and the permission for the Discalced to form new houses in Seville, Granada and La Peñuela (1573),[14] were the events that finally led to a widespread desire among the Mitigated for a complete suppression of the Discalced. Smet comments:

> It is difficult to conclude otherwise than that Vargas here exceeded his powers. Ample as his faculties were, they remained restricted to the Carmelite province of Andalusia.

---

[12] During this time, although Teresa's sisters were technically directly answerable to Rossi in Rome, Rossi's representative Fray Alonso González acted as the sisters' superior for all intents and purposes. Rossi appointed him 'Commissary and Rector of the Discalced nuns' in May 1569. (See Allison Peers 1954: 161). However, generally Teresa preferred to work with Fernández rather than González.

[13] Niccolò Ormaneto (d.1577), appointed Apostolic Nuncio to Spain in 1572, called these Andalusian friars 'wild horses.' *Documenta primigenia*: 83.

[14] The two founders of these convents, Baltasar de Jesús (Nieto) and Gabriel de la Concepción (de la Peñuela) were both embroiled in the disciplinary action of Rossi's earlier visitation to Andalusia that was discussed in Chapter 3.

He had no power over the friars of Castile (he had ordered friars from Castile to found the houses in Andalusia). It may also be questioned whether he had the right to found houses of the Order.

(Smet 1982: 1.60)

However, back at Avila in 1571 Teresa proceeded to quell the rebellious protests of many of the *Encarnación* sisters and impose some sort of order and structure into the old house. Visits of lay people were restricted and Teresa worked hard to ensure there was an adequate food supply for all the sisters, especially the poorest members. Fernández was pleased to write to the Duchess of Alba in January 1573:

At the Convent of the *Encarnación*, there are one hundred and thirty nuns and there is as much tranquillity and sanctity there as among the ten or twelve Discalced nuns in the convent at Alba. I was extraordinarily surprised and encouraged to find this. And it all comes from the presence of the Mother.

(Allison Peers LL: 1.113)

Meanwhile, in Andalusia, a new figure had entered the story of the Reform: the young charismatic friar Jerónimo Gracián (1545–1614). Born in Valladolid into a large family who had served the court faithfully, he studied at Alcalá where he was ordained priest in 1570. Although initially interested in joining the Jesuits he became enamoured of the Discalced life while staying at the newly established Discalced novitiate in Pastrana in 1572 (see F: 23, Tyler 2010 and Gracián *Obras*). Four months after his profession in August 1573, Baltasar Nieto, clearly still not entirely trusted in Andalusia, entrusted to Gracián the jurisdiction of the Carmels in Andalusia as decreed by Vargas. Of the early reformers Gracián from the beginning treated the Discalced reform as not being necessarily conjoined to the wider Carmelite body but worked more avidly for its separation as a distinct entity. In this respect he was able to use King Philip's interest in the young reform to his advantage, usually placing, as we shall see, the King's desire over that of the Carmelite General and authorities in Rome. This would help to hasten the final separation of the reform from the wider Carmelite family.

Rossi was, unsurprisingly, unimpressed by Gracián's work writing to him:

You are scarcely a novice, without knowledge of the institutions of the Order you may easily be led along ways and paths that are not good. I believe actions take their goodness from circumstances, and that the intention is not enough. Your intention is according to God, but because you act against obedience … I think you are not acting in the service of God. I am afraid that beneath the pretext of laudable zeal there lie suspicions and contention.

(*Documenta primigenia* 65 in Smet 1982: 62)

Teresa, on the other hand, was completely captivated by Gracián and in her many letters to him reveals a deep spiritual love and affection for the young man. The two met in April 1575 after Teresa had founded her latest convent in Beas and they immediately had a deep spiritual rapport (see F: 23–4):

And because at that time I had so much trouble, it seems that when I saw him the Lord showed me the good that was going to come to us through him. So during those days I went about with such consolation and happiness (*consuelo y contento*) that indeed I was surprised at myself.

(F: 24.1)

At this time, so she records in her *Testimonies*, she received a vision in which she made a vow always to obey Gracián.

When Vargas' time as Visitator to the Andalusian friars concluded in 1574 he handed over his task, with the agreement of the Nuncio Ormaneto, to Gracián, thus giving Gracián jurisdiction as Vicar Provincial over all the Carmelites, Discalced and Mitigated, in Andalusia in June 1574. Unfortunately, the existing Provincial, Agustín Suárez, was still in office thus helping to sow seeds for the calamity that was about to befall the Order as two rival jurisdictions were established (Suárez would continue in office until 1576, by which time the reform had been condemned by the Carmelite authorities meeting in Italy).

As Teresa moved to Seville in 1575 to begin her troubled foundation in that city Rossi wrote two letters to her, one in October 1574 and one in January 1575, asking for clarification of these latest developments in Andalusia. He was unhappy that friars previously disciplined were now roaming abroad in the reform and felt that that the new Discalced houses in Andalusia had to be closed. Sadly the letters did not reach Teresa until 17 June, by which time Rossi had convened a General Chapter of the Order in Piacenza, Italy in May 1575 to take action on the situation in Spain.

The Piacenza Chapter, taking the silence of the Reformers as an open act of defiance, agreed to forbid all new Discalced foundations, ordered Teresa to 'rest' in a convent of her choice, and appointed a General Visitor, P. Jerónimo Tostado (1523–82) to oversee the Reform of all the Order in Spain and the closure of the three Andalusian foundations made without approval of Rossi. As Teresa put it in *The Foundations*:

> The definitory gave me a command not merely to make no more foundations but not to leave the house in which I chose to reside, which would then be a kind of prison.
>
> (F: 27.20)

Mariano Azaro and Baltasar Nieto in particular were cited by the Council for their obdurance and were to be expelled from the Order if they persisted in their disobedience. The friars and nuns of the reform were not to go barefoot, or indeed call themselves 'discalced' but rather 'contemplatives' or 'primitives'. The idea behind the decrees was not to finish the reform but make sure it would continue within the structures of the Carmelite order as it stood rather than as a separate entity. In Crisógono's words, the Council 'was the signal, perhaps without anyone's being to blame, for a declaration of war among brethren' (Crisógono 1958: 90).

In May 1576 the decrees of Piacenza were published at the Castilian chapter of the Order at San Pablo de la Moraleja. In the absence of the Discalced brethren decrees were passed ordering the Discalced to wear the same habits as the Mitigated and to live in the same houses.

On his arrival in Spain in August 1576 Tostado immediately confronted King Philip and the Apostolic Nuncio, Nicolás Ormaneto. Meanwhile, Gracián began his first moves to create a separate province of Discalced using the logic that 'the faculties of apostolic visitators (i.e. himself) are greater than those of the Most Reverend Father General' (Smet 1982: 1.78). This included organising a chapter of the new Discalced Province at Almodóvar de Campo in August 1576 which was roundly condemned by Tostado. Tostado's view of the reform was not helped by the actions of that old reprobate Baltasar Nieto (de Jésus) who chose this point to abandon the reform, return to the Mitigated Carmelites in Madrid and present a letter to the King denouncing the reform in general and Gracían in particular.

Among the more lurid accusations were those that Gracián, while insisting on the abstinence of others, himself indulged in feasts of turkey, partridge and chicken; that he would get nuns to sing and dance for him and in Beas was indulged by a nun 'very young and beautiful' who dressed in the silks

of the sacristy 'so that she seemed more a prostitute than a nun.' Finally, the
old chestnut of *alumbradismo* was hurled at the reform, that constant threat
to all Teresa's activities (*Documenta primigenia*: 131 in Smet 1982: 2.83). To
compound the dire situation Ormaneto, who had protected Gracian and the
nascent reform from criticism died suddenly in June 1577 at the young age of
35. His replacement was Filippo Sega (c. 1537–96) who had been prejudiced
against the reform in Italy (although he would later soften in his attitude) and
it is to him we can attribute the famous denunciation of Teresa given to Juan de
Jésus in 1578:

> A troublesome, restless, disobedient and stubborn female, who under the guise of
> devotion invented bad doctrines, running around outside the cloister against the order
> of the Tridentine Council and prelates, instructing like a teacher in defiance of what St
> Paul taught, who ordered women not to teach.[15]

Capitalising on the appointment of a new nuncio unfavourable to the reform,
Tostado decreed that no new foundations of the reform were to be made
and that each Discalced house should replace their Discalced superiors with
Mitigated ones. If this had been enacted it would have probably meant the end
of the reform, however most Discalced houses were by this time *de facto* acting
autonomously taking their instructions from the leaders of the reform such as
Gracián and Teresa (Their correspondence at this point develops a increasingly
complex form of code and extra precautions are taken to ensure secrecy and
security in communication[16]).

As the situation deteriorated Gracián, in particular, found himself in a
difficult position caught between Pope and King. As he wrote in his memoirs
years later:

---

[15] '*Fémina inquieta, andariega, desobediente y contumaz, que a título de devoción inventaba malas doctrinas,
andando fuera de la clausura contra el órden del concilio tridentino y prelados, enseñando como maestra
contra lo que San Pablo enseñó, mandando que las mujeres no enseñasen,*' in Francisco de Santa María
*Reforma de los descalzos de Nuestra Senora del Carmen de la primitiva observancia, hecha por Santa Teresa
de Jesús* (Madrid 1644–55). 1:4:30

[16] Between December 1575 when she received news of Rossi's order of reclusion to June 1580 when the
separate Discalced province was announced, she had to be careful in her correspondence so developed her
own special code in her letters. Thus Gracián in the letters becomes 'Paul', 'Eliseus', 'Cyril' and 'Joannes'.
Teresa refers to herself as 'Ángela' or 'Laurencia'. The Grand Inquisitor becomes 'The Angel' or 'Archangel'.
The Discalced are 'the butterflies' or 'grasshoppers' while the Mitigated Carmelites become 'the cats', 'owls'
or 'Egyptians'.

Caught between King and Nuncio over this troublesome business of jurisdiction, the King said I was not to go to the Nuncio until a reply came from Rome. The Nuncio roared because I did not wait upon him, charging me with obstructing the Apostolic jurisdiction.

(Gracián, *Peregrinación de Anastasio* in *Obras*: 3.91)

As spring came in 1576 Teresa, who had been busy founding her convent in Seville, chose this moment to travel north to comply with the order of Piacenza to 'retire' to a convent of her choice. She arrived in Toledo around June 1576, travelling on to Avila the following summer around July 1577. As well as completing Chapter 27 of *The Foundations,* this stressful time saw Teresa embark on her last great masterpiece – *The Interior Castle* – begun in Toledo around June 1577 and completed in Avila a mere five months later in November 1577.

Due to the crises within the order both at Toledo and Avila, commentators suggest that she spent a mere three months in the actual writing of the text. This period included Teresa being re-elected Prioress of the *Encarnación* in October (which was later reversed by Tostado – his candidate, Ana de Toledo, eventually prevailed) and the appearance of a scurrilous pamphlet denouncing both Teresa and Gracián (see Kavanaugh and Rodriguez CW: 2.265). We shall return to the remarkable *Interior Castle*, written in such unpromising circumstances, in the following chapter. Teresa herself, however, wrote of this period in October 1577 from Toledo thus:

I have no trials now – it really seems too good to last! For they have given me a cell – and a very pleasant one – which is as solitary as a hermitage, and I am in good health, and a long way from my relatives, though they can still reach me by letter.

(Allison Peers LL: October 1577)

A peace that was denied her co-worker, John of the Cross, who, during this time had been living in a small workman's hut by the side of the *Encarnación* in Avila quietly going about the business which he was so skilled at: pastoral care of the nuns entrusted to his charge, spiritual direction and a life of austere prayer and penance. In early 1576 he had been temporarily deposed by a group of Mitigated friars and taken to Medina. Acting quickly upon the appointment of Sega, John and his companion F. Germán de Santo Matías, were arrested again on the night of 2 December 1577 by a group of Mitigated friars and taken to the Mitigated priory in Avila. Thence John was conveyed by night, blindfolded, to the Mitigated priory in Toledo to be held prisoner for nine months, finally escaping by a mixture of luck, skill and the seeming intervention of higher powers (see Tyler 2010).

Teresa, still a 'prisoner' in Avila, on hearing the news immediately wrote to King Philip:

> They are holding them prisoners in their monastery. They broke into the cells and took them and the papers they had. The whole place is highly scandalised that they should dare so much, when the place is so near where your Majesty is, it does not appear they respect either justice or God. As to me it grieves me greatly to see them in their hands. They have been longing for this for days. I should think them better off if they were among Moors, for perhaps they would have more pity.
>
> (Letter to King Philip II, 4 December 1577)

Thus, at what was probably the lowest point in the history of the reform, when all about seemed against them and their whole schema reduced to dust, we have the extraordinary phenomenon of both Teresa and John composing some of their greatest work. Teresa, the 62-year-old foundress, having already almost completed *The Foundations*, suddenly and quite unexpectedly is inspired to complete her writings on mystical prayer with the last great *Interior Castle*. John, on the other hand, the sensitive 35-year-old pastor, confined in his dungeon in the walls of Toledo begins his own remarkable writing career with the first stanzas of *The Spiritual Canticle* and the composition of many other of what would become his greatest poems (see Tyler 2010).

The Final Years

'I am not able to live in this world anymore' (Letter to Gracián, 17 April 1578) – so Teresa wrote in a letter to Gracián in 1578. As she entered her last half decade Teresa variously called herself a *pobre vieja* / 'poor old woman' or *una pobre vejezuela* / 'a poor little old woman' and there was clearly a sense that her work on this earth was coming to an end. Yet, as we shall see shortly, her letters and writings become filled with a new quality – peace and tranquillity. This, despite the turmoil and disturbance her 'little reform' had unleashed upon sixteenth century Spain.

In 1579 Sega had proposed what was increasingly becoming the only solution to the thorny problem in the Order – the formation of two separate provinces, one Mitigated and one Discalced (Letter to Gracián, 23 July 1579). This arose from a commission appointed by King Philip including the reform's old friend, Pedro Fernández. In April 1579 Sega issued a brief revoking the earlier brief that subjected the Discalced to the Mitigated and appointing a Vicar-General to the Discalced holding office 'independently of any Provincial' (see Allison Peers 1954: 60). This person was to be Ángel de Salazar (c. 1519–c. 1600), a mitigated Provincial of Castile.

Thus, on 15 July 1579, Sega and his four assessors entreated King Philip 'to command that of all the friars and nuns who profess the Primitive Rule of the Order there may be made a province distinct from those of the Mitigated, which shall embrace Castile and Andalusia ... to be subject to the General of the Order and to be governed by a Discalced Provincial' (Allison Peers 1954: 61). The final brief concluding the separation of the Provinces, *Pia consideratione,* was issued by Pope Gregory XIII in Rome in June 1580. The Discalced were to be an independent province, with their own superiors directly answerable to the General in Rome. In addition they were free to make foundations where they wished and independently of the Mitigated, who no longer had any jurisdiction over them.

Teresa received the news of King Philip's command to allow the creation of a separate province in Avila where she had settled after her enforced retirement. Her immediate response was to leave her birthplace in June 1579 and set off on the road again to continue her foundations. She had meantime suffered a nasty broken arm and needed a full time assistant, Bl. Ana de San Bartolomé, to help write her correspondence and attend to general domestic duties such as helping her to dress and undress. This was the time of her last foundations at Villanueva de la Jara (1580), Palencia (1580), Soria (1581) and Burgos (1582). However, from *The Book of Foundations* and her letters we can see that *la vejezuela* was ailing and finding it an increasing struggle to fight her old enemies: incompetence, complacency, arrogance and duplicity.

Yet, as we shall see, *The Foundations* retains to the last the sparkling gleam of Teresa's eye as she observes the passing pomp of petty squabbles and conceits. This is no more in evidence than in the final foundation of Burgos where she was thwarted by rainstorms, swollen rivers, a duplicitous Archbishop and unreliable contacts. All are described wonderfully in Chapter 31 of the book including this prize comment on her reception in Burgos:

Early that morning, Father Provincial (Gracián) went to seek the blessing of His Excellency (the Archbishop of Burgos, Cristóbal Vela), for we thought there would be nothing more to do. He found that the archbishop was very disturbed and angry because I had come without his permission[17] acting as though he had not ordered me to come or had never discussed anything about the foundation ... When finally he conceded that he had ordered me to come, he said that he meant I should come alone to discuss the matter – but I had come with so many nuns! ... He ended the visit with Father Provincial by telling him that if we did not have an income and our own house there was no way he would grant a licence and we could easily return to where we came from. And the roads were so good and the weather so charming!

(F: 31.21)

On 26 July 1582 she left Burgos with Bl. Ana and her niece 'Teresita'[18] in readiness for the latter's profession at Avila later that year. On the home journey the Duchess of Alba requested her attendance at the birth of her daughter-in-law's child. Obedient to the last, she obeyed this final request but found herself too ill to move from the convent at Alba. As well as her other symptoms, her letters in these final months tell us that she had been suffering from paralysing tonsillitis and sore throats throughout the long wet winter in Burgos, from which she never really recovered.

She died on the night of 4 October, the day chosen to introduce the new Renaissance calendar of Gregory XIII. Devised by his Jesuit astronomers to correct the problems of the older Julian calendar, 11 days were added to the calendar that night so that her feast day has henceforth been celebrated to this day on 15 October.

She left a vulnerable new reform movement with considerably more autonomy than anyone could have dreamed of even a few years before. However, the big personalities that had dogged the reform since its origins would continue to taint the smooth work of her successors.

For now, we shall conclude this chapter by looking at some of the vocabulary and style of *The Foundations* and *The Way* and how they manage to convey the

---

[17] The Archbishop had earlier shown enthusiasm but had only given oral permission not written permission.

[18] 'Teresita' was the usual name of this girl, Teresa de Jesús (1566–1610). She had been born in Quito, Ecuador, the daughter of Teresa of Avila's *conquistador* brother Lorenzo, whom we met earlier in the book. On returning to Europe, Teresita entered the Carmel at Avila where she was universally loved. She died as sub-prioress at *San José* in 1610.

message Teresa considered necessary at this later phase in her life and career as a foundress and spiritual guide.

The Language of *The Foundations* and *The Way*

The world view of *The Life* that we discussed in the previous chapter emerges from the Neo-Platonic and Dionysian schema of Teresa's 'master', Francisco de Osuna. In contrast to this beautiful world shot through with *eros* and ecstasy, *The Way* and *Foundations* offer a darker, perhaps more threatening, view of the cosmos. Teresa gives us an indication of this in the preface to *The Way* written in late 1565/early 1566. It was Teresa's fiftieth year and she senses that 'change is in the air'. Whereas the earlier text had been largely retrospective these new texts will map bold paths – *caminos* – to be taken in the future. *The Way* maps these paths through ethical desire, ascetic practice and, ultimately, the extended metaphor of the Lord's Prayer. *The Foundations* charts a more exoteric geography full, as we have seen, of the pitfalls of doubting companions, unreliable roads, the wiles of the devil and the perpetually adverse Spanish climate.

Teresa has become, in her own words, '*una romera*' (F: 3.3) – a word we can variously translate as 'gadabout', 'pilgrim', 'wanderer' or 'restless one'. Both of the routes laid out in *The Way* and *The Foundations* begin with a call articulated at the outset. In *The Way* it is a response to the 'world set on fire' / '*estáse ardiendo el mundo*' (F: 1.5) by 'the Lutherans'. In the case of the *Foundations*, it is the visit she describes to *San José* of a Franciscan friar, Fray Alonso Maldonado, who had recently returned from the King's Dominions in South America – the destination of her five brothers.

The good friar 'began to tell me about the many millions of souls that were being lost there for want of Christian instruction' (F: 1.7). Teresa describes herself as 'so grief stricken over the loss of so many souls that I couldn't contain myself' and that 'I went to a hermitage with many tears and cried out to the Lord that He may give me the means to be able to do something to win some souls to His service' (F: 1.7).

This new sense of mission as the great neo-Platonic palace of the medieval church collapses does not provoke *gustos* or *regalos*, but rather *devoción* and *ternura* (F: 1.7). For, unsurprisingly, this shift of Teresa's emphasis provokes a shift in the vocabulary she uses in these later works. *Gustos* and *Regalos* are there, but now she tends to be more circumspect in their use and holds up their appearance to the necessary hermeneutic of suspicion.

Thus in CV: 16.4 she describes how *gustos* and *regalos* can be given by the Lord to those 'who are completely lost' (*todo perdidos*). But, if they don't prepare themselves even these spiritual favours will be of no use to them: 'For myself I hold there are many to whom our Lord gives this test, but few who prepare themselves for the enjoyment of a higher grade (of prayer)'. This is a passage that differs in all three versions of *The Way* and it is clear that Teresa realized she was touching on a controversial area for in the earlier Escorial codex (CE: 26) she stresses that a soul in mortal sin cannot receive *gustos* and *regalos*. Teresa here approaches these phenomena with a much greater sense of detachment and suspicion than was ever present in the more ecstatic *Life*. The 'true contemplation', 'the higher grade of prayer', 'mental prayer/mindfulness' will rather come from 'the cultivation of the virtues' than a preoccupation with *gustos* and *regalos*.' At this crucial point she addresses 'her daughters' directly and challenges them:

> Therefore daughters if you want me to tell you about the way to arrive at contemplation, you will have to bear with me while I enlarge on some other matters (the practice of virtues) even though they may not seem important to you, for in my opinion they are. And if you don't want to hear about them or practise them, continue your mental prayer/mindfulness all your life, but in that case I assure you, and all persons who desire this blessing, that in my opinion you will not attain true contemplation (of course I can be mistaken but I am judging from myself, who sought it for twenty years).[19]
>
> (CV: 16.1)

Two chapters later in Chapter 18 of the Valladolid Codex she goes further in distancing herself from the importance of the *gustos* in the life of a Christian stressing that:

> What each of you will understand, daughters, if you are advanced, will be that you are the most wretched of all. And this understanding will be manifested in deeds (*obras*) done for your own good and the good of others, and not in having more *gustos* and raptures in prayer, or visions, or favours of this kind.
>
> (CV: 18.7) [20]

---

[19] In a typical Teresian move of unknowing in this passage she doesn't tell us that she acquired true contemplation, but simply that she has sought it (*procuré*) for twenty years.

[20] The 'distancing' from the *gustos* is even stronger in the later revised passages of the Valladolid Codex rather than the earlier redaction of the Escorial Codex.

For 'there are some people who seem to want to ask *regalos* from God as right'. On this she tartly comments 'what a pretty kind of humility that is!' (CV: 18.6). The same theme is found in *The Foundations* where Teresa outlines the temptation of relying too much on *gustos*, for this she sees, in her usual penetratingly psychological way, is at root a subtle form of self-love (F: 5.4) where we have become more obsessed with pleasing ourselves rather than others, or, above all, God: 'for clearly after a soul begins to taste how sweet the Lord is (*comienza a gustar cuán suave es el Señor*), it is more pleasing for the body to be resting without work and the soul to be regaled (*reglada el alma*)' (F: 5.4).

Such a rest she declares (F: 5.5) is a sham rest based on self-love rather than the true love of God and one's fellow humanity in suffering. In such work 'the soul loses its *regalo*' and counts the loss as gain for 'it is no longer concerned with its own satisfaction but how it can best serve the Lord.' In psychological terms she seems to be speaking of a 'decentred self' (we shall return to this in Chapter 8) where one is almost forgetting oneself in actions, works and deeds. Again, in this new language of *The Way*, 'the higher perfection' does not depend on *regalos interiores* (F: 5.10) and other visions and raptures, but simply on 'conforming our will to that of God'.[21]

To respond to the 'world in flames' not only is new behaviour required, but also, a new language which is developed in these later works. In this respect a key term that she begins to introduce more frequently from now on is *sosiego* – tranquillity, peace or calm. It is as though the more mature Teresa begins to increasingly associate God with this quality rather than the ecstasies and raptures of the young woman. One of the most striking, and beautiful uses of the word comes in Stanzas 14 and 15 of John of the Cross's 'Spiritual Canticle' where he describes the nature of the re-encounter of the soul with God after God 'has fled':

Mi Amado, las montañas,
los valles solitarios nemorosos

---

[21] See also letter to Gracián, 23 October 1576: 'The fact is that in these interior things of the spirit what is more acceptable and certain is what leaves the best effects (*la que deja mejores dejos*). What I mean by the best effects are those confirmed by works... Oh this is real prayer and not some *gustos* for the sake of nothing more than our own satisfaction (*¡Oh! Que ésta la verdadera oración y no unos gustos para nuestro gusto no más*) ... and often such a person is praying much more than the one who is breaking his head in solitude, thinking that if he has squeezed out some tears she is thereby praying.'

las insulas extrañas
los rios sonorosos
el silbo de los aires amorosos.

La noche sosegada
en par de los levantes del aurora,
la música callada,
la soledad Sonora,
la cena que recrea y enamora:

My Beloved, the mountains,
the lonely wooded valleys,
strange islands,
roaring rivers,
the whistling of love-filled breezes.

The tranquil night
at the time of the rising dawn,
silent music,
sounding solitude,
the supper that refreshes and brings love.

In these stanzas describing the 'divine union' John comments that the person:

> Sees and tastes abundance and inestimable riches (*Ve el alma y gusta en esta divina unión abundancia*) … She finds all the rest and recreation she desires, and understands secrets and strange knowledge of God, which is another one of the foods that taste best to her. She experiences in God a terrible power and force which sweeps away every other power and strength and tastes there an admirable sweetness and delight of the spirit (*y gusta allí admirable suavidad y deleite de espíritu*), discovers true tranquillity and divine light (*halla verdadero sosiego y luz divina*), and tastes sublimely the wisdom of God (*y gusta altamente de la sabiduría de Dios*) reflected in the harmony of his creatures and works.
>
> (CB: 14.4)

And on the *noche sosiego* itself he comments:

In this spiritual sleep in the bosom of the Beloved, the soul possesses and enjoys all the tranquillity and rest and quiet of the peaceful night (*posee y gusta todo el sosiego y descanso y quietud de la pacífica noche*); and she receives in God, together with this peace, a fathomless and dark divine knowledge (*oscura inteligencia divina*).

(CB: 14.22)

John's account of the *sosiego* is interesting on many levels and we must assume that he and Teresa would have discussed their interpretations of this spiritual language at some point. Teresa's *gustos* and *deleites* are present in John's account, however, he blends the Teresian ecstasy with the calm quiet of the *noche sosiego*. Also, in typical fashion, he introduces his favourite Dionysian language to link the *sosiego* with the *oscura inteligencia divina* in which he was so deeply immersed (see Tyler 2010). I suggested earlier that Teresa herself possessed this Dionysian framework to her writings, imbibed through the means of Osuna's 'Third Spiritual Alphabet',[22] however, in contrast to John, in Teresa's writing it is usually implied rather than explicit (however see my comments on the *Meditations on the Song of Songs* in Tyler 2010a).

Significantly, Teresa first uses *sosiego* in this later 'sublime' sense after the key Chapter 5 of *The Foundations* discussed above where she distances herself from the desire to seek *gustos* and *regalos* in prayer and meditation. In Chapter 6 she links this new sense of the spiritual life with another key theme for her introduced in *The Life* – the importance of *spiritual freedom*: 'From this we must learn that anything which gets the better of us to such an extent that we think our reason is not free must be considered suspect. Know that freedom of spirit (*la libertad de espíritu*) will never be gained that way' (F: 6.15). Anything else, she warns, is 'subjection of the spirit' (*sujeción de espíritu*) which for her is like being 'trapped in a bog or marsh' (*entran en un trampal u atolladero*). No matter what '*gustos* or *regalos*' we receive, how we act in the world will be the true vindication of these experiences, and this, she states, is to be discovered through '*sosiego del alma*', an adjunct for her, to humility.

From hereon the word occurs more frequently in her text and seems to presage her last letters where despite all the turmoils of these final years the word continually returns to her lips (see, *inter alia*, F: 16.5, 20.11 and 29.9).

---

[22] In *The Return to the Mystical* (Tyler 2011) I traced the 'mystical genealogy' of the Dionysian writing from its Victorine rediscovery in twelfth century Paris, through Gerson and eventually to Teresa via Osuna. For a summary of this see the following chapter in this volume.

Towards the end of her life, as the work of her reform seemed assured and the storms that had beset her for over a decade began to subside, she could write to Gracián on 26 October 1591, less than a year before her death, that '*estoy sosegada*' / 'I am now tranquil'.

This new linguistic framework will therefore enable Teresa to develop in these last works manuals to guide her sisters in the testing task of establishing the 'dovecotes of the Lord' in the demanding atmosphere of post-Reformation Europe.[23]

Summary

We have seen in *The Way* and *The Foundations* a subtle shift in Teresa's language from that of the early exuberant *Life*. Whereas the latter sought to find a 'mystical language' through interpretation of the *gustos* and *regalos* bestowed on the young nun, the later works reveal a calmer Teresa who is gently and firmly shifting the emphasis in her writing to the need for communal mutual respect, 'good works' and love to one's neighbours. This, in contrast to the ecstasies of old, will be replaced by the gentle *sosiego* that comes from union with the Divine will. As she embarks on her programme of reform, her response to the 'world in flames' of sixteenth century Europe, she realizes that the lords and ladies of earthly honour and wealth need to be treated carefully. In a letter to Gracián in 1581 she cries 'may God deliver me from these all powerful lords with their strange reversals'.

The language of *The Foundations* and *The Way* is about being affable, agreeable and pleasant to one another (*ser afables, agradar y contentar*): 'Do not cause offence!' she tells her sisters, 'so that everyone you talk to will love your conversation' (CV: 41.7). 'Don't let your soul retreat into a corner!' (CV: 41.8) she tells the sisters at the end of *The Way*. And in these later writings we get something of a sense of tiredness and occasional annoyance at having to deal with 'tricky customers' not only in the world but among her own brethren: 'as a rule nuns are discontented people/*descontentas*' (F: 20.11), 'I fear an unhappy nun more than many devils' (Letter to Gracián, 14 July 1581). Yet despite all her trials Teresa, the eternal 'gadabout', manages to pick a way

---

[23] We shall return to Teresa's 'programme of prayer' in these works in Chapter 8.

through the wreckage with grace and good humour keeping her wits about her while trying to keep in touch with that deep *sosiego* which, for the Foundress, would remain the ultimate prize of her crazy, wonderful pilgrimage to the Light.

6

Magistra Mystica: The Interior Castle

Introduction

We have one of the first references to the existence of a new work by Teresa in a letter written by her from Avila to Gaspar de Salazar[1] during the height of the persecution of her reform. Here, using the cryptic language that she often resorted to at this time, she suggests that if Father Gaspar were to come to Avila he may see a 'jewel' 'more precious' than *The Book of the Life*:

> For it treats of nothing else than Who He is; and it does so with more exquisite enamelling and craftsmanship. The jeweller did not know as much at that time, and the gold is of a finer quality, although the precious stones do not stand out as they did in the previous piece. It was done by order of the glassmaker,[2] and it appears good, or so they say.
>
> (Letter to Gaspar de Salazar, 7 December 1577)[3]

This theological masterpiece, in many ways the culmination of all her writing, was produced, as we have seen, in a breathless five month period in 1577 during the darkest hour in the history of the reform. Begun in Toledo early that year it was completed later in the year in Avila where she had moved to in July. As well as the original autograph held in the convent of the Discalced sisters in Seville

---

[1] Gaspar de Salazar (1529–93) was a Jesuit who, while at the College of St Gil at Avila, had helped Teresa enormously through many of her crises. At various times he toyed with the idea of becoming a Discalced Friar himself.

[2] That is, God.

[3] Teresa's autograph manuscript, now held at the Discalced Convent in Seville, begins with the inscription: *Este Tratado, llamado 'Castillo Interior' escrivió Teresa de Jesus.* At other times it is referred to as *Las Moradas*, literally 'The Mansions' or 'Dwelling Places'. Here I shall refer to it as *The Interior Castle* or sometimes simply *The Castle* and abbreviate with M.

there are several copies. The Toledo copy bears the date 1577 which seems to have been the copy made as Teresa wrote. The Discalced sisters of Córdoba hold a copy in Gracián's hand while the University of Salamanca possesses Ribera's copy (1588).

Gracián described her decision to write *The Interior Castle* in a conversation recorded after the event:

> Being her confessor and speaking with her once in Toledo about many things concerning her spirit, she said to me: 'Oh, how well that point is written in the book of my life, which the Inquisition has!' And I said to her, 'Well, since we can't recover it, write down what you remember, and other things, and write another book, and explain the basic doctrine without identifying the person who has experienced what you say there.'[4]

Which suggests that, like her other works, Teresa was well aware from the outset that this volume, too, must be prepared to withstand the gaze of the Inquisition as well as the general public.

We have seen how in *The Life* she developed a specific vocabulary and approach to the spiritual life that drew upon and developed the tradition of 'mystical theology' she had imbibed as a young woman. We also saw how in the later *Way* and *Foundations* she moved away to a more sceptical position especially with regard to the *gustos* and *regalos* she had so lovingly described in the earlier work.

This, as we have seen, was complemented by a new emphasis on the 'ethical', or indeed pragmatic dimension of the spiritual life with its concentration on the nature of the community life and the responsibilities and duties of her readers towards the wider world around them. The *Castle*, by contrast, can be seen as a final merging of these two positions as she produces a mature synthesis of the two. The pragmatic, ethical Teresa is there, but it is balanced with the old wisdom of the mystical theology she learnt from the books she had read in her youth. Before we look at her approach in the *Castle* it might be worth recalling her approach to the 'mystical theology' in the only book in which she refers to this – *The Book of the Life*.

---

[4] Quoted in Ahlgren (1996:61) from Gracián, *Anotaciones al P Ribera* in Antonio de San Joaquín *Año Teresiano, diario histórico, panegyrico moral, en que se descruben las virtudes, succesos y maravillas de la seráphica y mystica Doctora de la Iglesia Santa Teresa de Jésus*, Madrid 1733–69, 7.149.

The Mystical Theology

Recent research has begun to recover the significance and nature of mystical theology as a distinctive branch of theology in the middle to late Medieval period. We can now establish that from the twelfth/thirteenth centuries onwards we see in Europe the rise of a type of discourse that has been referred to as *Affective Dionysianism*.[5] Central to this movement was the group of theologians that arose around the Abbey of Saint-Denis near the schools of Paris (see Haskins 1957, Morris 1972, Knowles 1962). This group of writers and commentators associated with the abbey of St Victor in Paris[6] took particular interest in the Dionysian *corpus* which was in the process of being re-translated by theologians such as Sarracenus and Robert Grosseteste in a manner which replaced the deficiencies of the older translations by Hilduin and Eriugena.[7] The abbey grew with the schools of Paris and was open to the new theological developments of the university and from its inception it was concerned with questions on the relationship between the *intellectus* and *affectus*, which we can loosely translate as 'intellect' and 'affect'. The distinctive Victorine tradition established there combined 'a vigorous program of Bible study, serious and creative theological investigation and disciplined pursuit of contemplation all set in the context of a community orientated towards liturgical regularity and

---

[5] See, for example, Rorem 1993: 214–19 and McGinn 1998.

[6] The Abbey was founded by William of Champeaux, a master of the schools of Paris and described by Abelard as 'the first dialectician of his age', founding the abbey after retiring from the schools in 1108. He set up a small community at the site of an old hermitage on the left bank of the Seine just beyond the walls of Paris. Almost, it seems, by accident a community grew up around William who departed in 1113 to be made Bishop of Chalons. His disciple, Gilduin, was elected first Abbot of the community in the same year and under his leadership the abbey grew and flourished. Following the *Rule of St Augustine*, the community was at the forefront of clerical renewal through prayer, study and liturgy.

[7] Although circulating in the West from the eighth century onwards, the collection of writings attributed to 'Dionysius the Areopagite' (see Acts 17.34) had only received limited attention and irregular translation until the advent of the twelfth century Parisian schools. Sarracenus produced his version of the *corpus* in 1166–7, the first full translation since Eriugena, some three hundred years earlier. As Dondaine points out (1953: 64), Sarracenus used the glosses of Anastasius and Hugh of St Victor to perfect and advance his own translation. Generally Sarracenus in his translation smoothes out some of the inconsistencies and hard edges in Eriugena to present a more flowing Latin text. In particular, he avoided the strange Greek-Latin hybrid words that Eriugena often produced from his straightforward transliterations of Greek terms. Thus he renders θεοσοφίας in Dionysius's *De Theologia Mystica* (hereafter MT) as *divina sapientia (lit: divine wisdom)* rather than Eriugena's *theosophia (lit: theosophy)*. However, he does retain the *super-* terms introduced by Hilduin and Eriugena, however, ὑπέρθεε changes gender from *superdeus* to *superdea* in MT presumably in reference to the holy *Sapientia*, however the text remains ambiguous with the reference to *trinitas*.

shared experience' (Zinn 1979: 3). Within the texts of Dionysius the 'Victorines', as they became known, discovered a form of writing that allowed scholars to combine the intellect with the affect. This will go on to form the basis of much of the later medieval tradition of the 'Affective Dionysianism'. Here, as has been pointed out by commentators such as Rorem (1993) and McGinn (1998), the *affective* interpretation of Dionysius begins to surface, in contrast to what we may term the 'pure apophasis' of writers from, for example, the Rhineland School such as Meister Eckhart. In Victorine writings such as those of Thomas Gallus (which would ultimately go on to influence, among others, the English author of *The Cloud of Unknowing*), Dionysius' mystical union with God is now made through love (*affectus*) rather than intelligence (*intellectus*). It is this thread of interpretation of the Dionysian corpus made by subsequent writers that creates what I have called in this book the 'mystical theology' or *theologia mystica*.

As we have seen, Teresa herself received her education in the tradition from De Osuna's *Third Spiritual Alphabet* and Laredo's *Ascent of Mount Sion*. These two Spanish masters leant heavily themselves upon the work of Jean Gerson (1363–1429), sometime Chancellor of the University of Paris. In his writing Gerson informs us that there are two types of theology open to study. The first of these is the 'speculative theology' – the *theologia speculativa* – which is the theology of the *intellect* concerned with sharpening our understanding of the *logos* of Christian life. This would largely correspond to the type of theology taught in most universities today. However, in addition to this mode of theology he describes another, drawing upon Dionysius and the Victorines. This is the 'mystical theology'/*theologia mystica* which as the theology of the *affectus* is concerned with the *pathos* of Christian life – what we would often today refer to as 'Christian Spirituality' (see Tyler 2012).

Thus, in the *Tractatus Primus Speculativus* of Gerson's *De Mystica Theologia*, the Chancellor begins by asking: 'whether it is better to have knowledge of God through penitent *affectus* or investigative *intellectus*?' (GMT: 1.Prol.1).[8] After much discussion Gerson makes it quite clear which approach he will preference:

---

[8] My translation: *an cognitio Dei melius per penitentem affectum quam per intellectum investigantem habeatur.* From hereon I will abbreviate Gerson's *Theologia Mystica* to GMT.

Thus we see that it is correct to say that as *contemplatio* is in the cognitive power of the intelligence, the *mistica theologia* dwells in the corresponding affective power.

(GMT: 1.27.7)[9]

Therefore 'knowledge of God through mystical theology is better acquired through a penitent *affectus* than an investigative *intellectus*' (GMT: 1.28.1). For Gerson, this *theologia speculativa* resides in the *potentia intellective* – the intellectual potential – while the *theologia mystica* resides in the *potentia affective* – the affective potential. Thus, speculative theology uses 'reasoning in conformity with philosophical disciplines' (GMT: 1.30.2). *Theologia mystica*, on the other hand, needs no such 'school of the intellect' (*scola intellectus*). It is aquired through the 'school of the affect' (*scola affectus)* and (following Gerson's importance attached to the purfication of the affect) through the exercise of the 'moral virtues' that 'dispose the soul to purgation' (GMT: 1.30.3). This is acquired through the 'school of religion' (*scola religionis*) or 'school of love' (*scola amoris*). The acquisition of the *theologia mystica* does not therefore require great knowledge or extensive study of books. Rather, the mystical theology may be acquired by 'any of the faithful, even if she be an insignificant woman or someone who is illiterate' / '*a quolibet fideli, etiam si sit muliercula vel ydiota*' (GMT: 1.30.5). Concurring with St Bernard, Gerson suggests speculative theology can never be complete without mystical theology but the contrary can be the case: we all must acquire this 'affectivity' to reach right relationship with God. Therefore 'the language of mystical theology is to be hidden from many who are clerics or learned or who are called wise in philosophy or theology, so it can be conveyed to many who are illiterate and naïve, provided they have faith' (GMT: 1.31.1).

Thus, by the time Osuna and Laredo write the works of mystical theology that will so influence Teresa, this notion of the 'mystical theology' lying in the hands of the poor, the weak and 'the ignorant little old women' has taken deep roots in the soil of Spanish affective spirituality. Teresa, as we have seen, refers to herself frequently in these terms and, with her knowledge of this tradition, we cannot help but think she is doing so with more than an ironic half-smile.

Teresa herself only uses the term 'mystical theology'/*mística teología* four times in her work and these all occur in the later section on prayer introduced

---

[9] *Et cognoscamus quoniam, appropriate loquendo, sicut contemplatio est in vi cognitive intelligentie, sic in vi affective correspondente reponitur mistica theologia.*

into the *Book of the Life* on the command of García de Toledo.[10] Yet the ambience and style of the mystical theology pervades all her works, especially the later *Castle*.

Her first reference to the term is in Chapter 10 of *The Life* following, significantly enough, her description of how her life of prayer had gone astray once she had joined the Convent of the *Encarnación*. As she describes the sins into which her soul had fallen she makes a telling comment:

> And helping this was that as my sins grew, I began to lose the *gusto* and *regalo* in the things of virtue.
>
> (V: 7.1)[11]

For Teresa, one of the most distressing things at this time in her life was the loss of the *gusto* in her spiritual life. Deprived of this *gusto* she became 'afraid to pray' instead resorting to 'vocal prayer'. She clearly practised the outward virtues 'so that the nuns had a good opinion of me' while retaining this 'inner dryness'. She contrasts at this time her outer shows of piety and holiness (including instructing others on prayer) with her own interior sense of alienation from the source of her being – God. This period of unrest and unhappiness with her spiritual life dated from her profession at the convent of the *Encarnación* in 1537. Significantly, this period of physical collapse had coincided with the stay at the house of her uncle, Don Pedro de Cepeda, when, as we have seen, she first came across de Osuna's *Third Spiritual Alphabet*. As mentioned already the book remained 'her guide' for over twenty years as she found no spiritual director who could guide her as well as the book. 'During all those years, except after communion, I never dared begin to pray without a book' (V: 4.9). The experience of this time, she tells us, is one of recollection and dryness punctuated by another state of which she finds it difficult to speak (V: 4.8). This

---

[10] Throughout this discourse Teresa alters the spelling of the term from *mística teoloxía* (V: 10.1) to *mística teulogía* (V: 11.5, 18.2) to *mística teología* (V: 12.5). She also invariably prefixes her introduction of the term with the phrase *que creo se llama/creo lo llaman* – 'as I believe they call it' and surrounds it with her professed ignorance: 'I wouldn't know the proper vocabulary' (V: 18.2). In view of the greater argument of my book this dissembling seems clearly to relate to her desire to hide from censors her extensive (twenty years) study and knowledge of the subject. I shall refer to her use of the term with the more consistent phrase '*mística teología*'; however readers should see this merely as a cipher for her own more studied imprecision.

[11] *Y ayudóme a esto que, como crecieron los pecados, comenzóme a faltar el gusto y regalo en las cosas virtud .*

period ('of some twenty years' V: 8.2) she tells us was a time of neither 'pleasure in God' nor 'contentment with the world' / '*yo gozaba de Dios ni traía contento en el mundo*' (V: 8.2) for she is adamant that prayer is the source of *gustos* (V: 8.9) from the Lord, it is the place where 'the Lord takes delight in a soul and gives the soul delight' / '*entrar a regalarse con un alma y regalarla*' (V: 8.9).

In this place of deconstruction – without intellectual concourse (V: 4.7, 9.4, 9.5, 9.9) Teresa enters into a place to which she gives the name *mística teología*:

> It used to happen, when I represented Christ within me in order to place myself in His presence, or even while reading, that a feeling of the presence of God would come upon me unexpectedly so that I could in no way doubt He was within me or I totally immersed in Him ... I believe they call this 'mystical theology'.
>
> (V: 10.1)[12]

Teresa equates this 'mystical theology' with an indubitable sense of the presence of God:

> The will loves; the memory appears to me almost lost; the understanding does not discourse, so it appears to me – it is not lost, but, as I say, it does not work – however it is amazed at how much it can understand, because God wants it to understand how little it can understand of what God represents to it.
>
> (V: 10.1)[13]

The pull of the text here is as though she wants to declare the reason (*entendimiento*) ceases to work – the most extreme position of unsaying and apophasis – yet her uncertainty allows her to interject the milder *no discurre* / 'does not discourse'. Only the affective/the libidinal can function at this point, as she states in her short statement: *ama la voluntad* / 'the will loves'. As she describes in V: 12.5 this 'stopping of the intellect' is not something that is done by voluntary action, but something received from God, 'for otherwise we would

---

[12] *Acaecíame en esta representación que hacía de ponerme cabe Cristo, que he dicho, y aun algunas veces leyendo, venirme a deshora un sentimiento de la presencia de Dios que en ninguna manera podia dudar que estaba dentro de mí u yo toda engolfada en El ... creo lo llaman mística teoloxía.*

[13] *Ama la voluntad, la memoria me parece está casi perdida, el entendimiento no discurre, a mi parecer, mas no se pierde; mas, como digo, no obra, sino está como espantado de lo mucho que entiende, porque quiere Dios entienda que de aquello que Su Majestad le representa ninguna cosa entiende.*

be left like cold simpletons'. The intellectual should 'delight in God' (V: 13.11) rather than 'wear themselves out in composing syllogisms'.

Her next mention of the 'mystical theology' in V: 11.5 is to distinguish it from the beginning stages of prayer (or as she calls it 'mental prayer'/mindfulness) which will form the discourse from Chapters 11–22 – the famous analogy of the 'four waters' that we looked at earlier. The distinguishing element of the *mística teología* is, as we noted in Chapter 4 above, that it is the state of being able to 'enjoy' God's presence: *'lo más es gozar'* / 'the more to enjoy it' (V: 11.5). The beginning 'Mansions', as she will later call them in the *Interior Castle*, are places lacking in *gustos y ternera* – these are the special attributes of the *teología mística* (see V: 8.5, 9.9. 10.2 and 25.11). At this earlier stage the 'understanding' continues to 'work' and for this she recommends books such as Alonso de Madrid's *Arte de servir de Dios* (V: 12.2).The great delight in the Lord's presence in the soul (V: 14.2,14.9) reflecting the opening of the *Interior Castle*:

> This quietude and recollection is something that is clearly felt through the satisfaction and peace bestowed on the soul, along with great contentment and calm and a very gentle delight in the faculties.
>
> (V: 15.1)[14]

> Therefore in these times of quietude, let the soul remain in its repose, let them put their learning to one side … for he desires that the soul becomes a fool (*boba*), as indeed it is in his presence as His Majesty humbles himself sufficiently to allow us to be near Him despite what we are.
>
> (V: 15.8)

> I believe it will never attain true poverty of spirit, which means being at rest in labours and dryness and not seeking consolation or delight (*consuelo ni gusto*) in prayer – for those of the earth have already been abandoned – but seeking consolation in trials of love of Him who always lived in the midst of them.
>
> (V: 22.11)

As already mentioned, in *The Life* and *The Interior Castle* Teresa is always careful to avoid the term *dejamiento* when referring to these states because

---

[14] *Esta quietud y recogimiento del alma es cosa que se siente mucho en la satisfacción y paz que en ella se pone, con grandísimo contento y sosiego de las potencies y muy suave deleite.*

of the heretical association with the *Alumbrados* we discussed in Chapter 2. Throughout these works she is constantly conscious of the intense inquisitorial scrutiny surrounding such descriptions of the spiritual life – especially those given by 'idiots and little old women'! In fact, in all her works there is only one use of the term *dejamiento* and this is in *The Interior Castle* 3.1.8: '*No hay duda sino que si persevera en esta desnudez y dejamiento de todo, que alcanzará lo que pretende*' / 'there is no doubt that if we persevere in this nakedness and *dejamiento* from all things, we shall attain what we aim for.'

Thus, in these four references in the *Life*, *teología mística* is as much an *activity* as a state of mind or theological path. Yet, as I have already said, no sooner does she introduce the term in the early chapters of the *Life*, does she drop it never to reuse it. This may be, as we have suggested, to avoid inquisitorial scrutiny (hence her imprecision with its use and spelling) or, it may be that as she proceeds in developing her own spiritual theology she outgrows the term and its associations. It is striking that the term occurs nowhere in the last, great *Interior Castle*. Yet this work as a whole can be seen a commentary upon, or indeed apotheosis of, the long medieval tradition. As we shall see now, her genius in this work is to take this tradition and recreate it for her own specific needs before propelling it, in ways we shall describe in Part Three of this book, into future discourses of which she could have had no representational content.

The Entrance to *The Castle*

When we approach Teresa's final work, then, we must realize that apparent simplicity and naivety can artfully conceal many layers of sophisticated insight into the tradition of mystical theology that she had been inducted into. This is intertwined with more than twenty years' experience of writing as well as the extensive knowledge of the human psyche acquired from her duties as a foundress of a large flourishing religious congregation. At the same time she is also constantly alert to the possibility of inquisitorial scrutiny and endeavours to steer her discourse away from the problematic areas associated with *Alumbradismo* while giving 'her daughters' a feel for the 'rich treasures' of the spiritual life so necessary if her reform is to grow and spread.

In many ways *The Castle* is a mysterious, magical work and much ink has been spilt on deciphering its spirit and meaning. On one level the literary conceit of the book is simply put: the spiritual development of a person can be compared to seven descriptions of 'dwelling places' or 'mansions' which preoccupy the seeker.[15] However, there is a danger of oversimplifying this conceit. Teresa is sophisticated enough as a writer to know that the spiritual life can only be approached in writing by means of her elusive, elliptical *estilo* that we have analysed throughout this book. 'Hifalutin terms' for the spiritual life are dropped in favour of a simplicity and openness that can be deceptive. This is the mature exposition of her own mystical theology, but it is done in such a way as to confound 'learned men' and 'speculative theologians'. As with so much of Teresa's writing, the medium will become the message.

This approach is apparent from the very beginning of the book where Teresa presents her project in a magisterial opening passage:

While I was beseeching our Lord today to speak for/through me (*por mí*),[16] as I was unable to find a thing to say (*no atinaba a cosa que decir*),[17] or how to begin to comply with this obedience, what I will say now presented itself (*ofreció*)[18] to begin with this starting point: that we consider our soul to be like a castle, totally of diamond or very clear crystal, where there are many abodes (*aposentos*),[19] as in heaven there are many mansions. Now if we consider it carefully, sisters, the soul of a just person (*el alma del justo*)[20]is nothing else but a paradise where He says he takes his delights (*El tiene sus deleites*).[21] Well then, what do you think such an abode would be like where a King

---

[15] The conceit of seven 'mansions', 'dwelling places' or 'abodes' is an original one to Teresa and unlike anything else in previous Christian literature. However, Swietlicki (1986) and Green (1989), among others, contend that Teresa was consciously or unconsciously drawing on cabbalistic sources for the structure of her work. Other commentators (see, for example, López-Baralt, 1992) have hinted at Islamic Sufi origins. These sets of arguments have been well rehearsed in the publications in question and I do not intend to pursue them again here.

[16] Allison Peers gives 'through', Kavanaugh and Rodriguez give 'for'.

[17] Allison Peers gives 'I could find nothing to say', Kavanaugh and Rodriguez, 'I wasn't able to think of anything to say'.

[18] Allison Peers: 'a thought occurred to me', Kavanaugh and Rodriguez: 'there came to my mind'. I think both translations over-intellectualize the process that Teresa is conveying in this passage.

[19] Allison Peers: 'a rather more pretentious word than the English "room": dwelling-place, abode, apartment'. Kavanaugh and Rodriguez add: 'Teresa uses the Spanish words *moradas, aposentos y piezas* in approximately the same sense; they refer to rooms or dwelling places within the castle ... Most people today think of a mansion as a large stately home, not what Teresa had in mind with the term *moradas*. "Dwelling places" turns out to be a more precise translation of Teresa's *moradas* than is the classic 'mansions' and more biblical and theological in tone.'

[20] Allison Peers: 'the soul of the righteous man', Kavanaugh and Rodriguez:'the soul of the just person'.

[21] Allison Peers: 'He takes His delight', Kavanaugh and Rodriguez: 'He finds His delight' see also V14:10 and Excl. 7, allusion to Proverbs 8.31.

so powerful, so wise, so pure, so full of good things, takes his delight? I cannot find anything with which to compare the great beauty and capacity of the soul; and truly our intellects will no more be able to grasp this than they can comprehend God, no matter how keen they are, for He Himself said that He created us in his own image and likeness.

(M: 1.1.1)[22]

At first sight this seems an unpromising start for one of the greatest expositions of mystical theology in the Christian canon: 'While I was beseeching our Lord today to speak for/through me as I was unable to find a thing to say, or how to begin to comply with this obedience, what I will say now presented itself to begin with this starting point.' The by now familiar notes of uncertainty and self-deprecation are present from the start. Yet this stuttering voice also reveals the fact that our intellects (*nuestros entendimientos*) cannot grasp that which we seek – whether it be the nature of God or the nature of the soul (Teresa boldly implies that epistemologically they present the same situation to the intellect). Rather than presenting an intellectual or conceptual notion of the soul, something 'presents itself' to her.[23]

Teresa seems quite precise in her language that the image or trope of the Castle offers itself or presents itself rather than is thought, for, as she says, our intellects and understanding cannot grasp what is being presented. As she had said earlier in *The Foundations* and *The Way*: 'the soul is not thought' (F: 5.2) but is rather 'enjoyed without understanding' (CV: 25.2). So again, here she tells us that the self is 'enjoyed' (*se deleita*) by 'the King'. The dialectic of affectivity lies at the heart of this epistemology, just as it did in her earlier works. The true nature of ourselves, our relation to God, and God in God's self are described in terms of affectivity and delight. Just as Osuna quoted Proverbs 8.31 in his chapter on

---

[22] *Estando hoy suplicando a nuestro Señor hablase por mí, porque yo no atinaba a cosa que decir ni cómo comenzar a cumplir esta obediencia, se me ofreció lo que ahora dire, par comenzar con algún fundamento: que es considerar nuestra alma como un Castillo todo de un diamante o muy claro crystal, adonde hay mucho aposentos, así como en el cielo hay muchas moradas. Que si bien lo consideramos, hermanas, no es otra cosa el alma del justo sino un paraíso adonde dice El tiene sus deleites. Pues ¿qué tal os parece que sera el aposento adonde un Rey tan poderoso, tan sabio, tan limpio, tan lleno de todos los bienes se deleita No hallo yo cosa con que comparar la gran hermosura de un alma y la gran capacidad; y verdaderamente apenas deben llegar nuestros entendimientos, por agudos que fuesen, a comprenderla, así como no pueden llegar a considerar a Dios, pues El mismo dice que nos crió a su imagen y semejanza.*

[23] *Ofreció,* literally 'offers itself', it is not 'thought' as Kavanaugh and Rodriguez and Allison Peers translate it nor is it an 'idea' as other translators present it e.g. Benedictines of Stanbrook 1906.

the *sabrosa saber*, so again Teresa makes allusion to the same passage when she describes the soul as the place 'wherein our Lord takes delight'. As with Osuna, so with Teresa, knowledge is obtained from 'tasting' the delights of the *gustos espirituales;* this will become apparent as the reader moves through the 'castle'. The old language of *The Life* is never far from the surface.

The second thing to note about this paragraph is Teresa's use of symbol and metaphor. We shall return to this in the following chapter when we shall explore the role of symbol and metaphor from medieval and psychological perspectives. For now it is sufficient to note that Teresa presents a series of metaphors, one after another, for the soul – each one is piled one after the other: a castle, totally of diamond or other clear crystal, of many abodes, like the heavenly mansions, a paradise where He takes His delights, and like God in God's self. The effect leads to spatial and emotional disorientation which is another theme we shall explore in a later chapter.[24] This spatial instability continues throughout the chapter and indeed the whole book. As she states in M: 1.1.3, the aim of this disorientating metaphor is to illustrate the 'favours' which the Lord will grant:

> It is necessary that you keep this comparison in mind. Perhaps God will be pleased to let me use it to explain something to you about the favours (*mercedes*) He is happy to grant souls and the differences between these favours.
>
> (M: 1.1.3)

The recipients will be 'regaled and awakened' / *'se regalarán y despertarán'* (M: 1.1.4) by these favours for the castle itself is not just beautiful but 'full of delight' (*deleitoso* M: 1.1.5) to those who enter it. It defines itself in terms of 'delight' and *regalo*.

As well as the necessity for delight the first part of Teresa's *Castle* frequently mentions 'self knowledge' (*el propio conocimiento* M: 1.1.8, 1.2.8,[25] 1.2.9, 1.2.13[26]). This is not the 'head knowledge' of ideas and thought – the knowledge of the *letrados* and 'wise men' – but rather the 'experiential knowledge' of the affective medieval mystical theology closely connected to the libidinal springs of

---

[24] In M 1.2.1 more metaphors are introduced: 'this pearl from the Orient, this tree of life'. In M 1.2.8 it is a 'palmetto fruit'.

[25] 'Oh but if it is in the room of self knowledge! How necessary this room is – see that you understand me – even for those whom the Lord has brought into the very dwelling place where He abides.' (M 1.2.8)

[26] 'Self-knowledge is the most important thing for us.'

delight: the *affectus* of the Victorines, Gerson and Osuna. 'Without experience' /
'*si no hay experiencia*' (M: 1.1.9), she suggests, it is difficult to understand what
she is talking about. Experiential reflection is a necessary component of her
presentation – her 'offering'.

Self-knowledge, humility and delight are all presented in these dense first
pages of the *Castle*. The final element of Teresa's strategy – the 'transformational'
– is brought out towards the end of the first mansions. Here she notes that the
soul 'will not be able to enjoy' (M: 1.2.14) the pleasures of the Lord if there are
impediments in our outer life such as 'possessions, honour or business affairs'.

To proceed further, 'to enter the second dwelling place', the seeker 'must give
up unnecessary things and business affairs' (M: 1.2.14). Only by transforming
our 'outer' attachments can 'inner' attachments be altered. For Teresa, as she
has made clear countless times, has no desire to write an academic treatise on
theology or spirituality. Rather, the aim of her book is to *transform* the reader.
Just as that important influence on her, Ignatius Loyola, desired to write a book
of *Exercises* to be practised rather than read,[27] so Teresa's last great writing can
be seen to be as much a book of spiritual exercises as spiritual theology. Her
aim in writing the book is to transform her readers so that they too may enjoy
the same favours and gifts, *gustos* and *regalos*, that she herself has experienced.
Thence, as she outlined in the *Way* and *Foundations*, we shall be led to the
ethical action of the final 'mansions' of the *Castle*.

In M: 1.2.16 she describes the necessity of each individual sister making 'a
good beginning', observing faults and that which leads us from the interior
transformation to the exterior. This leads inevitably to her final paragraphs of
the First Mansions:

> Let us understand, my daughters, that true perfection consists in love of God *and
> neighbour* (my emphasis); the more perfectly we keep these two commandments the
> more perfect we will be.
>
> (M: 1.2.18)

She concludes her impressive opening chapter by giving an example to illustrate
the embodied, practical, ethical action she is recommending. In this case that
sisters, especially superiors, must be careful about admonishing one another

---

[27] See Hughes in Tyler and Woods 2012.

and how they upbraid others for not keeping convent rules, for 'much discretion is necessary'.

The First Mansion of *The Castle* is a *tour de force* of mystical strategy, combining as it does all the elements of unknowing and embodiment of the medieval mystical tradition that Teresa had imbibed in her reading as a young woman. The movement in the chapter from the opening passages saturated in metaphor and scriptural allusion, the subtle use of strategies of unknowing and embodiment, and the final presentation of a practical 'case study' will be typical of how she proceeds throughout the book. Each chapter will contain all three elements and, seemingly to emphasize the point, each chapter will end with a very practical example to illustrate the points that have been made. Mansion Four, for example, having discussed the 'prayer of quiet' and 'raptures' give some guidelines at the end for how to deal with nuns who appear to be suffering from such raptures but are simply physically ill. This is done with humour (an essential part of Teresa's programme, as we have seen), discretion and discernment:

> Since (these sisters) feel some consolation interiorly and a languishing and weakness exteriorly, they think they are experiencing a spiritual sleep (which is a prayer a little more intense that the prayer of quiet) and they let themselves become absorbed. The more they allow this the more absorbed they become because their nature is further weakened, and they fancy they are being carried away with rapture (*arrobamiento*). I call it being carried away in foolishness (*abobamiento*) because it amounts to nothing more than wasting time and wearing down one's health ... By sleeping and eating and avoiding so much penance the person got rid of the stupor.
>
> (M: 4.3.11)

The Remaining Mansions

In overview, the *Interior Castle* takes the basic form of three mansions which prepare the self in the way described for transformation. True to her roots in de Osuna and the *theologia mystica* she does not describe this transformation, but through the sort of verbal strategies we have explored suggests how this may come about for the person. Thus, after the preparations of the first three mansions, the fourth is essentially the 'mansion of transformation' where the change can occur. Thereafter the final three mansions discuss the consequences of the transformation with particular emphasis on the move from 'rapture' to 'works'/*obras* nicely summarized in this passage from the Fifth Mansion:

> When I see people very diligently observing the sort of prayer that they have and very wrapped up in it when they have it (for it seems that they will not let the thought move or stir in case they lose a small morsel of the *gusto* or devotion that they have had), I realise how little they understand of the road to the attainment of union. They think that the whole business lies in such things.
>
> No, sisters, no! The Lord desires works and that if you see a sick woman to whom you can give some help, never be affected by the fear that your devotion will suffer, but take pity on her: if she is in pain you should feel pain too; if necessary, fast so that she may have your food, not so much for her sake as because you know that the Lord desires it.
>
> (M: 5.3.11)

Thus, in the Second and Third Mansions she emphasizes (M: 2.1.7 c.f. V: 4.2, 11.10–15) that the *gustos* cannot be striven for: 'souls shouldn't be thinking about *regalos* at this beginning stage.' Our non-thinking extends towards not desiring the *regalos*. Once again she emphasizes that this is an *experiential* process and the reader cannot begin to recollect (themselves) by force but 'only by gentleness / *suavidad*' / '*y cómo no ha de ir a fuerza de brazos el comenzarse a recoger, sin con suavidad*' (M: 2.1.10). As always with this experiential learning 'it is very important to consult persons with experience.' It is a theme we shall return to in the next chapter when we consider Teresa and the role of the Spiritual Director.

In the Second Mansions Teresa talks of the disturbance of the intellect: 'Here the intellect (*entendimiento*) is more alive and the faculties (*potencias*) more skilled. The blows from the artillery strike in such a way that the soul cannot fail to hear' (M: 2.1.3). The devils 'represent the esteem one has in the world, one's friends and relatives, one's health a thousand other obstacles'. The power of intellectual representation is clearly a block to *recogimiento*, and in Teresa's language, is used by the devil for that purpose. The dangers of the intellect are clearly delineated here. In so far as the intellect is to be used it is to remind the person of the importance of persevering with *recogimiento* (M: 2.1.4) – it must not, however, be used as a critical tool in itself.

Even in these early mansions, the intellect is there to serve the function of helping the soul find *gustos, mercedes* and *regalos* within *recogimiento*, rather than striving after intellectual comprehensions. We are being prepared '*para gozar su gloria*' / 'to enjoy his glory' (M: 2.1.11).

Moving into the Third Mansions, she characterizes the people at this stage of the journey as being:

> Fond of doing penance and setting aside periods for recollection (*horas de recogimiento*); they spend their time well, practising works of charity towards their neighbours; and are very balanced in their use of speech and dress and in the governing of their households.
>
> (M: 3.1.5)

Clearly the *entendimiento* is well developed! To pass this level, which she compares with the rich young man of Matthew 19.16–22, we must pass into the place of unknowing and *gusto*:

> Let us prove ourselves, my Sisters, or let the Lord prove us, for He knows well how to do this even though we often don't want to understand it.
>
> (M: 3.1.7)

The action required 'must not be fabricated in our imaginations but proved by deeds' (M: 3.1.7): the person must move from interior reflection to embodied action. As she says in M: 3.1.9, a certain humility of intellect is required for this process to work: 'The Lord will give you understanding of them so that out of dryness you may draw humility – and not disquiet, which is what the devil aims after.'

The possession of the *entendimiento* is also connected with worldly success:

> After these years, when it seems they have become Lords of the world or at least clearly disillusioned in this regard. His Majesty will try them in some minor matters, and they will go about disturbed and afflicted that it puzzles me and makes me fearful.
>
> (M: 3.2.1)

She helps these people by 'compassion' / '*sentimiento*' and not 'contradicting their reason' (M: 3.2.2). The process of unknowing is not initiated through the intellect but the affect. For these people 'their reason is still very much in control. Love has not yet reached the point of overwhelming reason' (M: 3.2.7).[28] She exhorts us to 'let us abandon our reason (*dejemos nuestra razón*) and our fears into His hands' (M: 3.2.8).

---

[28] *Porque su razá muy en sí; no está aún el amor para sacar de razón.*

This 'letting go of the reason' and the move to the affect will occur in the all-important Fourth Mansions of transformation. At the beginning of this Mansion (M: 4.1.1) she once again returns to the dilemma that she had encountered in *The Life*: *how can the spiritual life be successfully described in simple language*, that is, what literary mechanisms, or indeed *strategies* can be employed to do this?[29]

She writes that she cannot *explain* the process but rather she will *show* it:

> As these mansions are much closer to where the King lives, they have great beauty and there are things so delicate to see and understand there, which the understanding does not have the capacity to grasp them, although something might turn out to be well put and not at all obscure to the inexperienced; those who have experience, especially a lot of it, will understand very well.
>
> (M: 4.1.2)[30]

By metaphor, disorientation and simple language she will demonstrate her transformative strategies. The power of the *gustos* and *regalos* will be an important part in that process of transformation until they too must eventually fall away in the last Mansions as the importance of embodied existence in ethical 'good works' takes over.

Consequently, as well as delineating the nature of the 'mystical strategy' as an unknowing-affective strategy Teresa goes into greater depth here than she has ever done before to map this affective territory. Teresa, of course, knows of the dangers here (The *Meditations on the Song of Songs* had not long been burnt, see Tyler 2010a) so she treads very carefully in defining the *gustos* in such a way as to retain their affective power but to protect her from unwelcome attention (and suppression) from the Inquisition.

As she begins Mansion Four she returns to the *gustos* of *The Life* but this time she is able to delineate their role with much greater precision:

> Well then, talking about what I said I would mention here about the difference between the *contentos* in prayer and *gustos*: *contentos* appear to me to be that which we can name

---

[29] 'Although I think I now have a little more light about these favours the Lord grants to some souls, knowing how to explain them is a different matter.' M: 4.1.1

[30] *Como ya estas moradas se llegan más adonde está el Rey, es grande su hermosura y hay cosas tan delicadas que ver y que entender, que el entendimiento no es capaz para poder dar traza cómo se diga siquiera algo que venga tan al justo que no quede bien oscuro para los que no tienen experiencia; que quien la tiene muy bien lo entenderá, en especial si es mucha.*

as having acquired from our meditation and petitions to our Lord, which proceed from our natural nature, although in the end God helps this.

(M: 4.1.4)[31]

In *The Life* this had been described as the 'beginning stages' of prayer in the first and second waters of the 'four waters'. In the earlier work, Teresa had not really named this experience, now she chooses the word '*contentos*.' They are, for Teresa, associated with the *entendimiento* (intellect) and their reception is linked with the work of the intellect described in the first three Mansions.[32] In this respect, for Teresa, they can be classified along with other 'warm feelings' that we receive in everyday life when, for example, we 'suddenly inherit a great fortune ... succeed in a large and important business matter or when you see your husband or brother alive after someone has told you he is dead' (M: 4.1.4). 'In sum', she concludes, these *contentos* 'have their beginning in our nature and end in God' (M: 4.1.4).

Although she states that the *gustos,* on the other hand, 'begin in God' (M: 4.1.5) she refuses to *say* what they are, but rather resorts to *showing* them to us through the use of metaphor and analogy, just as she did at the beginning of the *Castle* when referring to the nature of the self. The *gustos,* then, are like the words of the Psalmist '*Cum dilatasti cor meum*':[33] they are an enlargement of the heart. They are like a trough of water filled 'by a source of water right there, and ... without any noise ... There is no need for any skill, nor does the building of aqueducts have to continue; but water is always flowing from the spring' (M: 4.2.2–3).[34] This water appears '*con grandísima paz y quietud y suavidad*' /

---

[31] '*Los contentos me parece a mí se pueden llamar los que nosotros adquirimos con nuestra meditación y peticiones a nuestro Señor, que procede de nuestro natural, aunque en fin ayuda para ello Dios.*' Kavanaugh and Rodriguez translate this passage as 'the term consolations, I think, can be given to those experiences we ourselves acquire through our own meditation and petitions to the Lord'. Teresa, significantly, does not use this language of 'naming experiences', here as in many other passages Kavanaugh and Rodriguez show that they are tending towards an epistemological bias based on 'modern mystical' experientialism (see Tyler 2011).

[32] 'For we obtain them (the *contentos*) through thoughts (*con los pensamientos*), assisting ourselves, using creatures to help our meditation, and tiring the intellect (*cansado el entendimiento*).' (M: 4.2.3)

[33] Teresa actually writes 'Cun dilatasti cor meun', no doubt aware of the dangers of a woman writing on scripture described previously. The line is from Ps 118.32: 'When you did enlarge my heart.'

[34] Teresa has of course returned to her favourite metaphor of water. However here she reduces the four waters of *The Life* to the much simpler two: one filled by artifice and one from a natural spring. This fits better with her later contrast in *The Castle* between the *contentos* and *gustos*. The earlier *Life* did not emphasize such a contrast.

'the greatest peace, quiet and gentleness' and is associated with '*lo muy interior de nosotros mesmos*' / 'our most interior' state (M: 4.2.4) – an interior 'most unknown' to us.

Elsewhere, the *gustos* are like 'fragrance from a brazier giving off sweet smelling fragrances' somewhere deep in the self (M: 4.2.6). Or, like 'the whistling of the shepherd' (M: 4.3.2)[35] which wandering souls hear and return to with love and devotion. As she explains the draw of this whistle, which for her is at the edge of hearing and understanding, she makes one of her few explicit references to Master Osuna, whose thoughts on *recogimiento* and mystical theology are clearly with her here:

> I don't know in what way or how they heard their shepherd's whistling. It wasn't through the ears, because nothing is heard. But one noticeably senses a gentle drawing inward (*un encogimiento suave a lo interior*), as anyone who goes through this will observe, for I don't know how to make it clearer. It seems to me I have read that it is like a hedgehog or tortoise, when they withdraw into themselves; the one who wrote this must have understood it well.
>
> (M: 4.3.3)[36]

John, when expounding the passage of *El silbo de los aires amorosos* in the 14th Verse of *The Spiritual Canticle* (see footnote above), associates the phrase with 'the secret words that no-one is allowed to utter' (CA: 14.8). Faced with this ineffability John turns to poetry while Teresa turns to metaphor. Before the soul returns to the world of action at the end of the castle at this point in the journey it is simply suspended in love in the arms of the Beloved: 'the one who thinks less and has less desire to act does more' (M: 4.3.5).

To proceed on the spiritual journey, she says, we must 'not think much but love much... and so do that which best stirs you to love' / '*no está la cosa en pensar mucho, sino en amar mucho*' (M: 4.1.7, c.f. F: 5.2). 'Don't think this *recogimiento*', she writes, 'is acquired by the intellect (*entendimiento*) striving

---

[35] '*Un silbo tan suave que aun casi ellos mesmos no lo entienden*'/' a whistle so soft that even they (the courtiers lost outside the castle) almost fail to hear it.' An echo, surely, of John of the Cross' *silbo de los aires amorosos* in Verse 14 of the *Spiritual Canticle*. John makes reference here (CA: 14.7) to Elijah's encounter with the 'gentle breeze' during his flight from Jezebel in 1 Kings 19.12. John calls it the '*sutil y delicada comunicación del espíritu le nacía la inteligencia en el entendimiento*' (CA: 14.7).

[36] Osuna uses the same example in TA: 4.4. Teresa's *encogimiento* here is an interesting variant or development of *recogimiento*.

to think about God within itself, or by the imagination (*imaginación*) imaging Him within itself' (M: 4.3.3). However such 'unknowing' is accompanied by the increase of the affective and cannot exist on its own: 'love must already be awakened' (M: 4.3.4.). The *entendimiento* cannot be stopped without this:

> When His Majesty desires the intellect to stop, He occupies it in another way and gives it a light so far above what we can attain that it remains absorbed. Then, without knowing how, the intellect is much better instructed than it was through all the soul's efforts not to make use of it.
>
> (M: 4.3.6)

Thus the intellect moves into unknowing as the affect is quickened by the encounter with God. 'Without any effort or noise the soul should strive to cut down the rambling of the intellect (*el dicurrir del entendimiento*) but without suspending either it or the *pensamiento*' (M: 4.3.7). Teresa seems here to be treading the fine path between ending the discursive intellect and recognising the danger of an *Alumbradismo* like Quietism. Her compromise: 'cutting down the rambling' without suspending it, seems to suggest a way out. She has moved from Osuna's total reliance on the affect at the expense of the intellect. However, although this is what she states in M: 4.3 there are enough contradictory statements to suggest an alternative reading and that her position is not so far from Osuna's (and possibly the *Alumbrados*) as she would have us believe. The soul, she says, must 'enjoy' the new place without trying to understand it (M: 4.3.7).[37]

As we have seen, Teresa ends the Fourth Mansions with spiritual advice warning sisters who experience a sort of 'spiritual stupor' which she calls being carried away with 'foolishness' / '*abobamiento*'. Although there is an element of tongue-in-cheek here Teresa is of course strengthening her anti-*Alumbrado* credentials by these sort of remarks while using her well wrought humour. Unlike the *Life* which contained lengthy accounts of these practices, visions, levitations, locutions etc., the *Interior Castle* presents the considered views of a spiritual master on how such phenomena should be treated. We shall turn to those now.

---

[37] *Goza sin ninguna industria.*

Visions and Revelations

We have already seen in the 'third water' of the *Life* how Teresa felt the need
to discuss the extraordinary and supernatural phenomena that she associated
with a deepening spiritual life. There she was able to acknowledge these 'mad'
phenomena but also understand that 'the water is for the flowers' of 'good
works, good works, good works'. It is this relativization of the importance of
these phenomena which will be the hallmark of her most mature consideration
of them in the Sixth Mansion of the *Castle*.

Although the Sixth Mansion is her *Summa* on these phenomena, advice
and help for those undergoing these experiences is scattered throughout her
writings. Chapter 8 of *The Foundations* was devoted entirely to the subject which
she began with the memorable phrase: 'some people seem to be frightened by the
very mention of visions and revelations' (F: 8.1). I would venture to suggest that
the general misapprehension and incomprehension towards these phenomena
is as widespread today as it was in sixteenth century Spain. Perhaps an overly
rationalized culture will inevitably have problems with essentially a-rational,
libidinal phenomena such as the visions and ecstasies that Teresa (and her
co-workers) describe with such abandon. Whatever we may think of these
phenomena it is certain that they have existed throughout the two thousand
year history of Christianity and look set to continue to do so (see, for example,
Cartledge: *Charismatic Spirituality* in Tyler and Woods 2012). Indeed, they are
not confined to Christianity and similar phenomena may be found in Sufi Islam,
Tibetan Buddhism and various branches of Hinduism (see, for example, Samuel
1993 and Krishna 1971). As we heard recounted in her *Life*, Teresa herself experienced a great deal of misunderstanding and incomprehension from confessors
and friends alike in her early years in Avila, and it seems that in her last work she
felt the need to 'put the record straight' if only to give succour to future sisters
who have similar experiences. From *The Life* onwards her rule of thumb with
such experiences remained the same – were they leading us towards the *sosiego*
of 'good works' or were they leading to disharmony, distemper and disturbance?

In terms of Teresa's language at this point, she is very clear (M 6.2.2) that
these phenomena go beyond the *gustos* experienced in the earlier Mansions
(and earlier 'waters' of *The Life*):

(The experiences at this point) are very different from all that we can acquire here
below and even from the *gustos* that we talked about, for often when a person is

distracted and forgetful of God, His Majesty will awaken (the soul) like a bright comet passing quickly or a thunderclap even though one neither sees light nor hears noise; but the soul clearly understands that it was called by God, and understands such that sometimes – especially at the beginning – it trembles and even complains even though there is nothing that causes pain.

(M: 6.2.2)[38]

The enjoyment (*gozarse*) is clear and the pain is the old paradoxical pain of the Life – '*sabrosa y dulce*'. It is a *silbo tan penetrativo* like the one described earlier in the Fourth Mansion. We have returned to the ecstastic libidinal scene in Chapter 29 of *The Life* where Teresa encountered the cherub with the wounding spear:

Sometimes (when I was at this place) the Lord wanted me to see this vision: I saw an angel close to me on my left side in corporal form, something I only see occasionally. Although angels are represented to me many times I don't see them, at least not in the sense of 'vision' of which I spoke at first. It pleased the Lord that I should see this vision in the following manner: he was not large but small, very beautiful, the face so enflamed that he appeared to be one of the very high angels that appear to be totally aflame (I believe they are called Cherubim although they don't tell me their names, but I see clearly that there is a great difference between certain types of angels and others, and between these and others still, of a kind that I could not possibly explain). I saw in his hands a long golden spear (*un dardo de oro largo*), and at the end of the iron tip there appeared a little flame, this he seemed to put into my heart several times so that it reached my entrails (*y que me llegava a las entrañas*).[39] As he removed it, they seemed to be drawn with it so that I was left totally on fire with a great love of God. The pain I felt was so great that I uttered several moans, and so excessive was the sweetness (*suavidad*) caused by this pain that one would never want to lose it, nor would the soul be content with anything less than God. It is not a bodily pain, but spiritual, although the body

---

[38] Another difficult Teresian passage to translate. I have tried to keep Teresa's flow and sentence structure as she wrote it, although the subject of her verbs is obscure at some points. Unusually in this text '*relampago*' / 'lightning' is crossed out and replaced with 'thunderclap' (most of the text of *The Castle* is written without corrections). Efrén tells us that although Teresa uses the word *cometa* the sense of the word at the time (he quotes from a 1729 dictionary) is less that of a scientifically observed heavenly body but rather strange and unusual flashings of light in the night sky. Perhaps Teresa felt this was too near in meaning to 'lightning flash' and so subsequently deleted the latter.

[39] Allison Peers uses the more provocative 'penetrate' here, while Kavanaugh uses 'reach'.

has a share in it – considerably so. It is such a sweet love-exchange (*un requiebro*) which passes between the soul and God that I beg Him out of His goodness to give this *gusto* to anyone who thinks I am lying.

(V: 29.13)

This striking and justly celebrated passage is now recalled in the Sixth Mansion:

So powerful is the effect of this on the soul that it dissolves with desire and doesn't know what to ask for, for clearly it seems that it is with its God. You will ask me: Well, if it knows this, what does it desire or what pains it? What greater good does it want? I don't know. I do know that it seems that this pain reaches to the soul's entrails (*entrañas*)[40] and that when He who wounds it draws out the arrow, it indeed seems, in accord with the deep love the soul feels, that God is drawing these very entrails after Him. I was thinking now that it is as though, from this fire enkindled in the brazier that is my God, a spark (*un centella*) jumped out and so touched the soul that the flaming fire was felt by it and since it was not enough to set the soul on fire, and it is so delightful, the soul is left with that pain; and this produced by it just touching the soul.

(M: 6.2.4)

When the two passages are juxtaposed like this it is possible to interpret the passage according to Teresa's mystical theology. Bernini's statue at Santa Maria della Vittoria in Rome is, of course, a magnificent artefact of Baroque statuary, however the effect has been to take the passage from Chapter 29 of *The Life* entirely out of its mystical context so distorting its significance within her text. When the text is placed alongside that from the Sixth Mansion what is remarkable is the consistency of the language of the two passages written over ten years apart. The only word that does not reappear in *The Castle* is *gustar*. Following her development and clarification of the role of the *gustos* this is unsurprising and to be expected that it would be dropped in the later passage. The flame of the cherubim remains (so essential for the Victorine tradition, see, for example the 'dart of flaming love' mentioned in *The Cloud of Unknowing*). However Teresa introduces the all important word *centella* in the later passage. A clear reference to the *synderesis* of the medieval mystical tradition (literally; 'the little spark'): the place, according to Gerson, Bonaventure and Hugh of

---

[40] Matthew and Allison Peers give 'bowels' for *entrañas* which seems very appropriate.

Balma, where the divine touches the human in the soul. This little spark gently 'touches' the heart and causes the ecstasy of fire. It does not 'penetrate' as some translators suggest and although sexual connotations are present in the passage this sexualized interpretation cannot detract from the fact that these passages are referring to the workings of the heart rather than anything specifically sexual.

The other phrase that remains constant in the two passages is *las entrañas* – entrails or bowels. Teresa, as always, is circumspect in her descriptions of the nature of the 'centre of the soul' and this is another instant where she carefully uses language to indicate a source without clearly delineating the nature of the source. A theme we shall return to in Chapter 8 below. In their balance of Dionysian unknowing with libinal energization these passages are rightly celebrated as masterpieces of Teresa's mystical theology.

Union Through Action

The final three Mansions of *The Interior Castle* are concerned with showing how the living-out of the transformation she has described in the book is best effected through action in the world. What she is proposing is *union with God through action in the world* – essentially the thesis developed in the previous decade as she drafted *The Way* and *The Foundations*.

Thus, from the Fifth Mansion onwards she emphasizes 'service of the Lord' (*el servicio de nuestro Señor*) as much as 'self-knowledge' (M: 5.3.1). Through a virtuous life one affects others and so ultimately does God's work. She returns once again to her earlier theme, the importance of love of neighbour as much as love of God:

> The Lord asks of us only two things: love of His Majesty and love of our neighbour. These are what we must work for ... The most certain sign, in my opinion, as to whether or not we are observing these two laws is whether we observe well the love of neighbour ... The more advanced you see you are in love for your neighbour the more advanced you will be in the love of God.
>
> (M: 5.3.7–8)

Out of this she concludes her Fifth Mansion with the customary practical example of holy living: this time an exhortation on the need for 'good works'.

This, for her, 'is the true union with His will' (M: 5.3.11). Thus in these final mansions we notice a clear move from her preoccupations with mystical theology to that of ethical action in the world tempered by self-knowledge – the true source of all contemplation and spirituality.

The Sixth Mansions look back on the 'trials' of the previous mansions (and the previous forty years of Teresa's life, see M: 6.1.7) again couched in terms of the incomprehension of the intellect when faced with the stirrings of the affect (and, also, often the body): *'porque no estaba el entendimiento capaz'* / 'for the understanding had no capacity to comprehend' (M: 6.1.9). Looking back on her experiences she sees that intellectual comprehension was of little help in dealing with it:

> In sum, there is no remedy in this tempest but to wait for the mercy of God. For at an unexpected time, with one word alone or a chance happening He so quickly calms the storm that it seems there had not been even as much as a cloud in that soul, and it remains filled with sunlight and much more consolation (*consuelo*).
>
> (M: 6.1.10)

The process was one of suffering and difficulty, 'having seen itself totally incapacitated' to 'make it understand its nothingness' / *'nuestra nonada'* (M: 6.1.11). At such times, for Teresa, 'the best remedy is to engage in external works of charity' (M: 6.1.13). The *gustos* that led us to this place are now transcended, as we have seen, to allow the fullness of the life of 'action in union'.

Having clearly moved from the intellectual discernment of the earlier Mansions much of the rest of the book is given over to the question of discernment within the realm of unknowing and the affect. Thus in M: 6.3 she talks of locutions received, often 'when in darkness of intellect' / *'oscuridad del entendimiento'* (M: 6.3.5) and how they are to be discerned from God, the devil or 'melancholy' (Teresa's term for what we would now refer to as 'mental illness' – see Chapter 7 below).

As Teresa points out in M: 6.7.13, the *gustos* of the 'prayer of quiet' are not an end in themselves and although she uses the mystical strategies we have delineated they are for her a 'means to an end', in this case 'the prayer of union' or *'vista'* that she mentions at the beginning of the Sixth Mansions. These moments of union involve the theological entrance into relation with Christ and the Trinity in the presence of the Mother of God and the saints. Throughout it all, however, the faculty of the intellect has to be circumvented and the strategy of unknowing remains:

You will ask how if nothing is seen one knows that it is Christ, or a saint, or His most glorious Mother. This, the soul will not know how to explain, nor can it understand how it knows, but it does know with the greatest certitude.

(M: 6.8.6)

Teresa stipulates throughout a 'divine unknowing' – the Dionysian *stulta sapientia* she inherited from the medieval tradition – this, for Teresa, is the 'realm of the supernatural' (see M: 6.9.18). She concludes these extraordinary Sixth Mansions by suggesting two aspects that remain from the states she has mentioned here: the one is pain, the other is 'overwhelming joy and delight' / '*muy excesivo gozo y deleite*' (M: 6.11.11). Through it all, and the discussions of the supernatural unknowing of these states, she returns to the epistemology of delight. Although mixed with pain, as we shall see in the Seventh Mansions, that delight remains to the end, long after the pain has dropped away. The pain of this union is that which achieves the 'true union' rather than the 'delightful union'. This 'true union' – the union with God in the world, is achieved by transcending the *gustos* and so reaching true embodied service in the world. For Teresa, this can only be achieved through identification with Christ.

Therefore the final Seventh Mansions present both the strategy of embodiment/affect combined with the newer 'true union' of action in the world. This, of course, all happens through her theological eyes in union with Christ in Trinitarian perspective.

Thus, at the beginning of these Seventh Mansions, Teresa repeats her phrase from the beginning of the First Mansions where she reflected the Book of Proverbs, stating that the soul is the place where 'The Lord finds his delight' / '*almas con que tanto se deleita el Señor*' (M: 7.1.1). However, in contrast to the earlier mansions she seems to imply that in this 'spiritual marriage' / '*el matrimonio espiritual*', as was the case implied with the raptures and the prayer of union in the previous Mansions, there is here a passing over of the strategies of affect and unknowing 'for all the faculties are lost'. There is a vision of the Trinity and a 'certain representation of the truth'. At this point Teresa has moved completely into the theological realm – a realm of 'theological' not 'intellectual' knowing (e.g. M: 7.3.8, what Howells refers to as the 'mystical knowing' of Teresa, see Howells 2002). It is a time of quiet 'like the building of Solomon's temple when no sound was heard' (M: 7.3.11). 'There is no reason for the intellect to stir or seek anything … the faculties are not lost here, but they do not work, remaining as though in amazement.'

The theological content is at its strongest here which fits with Teresa's theological strategy of returning us to Christ through the processes of the *theologia mystica*. Yet, as commentators such as Howells point out (Howells 2002: 117) Teresa must 'work hard' to bridge philosophico-psychological divides in her picture of the self with theological imagery and thought, centred on the resemblance of the self to Christ's own union of two natures – the divine and the human.

Yet although Teresa insists that the soul has now 'gone beyond delight' she persists in using the language of delight to describe this place: M: 7.3.13 'Here one delights (*se deleita*) in God's tabernacle.' To the end she seems happy to use paradox as a linguistic strategy to *show* rather than *say* what she is trying to express in these last mansions. Yet, as has been stressed repeatedly, for Teresa, the end-point of her *theologia mystica* are the 'good works, good works' / '*Obras, Obras*' which will enable action in the world:

> This is the reason for prayer, my daughters, the purpose of this spiritual marriage: the birth always of good works, good works ... I repeat it is necessary that your foundation consist of more than prayer and contemplation. If you do not strive for virtues and practice them, you will always be dwarves.
>
> (M: 7.4.6)

These 'good works' and the 'practice of virtues' are for her the means of discerning the authenticity of the spiritual path that has been followed: 'Let us desire and be occupied in prayer not for the sake of enjoyment but so as to have this strength to serve' (M: 7.4.12).

Yet, despite it all, and though the end of the journey is clearly the creation of good works, twice in the epilogue Teresa exhorts her sisters to 'delight in the castle' (M: Ep.1–2: '*a gozar de esta castillo*'). Even though ultimately the strategy of affect must fade away Teresa clearly intends it as a key strategy in bringing her daughters (allied with the strategy of unknowing) to the place of theological union with the Trinity that she herself underwent. She concludes with the reflection of those verses from Genesis and Proverbs with which she began and which we have seen re-echo throughout the lines of the *Castle*, forming, as it were, a counterpoint to the strategy of desire throughout the castle:

> Although no more than seven dwelling places were discussed, in each of these there are many others, below and above and to the sides, with lovely gardens and fountains

and labyrinths, such delightful things (*cosas tan deleitosas*) that you would want to be dissolved in praises of the great God who created the soul in His own image and likeness.

(M: Ep.1)

Teresa's remarkable achievement in the *Interior Castle* is to blend the linguistic strategies of the *theologia mystica*, to which she was heir, with theological imagery to present a radical proposal of how the Christian should act in the world through 'embodied unknowing' in selfless action. The final result is a sophisticated text with an unprecedented experiential force in the literature of Western Christian spirituality.

Summary

Written rapidly in a few short months and with hardly any corrections Teresa's *Interior Castle* remains her masterpiece. As has been argued in this book, the building blocks for the castle were already prepared before that dreadful summer of 1577: the libidinal language of delight, *regalo* and *gusto* from *The Life* and the ethical summation of mystical prayer so clearly delineated in *The Way* and *The Foundations*. Apart from its conceit of the literary seven mansions, one could argue that *The Interior Castle* adds little that is new to the Teresian panorama. However, the importance of the book lies in its value as a *Summa* of all Teresa's thought, combining, as it does, her lifelong preoccupation with and desire to develop her own mystical theology with the need to produce books that will not just be read as textbooks but actually change the lives of those who read them. In this respect, as a classic example of transformational spiritual literature, it is unparalleled.

Reading *The Interior Castle* is like reaching the summit of the mountain of Teresa's literary output. We have arrived at Carmel itself and it returns to us 'all glittering, like a bride ready for the bedchamber'.

PART THREE

The Interpretation

7

Teresa, Jung and the Psychological Self

Introduction

So far in this book we have given an account of Teresa's life and context and used this to justify a reading of her works which listens as much to the cadences of *how* she writes as much as *what* she writes. In this final part of the book I shall broaden the conversation by enabling Teresa to speak with two contemporary discourses that have emerged in the past one hundred years on the horizon of interpretation of humanity's spiritual search.

The first, which we will explore in this chapter, is that which arises from the twentieth century psychological schools. As the area is so wide I have decided out of necessity to concentrate on one school in particular – that which arises from the work of the Swiss analyst Carl Gustav Jung (1875–1961).[1] In choosing this body of work as a conversation partner I want to first demonstrate how Teresa's work will stand up to the scrutiny of such a school, and secondly show the synchronicities between a contemporary and late medieval 'spiritual anthropology'. In doing this I approach the work of Jung, as I have done that of Teresa, with a certain amount of critical openness so that hopefully the reader will not be seduced by the more 'purple passages' to be found in the literature of analytical psychology, but also will not dismiss the contributions of Jung and his later school to the ongoing debate about the expression of the psycho-spiritual in a transpersonal context.

My second conversation partner will come from Buddhist anthropology and will place particular emphasis upon the contemporary rediscovery of the practices of mindfulness in Western pastoral situations. Again, I shall approach the dialogue with critical respect in an attempt to allow Teresa's voice to be held

---

[1] In a later work I hope to analyse Teresa's relation to the Freudian and Object Relations school.

up to those emanating from this school. I shall conclude the book by summarising what form a contemporary 'language of the soul' derived from Teresa
may take.

The Mansion of Self Knowledge

We have seen from Teresa's writings how she constantly emphasizes the need
for self-knowledge in our spiritual search. Yet it is a self-knowledge which
embraces the very unknowing and libidinal side we have explored in the last
few chapters. As she writes in a letter to the Discalced Sisters in Seville:

> Often the Lord allows a fall so that the soul will be more humble and when it returns to
> the right way of acting and grows in self-knowledge (*conocimiento*) it advances further
> in the service of the Lord.
>
> (Letter to Discalced Sisters of Seville, 13 January 1580)

Or, as she put it in *The Interior Castle*:

> Oh, but if it is in that (the room) of self-knowledge! (*U, que si es en el propio
> conocimiento*). How necessary this room is – see that you understand me – even for
> those whom the Lord has brought into the very dwelling place where he abides. For
> never, however exalted the soul may be, is anything else necessary for it, and this it will
> never be able to neglect even if it desire to do so.
>
> (M: 1.2.8)

For Teresa the nature of spiritual progress is a complicated one requiring a
delicate choreography of knowing and unknowing, saying and showing. Just
when we think we are achieving something the opposite effect will occur –
what Jung will later call the *enantiodromia*. We are clearly moving here into
the territory we would nowadays call the 'psychological'. As we relate sixteenth
century approaches to twenty-first century approaches to the psyche we must
move with a certain amount of caution. As I put it in my earlier book on St John
of the Cross:

> The ideas of Marx, Freud and Darwin, although nineteenth century in origin, have
> required over a hundred years to be assimilated by secular society to an extent that they

invisibly mould our thinking and action today. This scientific and cognitive revolution has shaped our present world and creates what we nowadays call the 'psychological mindset'. Today the 'talking cure' initiated by Sigmund Freud (1856–1939) has spawned a whole subsection of culture that embraces as well as Freud's original psychoanalysis, a whole range of transpersonal therapies, counselling, cognitive and behavioural therapies, the psychiatric and psychological sciences and many more too numerous to mention.

(Tyler 2010: 80)[2]

Yet it is understandable that we throw this hermeneutical caution to the wind when reading Teresa as so much of her writing emphasizes the 'quest for self' that we find in particular in the 'founding fathers' of psychology such as Freud and Jung. This is no better revealed than in Teresa's letters. As she says, for example, to Gracián in 1579: 'Oh good God, how true it is that we do not know ourselves!' (Letter to Gracián, mid-April 1579). When comparing the work of Teresa with, say, Jung, it is important to explore the significant themes that link the two thinkers while hopefully steering away from a syncretism that denies the validity of each thinker's approach on its own terms.[3] To set about this task it will be necessary to introduce the main avenues of Jung's thought that I will bring into conversation with Teresa before eliciting a response from her perspective.

Jung and the Christian Way

Jung once wrote:

> Among all my patients in the second half of life – that is to say, over thirty-five – there has not been one whose problem in the last resort was not that of finding a religious outlook on life. It is safe to say that every one of them fell ill because he had lost what

---

[2] For a lengthier discussion of this subject see Chapter 4 of 'St John of the Cross'. I do not propose to reiterate these arguments here.

[3] An excellent example of this sort of work is John Welch's *Spiritual Pilgrims: Carl Jung and Teresa of Avila* (1982). Welch himself admits that he has not been able to avoid 'twisting Teresa's words to fit certain (Jungian) theories' (126). His pastoral approach is second to none and it remains an exemplary book. In this chapter I propose to give Jung's theories a more sceptical examination than Welch allows, especially in the light of the recently published 'Red Book' (Jung 2009) which gives us greater insight into many of Jung's 'hidden views' on religion, and especially Christianity.

the living religions of every age have given to their followers, and none of them has been really healed who did not regain his religious outlook.

(Jung CW: 11.509 published originally as *Die Beziehungen der Psychotherapie zur Seelsorge,* Zurich 1932)

In the same work he went so far as to suggest that anyone he encountered at this stage of development who was experiencing mental crisis and who had had some previous religious formation should be encouraged to return to their religious roots if they were to stand a chance of being mentally healed. Thus, from its beginnings Jungian analytical psychology has preferenced the transcendent and the need for each individual psyche to make friends with the transcendent, for not doing so, warns Jung, will lead to severe psychological problems.

There is no doubt that there is much in Jung's writing that is inimical and downright erroneous for a straightforward Christian seeker trying to reconcile her faith with Jungian transpersonal analysis. Yet, despite some of the excesses that are to be found in his work, there is no doubt that his map of the soul provides a corrective to the rising tide of materialism that has swamped early twenty-first century culture. As Dueck puts it in his perceptive short book on the relationship between Jung and Christianity, *The Living God and Our Living Psyche: What Christians Can Learn from Carl Jung* (2008):

> Rising through the last several centuries, modernity had reached an apex of its power in the first half of the twentieth century, and its capitulation to science had drained away much of the healing power of Christian practices. Jung sought to recover this vitality.
>
> (Ulanov and Dueck 2008: 5)

Thus, suggests Dueck, Jung attempted 'a pastoral attempt to counter the personally debilitating effects of modernity'. His primary concern was healing. Not only the healing of the individual psyche but the healing of the collective psyche. Accordingly, his 'epistemology is not positivist, but diverse enough to include narrative, dreams, fantasy, propositional truth and ethical pronouncements' (Dueck 2008: 9).

'To a drunken feast of joy'

Despite the help that Jungian psychology can provide the contemporary seeker of the transcendent I think it is important to point out in a book such as this where we are seeking to create a dialogue between the Christian outlook of a pre-modern writer such as Teresa of Avila with the postmodern culture that surrounds us, that the position of Jung with regard to Christianity was never a straightforward matter. Very early on, before his split with Freud, he could write to his colleague in 1910:

> Religion can be replaced only by religion. Is there perchance a new saviour in the International Fraternity – we need the eternal truth of myth
>
> (Jung to Freud 11 November 1910 in Bishop 1995)

Thus, from its very beginnings, psychoanalysis explicitly saw itself as replacing Christianity: 'Christianity must be replaced by something equivalent' (ibid). Psychoanalysis, writes Jung to Freud (or as they refer to it, from its Greek fore letters: ψα) will provide a new phenomenon to replace religion, and in particular Christianity. To effect this psychoanalysis will draw on the Dionysian spirit popularized by Nietzsche in works such as *The Birth of Tragedy from the Spirit of Music*:

> I think we must give ψα time to infiltrate into people from many centres, to revivify among intellectuals a feeling for symbol and myth, ever so gently to transform Christ back into the soothsaying god of the vine (*in den weissagenden Gott der Rebe*), which he was, and in this way absorb these ecstatic instinctual forces of Christianity (*jene ekstatischen Triebkräfte des Christentums*), for the one purpose of making the cult and the sacred myth (*den heiligen Mythos*) what they once were – a drunken feast of joy (*zum trunkenen Freudenfeste*) where mankind regained the ethos and holiness of an animal. This way the beauty and purpose of classical religion which from God knows what biological need has become a *Jammerinstitut* (literally, 'an Institute of Woe'). Thus Analysis should be a means to help people get in touch with these Dionysian libidinal impulses.'
>
> (Jung to Freud 11 November 1910 in Bishop 1995)

Thus, as Bishop points out instead of the '*Dionysos gegen den Gekreuzigten*' that we find at the end of Nietzsche's last published work,[4] Jung will 'transform the Crucified back into the God of the grape' (Bishop 1995: 64). This 'Dionysian

---

[4] Nietzsche's final written words in *Ecce Homo*: '*Hat man mich verstanden: Dionysos gegen den Gekreuzigten.*'/ 'Have you understood me: it is Dionysos or the Crucified One...' (In *Warum Ich ein Schicksal Bin*: 9)

element' is one to which Jung would constantly return, even after the break with Freud:

> The Dionysian element has to do with emotions and affects which have found no suitable religious outlets in the fundamentally Apollonian cult and ethos of Christianity.
>
> (Jung CW: 12.182)

'Intoxication', he writes in the same essay, 'that most direct and dangerous form of possession, turned away from the gods and enveloped the human world with its exuberance.' Thus, for Jung, Christianity was not to be destroyed (how far this remained on Freud's agenda remained and remains a moot point), but rather to be transformed by helping people to return to the springs of the libidinal – the *ekstatischen Triebkräfte des Christentums* – which Jung felt had been abandoned.[5] Could it be that in reading a pre-modern writer such as Teresa we catch a glimpse of these *ekstatischen Triebkräfte* for one last time before they get subsumed into the 'Apollinian religion' of the moderns? Teresa's *gustos* suggest the return of such *Triebkräfte*.

So, in Jung, we don't have the destruction of Christianity, but rather the *transformation* of Christianity. Jung is a reformer, in as much as Luther was a reformer. He sees much that is good in Christianity but that it has lost its connection with the libidinal. Thus, he will emphasize two main things in his future reform of Christianity: the return to the libidinal and the importance of the symbolic function.

The Descent to the Mothers

Jung's 'return to the religious' is thus quite unlike anything similar we can find in comparable late modern writers. In many respects his writings mark the end of the modern and the return to the pre-modern as post-modern phenomenon. In this respect his writings, especially after his break with Freud, mark a serious attempt by a late modern thinker to engage with medieval thought patterns on a deeply existential level.

---

[5] It is worth contrasting Jung's view here with that of the post-Freudian, Julia Kristeva. In *This Incredible Need to Believe* (Kristeva 2009: 84) she contrasts Nietzsche's 'Dionysius's drunkenness' with the suffering 'God-man' of Christianity. She preferences the latter.

After Jung's break from Freud in 1913 Jung himself was plunged into a disso-
ciative state and as the First World War raged in Europe, Jung fought his own
internal wars as he tried to make sense of the caverns and hells of psychic space.
Until 2009 much of our understanding of this process was hidden from view and
had to be pieced together from scraps in his later published work. All we knew for
sure was that Jung had undergone some sort of psychotic breakdown which had
resulted in a complete restructuring of his psyche. The publication of the *Red Book/
Liber Novus* in 2009 (Jung: 2009) has since allowed us an insight into the processes
that Jung underwent during those turbulent years. As he wrote of this period:

> The years ... when I pursued the inner images, were the most important time of my
> life. Everything else is to be derived from this. It began at that time, and the later details
> hardly matter anymore. My entire life consisted in elaborating what had burst forth
> from the unconscious and flooded me like an enigmatic stream and threatened to break
> me. That was the stuff and material for more than only one life. Everything later was
> merely the outer classification, scientific elaboration, and the integration into life. But
> the numinous beginning, which contained everything, was then.
>
> (Jung 2009: Preface)

From this would emerge all the main innovative elements with which Jung would
chart the psyche and develop his own form of what he termed 'analytical psychology'.
The 'descent to hell' charted in *The Red Book* is prefigured in his correspondence with Freud when he used the phrase: 'the descent to the realm of the
mysterious Mothers' derived from Goethe's *Faust*, Part Two 6287–90. After his
break with Freud in 1913 Jung will call his psychological research a 'descent to
the underworld', a *katabasis* or descent to *das Reich der Mütter*. From this 'spirit
of the depths' / '*geist der tiefe*' (RB: 243) he will discover, as he says in the *Red
Book*, the 'birth of the new god' (*des neu-gottes*). Here he tells us that 'Christ
journeys to Hell and becomes the anti-Christ' (RB: 243) – 'no one knows what
happened during the three days Christ was in Hell. I have experienced it' / '*ich
habe es erfahrt*' (RB: Folio V). After the events described in the *Red Book*, Jung's
conception of Christianity can never be the same again.

This became apparent in the celebrated correspondence Jung had with the
English Dominican priest, Victor White from 1945 until White's death in 1960.[6]

---

[6] The complete correspondence was published in 2007 as *The Jung-White Letters*, A. Conrad Lammers and
A. Cunningham (eds). London: Routledge.

Initially keen to incorporate Jung's psychology into his Catholic theology and approach to pastoral care, White realized during the course of his relationship with Jung that the block towards this would be Jung's attitude to evil in general and the Catholic doctrine of *privatio boni* in particular.[7] We shall return to this conflict shortly.

White, in his last two books, *God and the Unconscious* (1952) and *Soul and Psyche* (1960) rather neatly summarizes his attitudes to Jung and Jung's approach to Christianity in general. Here he makes explicit reference to Jung's 'descent to the mothers' (White 1952: 210). This he characterizes as the essential call of the Gnostic: 'essentially the attitude of magic, seeking to subject the mystery to the comprehension of the Ego, and utilizing transcendent power and knowledge for its own ends and aggrandizement' (White 1950: 210):

> The enlargement of consciousness, inward-turned to the Realm of the Mothers, the *'mysterium tremendum et fascinans'* of the archetypes, away from the chaos of the hard, cruel world of fact and human history and society: there lies salvation. Know the names and origins of the archetypes and projections of the unconscious; know their conflicts and triumphs and falls and recoveries; and you will be their master and will be saved.
>
> (White 1952: 210)

White in 1952 contrasts this conception of 'Gnosticism' with 'faith' which he describes as 'humbly accepting a Divine revelation it knows it cannot fully comprehend'. This 'unknowing' for White (as it did for Dionysius and the medieval practitioners of 'theologia mystica', including, I argue here, Teresa of Avila) lies at the heart of Christian belief and stands in complete contrast to the 'knowing' of Gnosticism. In 1952 White explained the problem very well but at this time he was still very close to Jung's project of analytical psychology and so refused to go so far as to class Jung himself as presenting the Gnostic position. However, after his conflict with Jung over the *privatio boni* he became more critical of Jung's position. In his last book, *Soul and Psyche* (1960) White comes closer to describing Jung's position as essentially that of the Gnostic early Christians.

---

[7] Literally, 'the privation of good', St. Augustine's early attempt to formulate a Christian response to the problem of evil and later systematized by St. Thomas Aquinas in his *Summa Theologiae*. The teaching suggests that evil is ultimately caused by an absence of good and has no ontological status in itself.

'The Primitives'

One of the characteristics laid at the feet of Gnosticism by White was its tendency to elitism – it was for him the preferred spirituality of the 'moneyed, leisured classes'. In this respect some of Jung's criticisms of institutional religions (including White's religious order) had the aroma of this elitism. This is no more apparent in this apparent distaste for certain forms of 'primitive' Catholicism.

In the discussion of Eckhart and medieval mysticism in Volume Six of the *Collected Works* of Jung we encounter the idea that the medieval mystics are equated with 'primitives' (CW: 6.414). This may seem an isolated reference but it is a theme that Jung returns to repeatedly. That is, that certain forms of religion – and in the case of Western religion this is manifest in Roman Catholicism – are more 'primitive' or 'chthonic'. Now Jung doesn't necessarily mean this as a bad thing (no matter how insulting it may sound to the members of that denomination) but rather he seems to mean it as other moderns would talk of the 'noble savage' with all its pejorative associations, i.e. that Roman Catholics, for example, have access to some sub-cultural magic which the more sophisticated or thinking Protestants have somehow lost:

> (Catholics) have at their command a rich and palpably ritualistic symbolism which fully satisfies the demands as well as the obscure passions of simpler minds.
>
> (Jung CW: 11.548)

Or as we find in *Psychological Types*:

> Almost everywhere on the lower human levels the idea of God has a purely dynamic character; God is a divine force, a power related to health, to the soul, to medicine, to riches, to the chief, a power that can be captured by certain procedures and employed for the making of things needful for the life and well-being of man, and also to produce magical or baneful effects.
>
> (CW: 6.414)

Therefore, the forms of medieval mysticism described become 'a regression to a primitive condition' (CW: 6.415). Nothing, in a way, could be further from the spirit of the *theologia mystica* as expounded in this book.

The Creation of the Symbol

It would, however, be unfair and misleading to end this analysis of Jung's interpretation of Christianity on such a negative note. As we have seen above many contemporary commentators have found much that is useful in Jung's approach and he still finds many enthusiastic followers from within Christianity. For the purposes of our study of Teresa here I think the most important lessons we can derive from Jung are from his investigations of the medieval psyche, and the general deconstruction of the rational 'I'. As we have stated throughout this chapter, one of Jung's primary concerns, certainly after the expression and style of the *Red Book*, was to recapture key elements of the style and process of medieval thinking for the (post-) modern reader/ seeker. In respect to our discussion of Teresa within this book I feel the most important revived aspect of Jung presented from this perspective is the impor- tance of the symbol.

In the recovery of the symbolic Jung was not alone. While his own researches into the nature of the symbol were to prove so important, other mid-twentieth century *ressourcement* writers such as Marie-Dominique Chenu (1895–1990) had also begun to appreciate the significance of the symbolic for interpreting the medieval mindset. In his perceptive essay on Victorine spirituality *Nature, Man and Society in the Twelfth Century* (Chenu 1997), Chenu alludes to the role of the symbolic for the medievals as being largely anagogical, i.e. the symbol is the means whereby the heavenly order is reflected in the earthly order:

> Creation was a theophany, a manifestation of God, and symbolism was the means appropriate to that manifestation; even granting a dialectical tension between the power of creation to manifest God and its complete inferiority to God, symbolism revealed nothing less than God's transcendence
>
> (Chenu 1997: 128)

As well as this anagogical element, the symbolic for the medievals was another mode of thought, in contradistinction to, for example, the dialectics of the Schools. In this respect, the symbolic for the medievals was not considered another form of logic but a different way of 'showing' truth. As Chenu states:

To bring symbolism into play was not to extend or supplement a previous act of the reason; it was to give primary expression to a reality which reason could not attain and which reason, even afterwards, could not conceptualize.

(Chenu 1997: 103)[8]

It is therefore apparent how this 'alternative to logic' would appeal to the medievalist (or at least contra-modern) Jung. For him the symbol will become the means whereby the 'meta-rational' components of the greater 'Self'/*Selbst*, will become accessible to the more circumscribed 'I'/*Ich*. The symbol, in Jung's hands will become the linking point between the known 'I' and the unknown 'Self', thus performing a crucial function in his psychology:

In practice, opposites can be united only in the form of a compromise, or irrationally, some new thing arising between them which, although different from both, yet has the power to take up their energies in equal measure as an expression of both and of neither. Such an expression cannot be contrived by reason, it can only be created through living.

(Jung CW: 6.169)

The mediating axis for this process is the symbol:

The mediating position, between the opposites can be reached only by the symbol

(Jung CW: 6.162)

This symbol will therefore represent 'something that is not wholly under-standable, and that it hints only intuitively at its possible meaning' (Jung CW: 6.171). This function will also be a 'playful' function:

Schiller calls the symbol-creating function a third instinct, the *play instinct*; it bears no resemblance to the two opposing functions, but stands between them and does justice to both natures.

(Jung CW: 6.171)

---

[8] See, for example, Hugh of St Victor: 'Symbolum, collatio videlicet, id est coaptatio visibilium formarum ad demonstrationem rei invisiblis propositarum' /'A symbol is a juxtaposition, that is a gathering together of visible forms in order to demonstrate invisible things', Hugh of St Victor 'On the Celestial Hierarchy'iii. PL CLXXV 960D.

So, the symbolic function is, for Jung:

- Neither rational or irrational.
- Playful and creative.
- Allowing the conscious to grasp the unconscious.
- A gateway to the Gnostic/Dionysian Jungian god.

Therefore religion, for Jung, becomes the acceptance of the reality of the symbol (Jung CW: 6.202). For him, the *symbolic* and the *religious* (whether that is represented by Christianity, Hinduism or Taoism is irrelevant) are coterminous:

> The solution of the problem in *Faust*, in Wagner's *Parsifal*, in Schopenhauer, and even in Nietzsche's *Zarathustra*, is *religious*
>
> (Jung CW: 6.324)

Jung – Friend or Foe?

To conclude this survey, we must perhaps ask ourselves the question: 'Is Carl Jung a friend or foe of Christianity?' Well, if we understand Christianity in terms of the doctrines or creeds of Orthodoxy then he is no foe, but rather someone who fails to understand the implications of Orthodox Christianity for an interpretation of the nature of Christ and ultimately of Christian life. If we follow the version of Christianity presented by Jung we are no longer following Orthodoxy but rather a late Gnostic version of Christianity. Is that such a bad thing?

In a world almost swallowed up in reductive materialism Jung saw his fundamental task as preserving the spiritual from the ravages of reductive empirical materialism. This he termed the 'religious outlook to life' which he felt was fundamental in preserving good mental health (see Jung CW: 11.509). His spiritual life was as much for 'unbelievers' as 'believers' to the former of which he explicitly claimed to be addressing his writing:

> I am not … addressing myself to the happy possessors of faith, but to those many people for whom the light has gone out, the mystery has faded, and God is dead. For most of them there is no going back, and one does not know either whether going back

is always the better way. To gain an understanding of religious matters, probably all that is left us today is the psychological approach.

(Jung CW: 11.148)

In this respect, for Jung all religions are equal. None has the monopoly on the 'cure of souls':

> Yes, I agree, the Buddha may be just as right as Jesus. Sin is only relative and it is difficult to see how we can feel ourselves in any way redeemed by the death of Christ.
>
> (Jung CW: 11.518)

As with his views on god/God, Jung betrays his theological naivety. He does not seem to understand that, for example, Christianity and Buddhism have fundamentally mutually exclusive views on the metaphysics of human salvation. Be that as it may, if we see reductive materialism as the enemy of Christianity then on the theory that an enemy's enemy is a friend, Jung therefore belongs on the side of the angels and a guardian of Christianity in a world that has rapidly become a stranger to the spiritual – or at least the ability to express that spiritual life in a comprehensible language. In *Seelsorge,* for example, he is quite bullish about the rights of the clergy to trespass on to the realm of the materialist psychologist:

> I therefore hold that psychological interest on the part of the Protestant clergy is entirely legitimate and even necessary. Their possible encroachment upon medical territory is more than balanced by medical incursions into religion and philosophy, to which doctors naively believe themselves entitled (witness the explanation of religious processes in terms of sexual symptoms or infantile wish-fantasies).
>
> (Jung CW: 11.548)[9]

There is no doubt that Jung's transpersonal psychological language has given a means for a whole generation to communicate its unease with the astringent materialism of our time. For this, perhaps, Christianity owes him a debt. Although we might want to baulk at awarding him the title 'Defender of the Faith' he certainly deserves the title 'Defender of Faith'. White recognized this

---

[9] We can also perhaps hear here a gentle criticism of Freud's 'explanation' of religion.

when he saw that Jung was a prophet warning against a collapse of the Western psyche brought about by one-sided materialism. In the opening of his 'God and the Unconscious' he quotes with approval Jung's words from 'Psychological Types':

> Our age has a blindness without parallel. We think we have only to declare an acknowl-
> edged form of faith to be incorrect or invalid, to become psychologically free of all
> the traditional effects of the Christian or Judaic religion. We believe in enlightenment,
> as if an intellectual change of opinion had somehow a deeper influence on emotional
> processes or indeed upon the unconscious! We entirely forget that the religion of
> the last two thousand years is a psychological attitude, a definite form of adaptation
> to inner and outer experience, which moulds a definite form of civilization; it has
> therefore created an atmosphere that remains wholly uninfluenced by any intellectual
> disavowal.
>
> (Jung CW: 6.313)

Jung's critique was as much a critique of Christian culture and mindset as it was of Christianity itself. For him, the 'Christian mindset' still continued to mould and shape our everyday realities, even in the twenty-first century, perhaps more than we would care to admit:

> Everything we think is the fruit of the Middle Ages and indeed of the Christian Middle
> Ages. Our whole science, everything that passes through our head, has inevitably gone
> through this history. The latter lives in us and has left its stamp upon us for all time and
> will always form a vital layer of our psyche, just like any phylogenetic traces in our body
> ... The Christian *Weltanschauung* is therefore a psychological fact which does not allow
> of any further rationalization; it is something which has happened, which is present.
>
> (White 1960: 67 quoting an address by Jung given in 1934)

Jung's analysis of the individual, of religions such as Christianity and ultimately of Western Cultural Patterns emphasizes the need for a correction. Or as he calls it an 'enantiodromia' – a new openness to the transcendental and a balance to the hard ossification that has clearly happened on both sides of the religion/materialist divide over the past century. His psychology, with all its ambiguity and slipperiness, does offer an alternative for the psyche to breathe and rearrange itself in a time of change and realignment of priorities. Jung seems to say that religion may choose to stay on the sidelines of that realignment, but no-one, least of all the psychologists, will in the long term thank it for its self-immolation.[10]

Psychoanalysis for Jung became the arena whereby one person helped another to link again with the 'sources of psychic life' (CW: 11.534). This, for the late Jung, would require unknowing on behalf of the analyst as much as the client. In this clinical sense of unknowing Jung perhaps comes closest to the 'unknown God' of Orthodox Christianity and the medieval mystical theology which we have discussed throughout this book.

'The Seasons of the Soul'

Having reviewed Jung's influence upon transpersonal psychology it is necessary to return to Teresa. It is clear from her writings that she had a sense of the 'interior life' every bit as strong as a psychologist such as Jung. Within this she was aware of what she once called 'the seasons of the interior life', as she wrote in a letter to Don Antonio Gaytán in the final months of 1574: 'On this earth there are different seasons, so it is with the interior life.'[11]

Within her own 'interior life' there had of course been many different seasons. We have explored earlier in this book the ecstasies and consolations felt by the young Teresa and described so lovingly in *The Life*. But, as we saw in the later mansions of *The Interior Castle*, Teresa was not immune to receiving the darknesses and aridities more commonly associated with St John of the Cross. As a mature woman she had a particularly difficult period of this while undergoing the foundation of the convent at Segovia. In the *Book of Foundations* she recalled:

> There is never a foundation in which there is not some trial. And the trial came in addition to the fact that I went there while suffering from a high fever and nausea, and from interior ills of very great dryness and darkness of soul (*males interiores de sequedad y escuridad en el alma grandísima*).
>
> (F: 21.4)

---

[10] As he says in Jung CW: 12.17: 'Psychology thus does just the opposite of what it is accused of: it provides possible approaches to a better understanding of these things, it opens people's eyes to the real meaning of dogmas, and, far from destroying, it throws open an empty house to new inhabitants.'

[11] *En este mundo hay tiempos diferentes, ansí en el interior.*

An account confirmed in a letter to Don Teutonio de Braganza written in the middle of June 1574 shortly after the dark episode described in *The Foundations*: 'The extremely serious illness lasted two months and it was of a kind that had repercussions on my interior life so that I felt as though I had no being (*para tenerme como una cosa sin ser*)'.[12] She refers to it as her '*tormento de melancholia*' (Letter to Madre María Bautista, 14 May 1574), a term we will return to shortly.

In the work of her foundations Teresa not only had to be aware of her own 'seasons of the soul' but also of those around her. We cannot accuse Teresa of being blasé or naïve about the challenges of community life. She is painfully honest about her fellow nuns and writes rather candidly in *The Book of Foundations*: 'as a rule nuns are discontented people' (F: 20.11).[13] And again, in a letter to Gracián on 14 July 1581: 'Believe me I fear an unhappy nun more than many devils.'[14] In this sometimes fevered atmosphere (and we remember her early training in religious life in the *Encarnación* – that hotbed of intrigue and gossip) it is no surprise that Teresa had to learn the skill of dealing with awkward psychological temperaments with tact and skill. None more so than with how she deals with what she terms 'melancholia'.

Imagination, Bad Humours and Melancholy

As with her co-worker, St John of the Cross, Teresa had a keen sense of what we would now call 'mental illness' with its manifestations such as clinical depression. Both writers are at pains to distinguish this pathology from the movements of the spiritual life.[15] Teresa is particularly harsh on spiritual directors who 'misdiagnose' spiritual aridity as mental illness in Mansion Six of *The Interior Castle*:

> He fears everything and finds in everything something to doubt because he sees these unusual experiences ... everything is immediately condemned as from the devil or melancholy. And the world is so full of this melancholy that I am not surprised. There

---

[12] 'It held me like a thing without being,' Allison Peers.

[13] *Las monjas, las más estavan descontentas.*

[14] *Crea que una monja descontentada yo la temo más que a muchos demonios.*

[15] John gives detailed guidelines for distinguishing mental illness from spiritual aridities in *The Dark Night of the Soul* Book 1, Chapter 9. For more on this see Tyler 2010, Chapter 4.

is so much of it now in the world and the devil causes so many evils through this means that confessors are very right in fearing it and considering it carefully.

(M: 6.1.8)

Such a soul suffering from this torment, as Teresa had herself done,[16] requires compassion and love from the spiritual director. Indeed, she is critical of directors who condemn or judge their wards for experiencing this torment. As with John, she emphasizes the need to be able to 'keep in words' with the confessor: it is as though that which isn't expressed or verbalized takes on a power of its own to overwhelm the person:

All this would be nothing were it not that on top of this comes the view that she doesn't know how to explain herself to her confessors and is deceiving them.

(M: 6.1.9)[17]

Yet it would be false, I believe, to think that Teresa is advocating the role of the Director (or therapist for that matter) as one who must *articulate everything*. As I have argued throughout this book, for Teresa, the choreography of listener and speaker requires as much a space for *non-saying* as it does for saying. As she writes later: 'Is it true that she will know how to explain what has occurred? It is unspeakable (*indicible*)[18] because they are spiritual grips and pains (*apretamientos y penas espirituales*)[19] of which one cannot give names' (M: 6.1.13). The role of the spiritual director, confessor, or indeed in contemporary terms the psychologist, will be to accept the unnameability of these conditions. As she says 'the best remedy (I don't mean of getting rid of them, because I don't find any, but so that they may be endured), is to engage in works of charity and external affairs (*obras de caridad y esteriores*) and to hope in the mercy of God who never fails those who hope in him' (M: 6.1.14).

---

[16] From a clinical point of view, Teresa, and so it appears many of her contemporaries, saw 'melancholia' as a more transitory or impermanent state to how we would understand 'clinical depression' today. Sufferers could pass in and out of it quite frequently.

[17] *Todo no es nada, si no es que sobre esto venga el parecer que no sabe informar a los confesores y que los trai engañados.*

[18] Allison Peers 'inexpressible', Kavanaugh 'indescribable'.

[19] Again, more colourful Teresian language. *Apretar* is literally 'to tighten up, squeeze or grip.' It is close to the *arrinconcar* we shall discuss in the following chapter. Allison Peers gives 'distress and oppression,' Kavanaugh 'afflictions and sufferings.'

This solution of occupational therapy and the cultivation of patience for the passing of this season of the soul is Teresa's mature response to the problem posed by 'melancholia'. Rather than attempting to 'name' or 'pin down' these spiritual conditions, Teresa suggests in her mature response in the *Castle*, we should accept the choreography of the unnameability that goes with the spiritual dimension and concentrate rather on the ethical action in the world as developed in the *Way of Perfection* and the *Book of Foundations*.[20]

Yet, in her earlier works she is less pastoral in her response, suggesting that the response of the *Castle* was one hard-won through many years of searching. In the *Book of the Foundations* she concentrates more on the harm the illness can cause both to the individual and the community around the sister and the 'troublesome' nature of the ailment. While she accepts that 'not all who have this humour are troublesome' (F: 7.2) (for there are 'greater and lesser degrees of this humour'), 'if reason is lacking madness results' / '*parece que si no hay razón que es ser locos*'. Accordingly, the superior should deal with the problem by 'putting fear into them' (F: 7.3): 'the prioress must use penances of the order and strive to bring these persons into submission in such a way as to make them understand they will obtain neither all nor part of what they want.'

For, 'that which interests these melancholic persons most is getting their own way, saying everything that comes to their lips, looking at the faults of others with which they hide their own … in sum they are like a person who cannot bear anyone who resists her.'[21] In this condemnatory way Teresa even suggests 'melancholia' may even be used as an excuse and should be banned as a term from the houses:

> Nowadays the term is used more than usual and it happens that all self-will and freedom go by the name melancholy. Thus I have thought that in these houses and in all Religious houses, this term should not be uttered. For the term seems to bring along with it freedom from any control.
>
> (F: 7.8)

---

[20] Paraphrasing Wittgenstein again, paraphrasing Goethe: 'In the beginning was the Deed!' (see *On Certainty*: 402).

[21] Teresa adds: 'If light punishment is not enough, try heavy; if one month in the prison cell is not enough, try four months'(F: 7.4), and 'if the insane are bound and chastised so that they will not kill others, and this is right and even seems to be a very compassionate thing to do since they cannot control themselves, how much more must one be careful and not to allow these melancholic persons liberties by which they could harm souls' (F: 7.7).

These passages convey the distance our own understandings of mental illness would have from the prevailing sixteenth century view. Teresa's interpretation seems to have a moral dimension lacking from our twenty-first century views of psycho-pathology. In this respect the prescriptions of the later *Interior Castle* seem more acceptable to us today than the somewhat harsh reprimand of *The Foundations*. Perhaps Teresa herself, in this later work, is able to transcend the prescriptions of her own culture and age to present a more nuanced view of psycho-spiritual pathology closer to our own. However, even in these earlier passages from *The Foundations*, Teresa admits a contradiction in her advice between strict discipline and compassion. Ultimately the prioress 'should lead them with all the skill and love necessary so that if possible they submit out of love ... she should show that she greatly loves them and this known through words and deeds' (F: 7.9). And as in the later *Castle* she concludes that the superior 'strive that they do not have long periods of prayer (and use of the imagination) ... for practical occupations are better.'

Spiritual Direction and Discernment of Spirits

As we heard before, Teresa herself suffered a great deal from the lack of a spiritual director, essentially the person who could help her articulate these inner experiences and give them shape in her own language and discourse. As we saw above, the greatest danger she sees in this relationship is when the director or confessor feels that they have somehow a deep insight into the nature of the soul before God. Rather, she says, leave the understanding of the soul to God. As she says in *The Foundations*:

> A prioress must not think that she can understand a soul immediately: let her leave this to God, for it is He alone who can understand (the soul), and let her try to guide each soul in the way in which His Majesty is leading it.
>
> (F: 18.9)

Rather, the aim of the director is to lead the soul gently by offering what we would today call a 'safe space' in which the expression of the spiritual relationship can be articulated. As she wrote on 3 July 1574 to Don Teutonia de Braganza:

It is necessary that we bear our weakness and not try to constrain our nature. Everything (we do) is seeking God (*Todo es buscar a Dios*), since it is for Him that we search out every kind of means, and the soul must be led gently (*Por él andamos a buscar medios, y es menester llevar el alma con suavidad*).

Indeed, as Teresa grew in stature friends, relatives and high officials would seek her advice so that her correspondence in these later years often turns into a form of direction by post. Yet throughout it all she refused to be prescriptive in this ministry, preferring rather to offer gentle succour to her 'directees' and leaving the rest to God's mercy. As she wrote to Gonzalo Dávila in the summer of 1578, a few years before her death:

One of my great errors is to judge these matters of prayer from my own perspective, (*Una de las grandes faltas que tengo es juzgar por mí en estas cosas de oración*) and so you don't have to pay any attention to what I say … the soul is not obliged to attend to any other cares but only to the One to whom she is present (*más que al que tiene presente*) … Thus it seems the soul remains freer.

But whenever she did give advice she never strayed far from the lessons she had picked up from her first Jesuit confessors such as Baltasar Álvarez. In particular, advice based on St Ignatius of Loyola's *Rules for the Discernment of Spirits* from his *Spiritual Exercises*.[22] The notion of discernment, as we have seen, pervades all her writings and is especially strong in the later *Interior Castle* where she gives clear guidelines for, among other things, discerning 'charismatic phenomena' from God and from the diabolic (Mansion Six) and the discernment of actions that lead to peace and spiritual progress and those of a more selfish or worldly origin (Mansion Three). In the *Way of Perfection* she makes explicit reference to an earlier account of discernment from the Desert Tradition given in the *Conferences* of John Cassian. Here she tells us that:

The account is given, I believe in Cassian,[23] of a hermit who lived a most austere life. The devil made him think that by throwing himself into a well he would see God

---

[22] However, see her rather caustic comments about Ignatius and his *Exercises* in the *Vejamen*: 6.

[23] Another example of the post–1559 Teresa being very careful to express inexactitude in the knowledge of her sources. The precise description of Cassian's example suggests she knew, and had access to, the text quoted.

more quickly. I truly believe that this hermit could not have served with humility or goodness; for the Lord is faithful, and His Majesty would not consent that one be blinded in a matter so obvious ...

Thus the time of prayer should be shortened, however delightful (*gustosa*) the prayer may be, when it is seen that the bodily energies are failing or that the head might suffer harm. Discretion is very necessary in all (*En todo es muy necesario discreción*).

(CV: 19.13)

Her reference is to Cassian's description of Abba Moses in his second *Conference*. Kavanaugh suggests her source was probably the *Vida de los Santos Padres* published in Zaragosa in 1511 (Kavanaugh and Rodriguez CW: 2.467). During the process of Teresa's Beatification, Petronila Bautista declared that:

She was very devoted to the *Conferences* of Cassian and of the Fathers of the Desert, and so when this witness was with her the Holy Mother asked her to read two or three accounts of those saints each day and at night tell her about them since she herself didn't have the time to do so because of her just and holy occupations.

(BMC: 19.591)

This 'desert tradition' of 'discernment of spirits', *diakresis* or *discernio*, was clearly important to her and it is worth looking at the source she refers to in *The Way of Perfection*. Drawing on the apostolic tradition of Ss Paul and John, Cassian, in his second *Conference*, places discernment as central to the spiritual quest and the attribute most prized in the spiritual elder. Here he builds on references to the discernment of spirits in St. Paul's first letter to the Corinthians (I Cor. 12) as well as St John's advice in his First Letter: 'Do not believe every spirit, but test the spirits to see whether they are from God, for many false prophets have come into the world' (1 Jn 4.1).

In Cassian's hands discernment becomes a tool for distinguishing between general trends of virtue or vice. It is a 'discernment of passions', not an attribute of 'grey hairs' or 'many years' but rather a gift or charism that can be imparted to anyone (see *Conferences*: 2.8). He also states that the monk without *discernio* is like a person wandering in a desert at night: they may fall down a precipice themselves and take others with them.

'Not only all our actions', writes Cassian 'but even all our thoughts should be offered to the inspection of the elders' (*Conferences*: 2.10.1). Which is the point in the narrative where Cassian refers to the incident mentioned by Teresa: the elder Heron who was revered by many disciples yet finally took his own life jumping down a well, for a devil 'disguised as an angel of light' had tricked him into thinking God's angels would protect him as he jumped in the well and the miracle would bring many more to the faith. As Cassian states:

> Just as all young men are not similarly fervent in spirit and instructed in discipline and the best habits, so neither in fact can all the elders be found to be similarly perfect and upright. For the riches of elders are not to be measured by their grey hairs but by the hard work of their youth and the deserts of their past labours.
>
> (*Conferences*: 2.13.1)

Therefore the elderly are as much prone to deception as the young (*Conferences*: 2.8.1).

One can see how this tale would have appealed to Teresa, having suffered as she had and continued to do so at the time of writing *The Way*, at the hands of superiors or guides who often seemed befuddled by the tricks of the diabolic. The old, says Cassian, are as susceptible as the young, if not more so. Within this tradition, then, *everything* we experience must be explored with another, nothing should be left out of the account of the seeker to their director. Again, the saying must go alongside the showing:

> Everything that is thought of is offered to the inspection of the elders, so that, not trusting one's own judgement, one may submit in every respect to their understanding and may know how to judge what is good and bad according to what they have handed down
>
> (Abba Moses in Cassian's *Conferences*: 2.10.1)

For 'as soon as a wicked thought is revealed it loses its power' (*Conferences*: 2.10.1). As Jung and the early psychologists were to rediscover at the beginning of the twentieth century, the act of telling a secret or desire can often kill its power over us. Teresa was thus heir to a tradition of spiritual direction which realized that the *act of speaking* holds its own power over the passions of the soul. In this way spiritual direction becomes a choreography between what is said and what is unsaid.

Conclusion

In her dealings with her sisters and herself Teresa invariably displays compassion and gentleness that reflects the spiritual tradition to which she is heir. I began this chapter by suggesting that much light can be shone on the processes of psycho-spiritual formation in Teresa's writings from the life and work of the psychologist Carl Jung. Having surveyed his contributions and related them to Teresa's work what comes to light is the subtle interplay of light, darkness, *jouissance* and the symbolic in Teresa's approach to the interior psychological world. Her writings are as convincingly pastoral and perceptive as anything by Jung. Where they differ significantly, however, is in the theology that underpins both.

In the case of Jung we detected a Gnostic undertow that seems to wash his thoughts away from the locus of apophasis that lies at the heart of the Christian project. Teresa, on the other hand, prefers to place a discrete distance between herself and the action of God in the soul so that within this cordon of unknowing the Holy Spirit can act without the prying eyes of the intellect hovering over it.

While Teresa appreciates the need for the process of spiritual direction to 'name' the passions of the soul (especially in the case of mental disturbances such as melancholia) she also understands that the apophatic basis of Christian theology will not allow for the stronger brand of Gnosticism that seems to occur in many of Jung's writings, especially in the *Red Book*. Her own approach to spiritual direction, and by extension what we would now call 'psychology', places a significant pool of 'non-saying' at the centre of interpersonal interaction, the locus, for her, of the action of the Holy Spirit in one's encounters with self, the other and the world.

Having discussed Teresa in the context of the postmodern stream of psychoanalytic thought centred on Jung in this chapter, the following chapter will go deeper into this perceived 'apophasis' and 'non-saying' that lies at the heart of Teresa's understanding of self as we enter into dialogue with contemporary Buddhist understandings of mindfulness and 'non-self'.

8

Mindfulness, Mental Prayer and
'The Centre of the Soul'

Introduction

So far in our account of Teresa and her writings we have discussed some of her discourse on prayer, contemplation and the nature of the soul. In this penultimate chapter I would like to concentrate in particular on one aspect of her discourse: what she refers to as '*oración mental*', which has usually been translated into English as 'mental prayer'. My aim in this chapter is to relate her discourse here to the increasingly frequent contemporary discourse on 'mindfulness', especially as adapted from its Buddhist roots. Accordingly, I shall introduce some aspects from the Buddhist tradition and how it is used today before cross-referencing this account with Teresa's own accounts of her 'mental prayer', or as I will often render it, 'mindfulness'.[1]

To complete this 'Buddhist' chapter I shall conclude by giving a description of Teresa's account of the 'centre of the self' and see how this relates to Buddhist notions of personal anthropology and its contexts. I will be especially concerned to relate aspects of Teresa's account with Buddhist notions of *anattā* or 'no-self'; even if this notion may be seen as a major difference in the approaches of the two to contemplation and mindfulness. I hope that this chapter may stimulate contemporary practitioners of mindfulness to give some more thought as to the phenomenological bases of the practices that are presently being developed.[2]

---

[1] I shall give my reasons for introducing this translation as we go along.

[2] As a scholar of Christian literature I have had to rely on the help of my colleagues in formulating this chapter, especially in respect to the use of the Pali and Sanskrit terms. I am therefore very indebted to the generous assistance of Paul Trafford and Federico Filippi. Occasionally I will refer to their comments in footnotes.

The Discourse of Mindfulness

As the discourse of mindfulness has developed in contemporary healthcare, psychological and educational settings there has been a tendency to draw on non-Christian, especially Buddhist, sources. In this respect, the first thing to be said is that when we talk about 'mindfulness' in the Buddhist tradition, writers are usually referring to *sati*, an Indic term from the Pali for which there is no straightforward or simple definition. The term was first translated into the English as 'mindfulness' by Thomas William Rhys Davids in 1881 (Rhys Davids 1881: 107),[3] who noted that:

> *Sati* is literally 'memory' but is used with reference to the constantly repeated phrase 'mindful and thoughtful' (*sato sampagâno*); and means that activity of mind and constant presence of mind which is one of the duties most frequently inculcated on the good Buddhist.
>
> (Rhys Davids 1881: 145)

The equivalent term in the Sanskrit canon is *smriti* which literally means 'that which is remembered'.[4] In the *Satipaṭṭhāna Sutta, sati* is paired with two other qualities. First, *sampajañña* – watchfulness or alertness – which is seen as complementing the condition of mindfulness and secondly *atappa* or ardency 'being intent on what you're doing, trying your best to do it skillfully' (Thanissaro Bhikku 2010: 2). From all three together – mindfulness, watchfulness and ardency – we aspire to *yoniso manisikara* or 'appropriate attention'. The term 'appropriate' is apposite as, the Buddha suggests, it precludes useless metaphysical wondering of the mind into questions such as 'Is there a self?' Thus, in this context we can see how (dogmatic) notions of 'non-self' as much as 'self' would not be appropriate to the spirit of the Buddha's gentle and practical enquiry into the nature of delusion and ignorance. Thus, in the *Cūḷamālunkya Sutta*, the Buddha states that all speculation as to whether there is 'soul' or how it relates to body is to cease:

> Therefore, remember that I have left undeclared as undeclared and remember what I have declared as declared.

---

[3] 'Right Mindfulness: The active, watchful mind.'
[4] Here we are close to the Spanish term *recogimiento*.

- I have left undeclared 'The soul is the same as the body'
- I have left undeclared 'The soul is one thing and the body another'
- I have left undeclared 'After death an enlightened one exists'
- I have left undeclared 'After death an enlightened one no longer exists.'

(Cūḷamālunkya Sutta: 7 in MN: 1.432)

Further, the Buddha is specific as to why these questions must remain undeclared:

Why have I left it undeclared?
   Because it is unbeneficial. It does not belong to the fundamentals of the holy life, it does not lead to disenchantment, to dispassion, to cessation, to peace, to direct knowledge, to enlightenment, to *Nibbāna*. That is why I have left it undeclared.

(Cūḷamālunkya Sutta: 8, in MN: 1.432)

As he famously puts it in the same Sutta, our state is that of a wounded patient with a poisoned arrow in them. Would such a person, when presented with the surgeon for the removal of the arrow, hesitate to say:

"I will not let the surgeon pull at this arrow until I know the name and clan of the man who wounded me … Until I know whether the man who wounded me was tall or short of middle height … Until I know whether the bowstring that wounded me was fibre or reed or sinew or hemp or bark …"
   All this would still not be known to the man and meanwhile he would die.

(Cūḷamālunkya Sutta: 5, in MN 1.429)

Thus as well as specific exercises arranged around practices such as breathing, mindfulness in this early sense can be seen as encompassing a whole sphere of what we may term 'attentiveness' on various aspects of life including our day to day practice in the world. However, a great deal of Buddhist practice and teaching throughout its long history has been a wholesale critique of 'attempts to attain permanence, independence and self-subsistence by identifying with transient, conditioned phenomena – whether mental, psychological or conceptual' (Waldron 2005: 1). The sense of self as a permanent unchanging 'I' existing against a backdrop of an objective 'other' is constantly critiqued in all Buddhist traditions and cultures. That is, the notion of 'an enduring subject which exists independently of the external objects around it, which is can possess and enjoy' (Waldron 2005: 2). Mindfulness, then, should be regarded as a tool for disentangling us from the matrix of delusion within which we find ourselves. This will therefore not just be through the statutory period of sitting meditation but will last beyond into all aspects of living. As the Buddha states in the *Prajnāpāramita Sutta*:

> Subhuti, in what way does a Bodhisatva-Mahāsattva, being aware that he has a body, practise perfect conduct? Subhuti, a Bodhisatva-Mahāsattva, when walking is fully mindful that he is walking, when he stands up is fully mindful of standing up, when sitting is fully mindful of sitting, when sleeping is fully mindful of sleeping, and if his body is well or ill, he is fully mindful of either condition.

(Namkhai Norbu 1986: 147)

'Mindfulness' or *smriti* in the Sanskrit tradition is therefore 'a total awareness of the immediate situation. This is however, a detached noninvolved awareness, free from desire or aversion' (Samuel 1993: 375). For Desire and Aversion are two of the three root causes of delusion or *samsāra*.

The Purpose of Mindfulness: The Agnostic Self

What then is the purpose of mindfulness in this Buddhist context? Essentially it can be seen as the need to develop freedom from entanglement with things as they seem. Desire, craving and its consequences will create the illusion of 'self' and 'I' that will further drive craving, desire and unhappiness (*Dukkha*).[5] The Buddha wrote of the delusion of self resting on our grasping of the five 'aggregates' or 'heaps' of 'grasping' (Pali *khandha*/ Sanskrit *skandha*).These aggregates are not to be seen as irreducible elements of the personality, but rather as 'the most prominent functions that are involved whenever the human personality is the subject of discussion' (Kalupahana 1992: 21). They are traditionally classed as:

1. *Rūpa* – material form
2. *Vedanā* – feeling or sensation (that which is pleasant or unpleasant)
3. *Saññā* – perceiving/recognition

---

[5] 'This delusion is the basis of *māna* (conceit of 'I am'), one of the *samyojanas* (fetters) that bind us to the wheel of rebirth.' Paul Trafford: Note to author, 2012.

4. *Sankhārā* – disposition or karmic formation/volition
5. *Viññāna* – consciousness[6]

The work of mindfulness is therefore the work of awareness of these elements of existence so that the shifting bases of personality will inevitably be revealed. Therefore, through the practice of mindfulness the essentially shifting nature of the self will be revealed (Kalupahana 1992: 75). Against this, write the Buddhist commentators (see Kalupahana 1992: 40), there are two human tendencies, viz: to essentialize the self (largely speaking the contemporary Western view of personality) or to dissolve the self into nothingness (such as is found in wrong notions of 'non-self'). For Kalupahana 'the middle way consists of neither succumbing to essentialism or nihilism. Absolute self negation as well as absolute self cessation are not only morally repugnant but also epistemologically unwarranted' (Kalupahana 1992: 40).

Mindfulness will accordingly assist us in moving from the grasping illusion of an 'essential self' to the flexibility of a de-centred or agnostic self. In the Buddha's terms we remove our attachment to the aggregates to realize that over-identification with them is the source of delusion:

> He regards feeling as self ... perception as self ... volitional formations as self ... consciousness as self, or self as possessing consciousness, or consciousness as in self, or self as in consciousness. That consciousness of his changes and alters. With the change and alteration of consciousness, his consciousness becomes preoccupied with the change of consciousness. Agitation and a constellation of mental states born of preoccupation with the change of consciousness remain obsessing his mind. Because his mind is obsessed, he is frightened, distressed and anxious, and through clinging becomes agitated.
>
> (BS: 3.16)

> A well taught, noble disciple ... regards material form thus: "This is not mine, this I am not, this is not my self." He regards feeling thus, "This is not mine, this I am not, this is not my self." He regards formations thus, "This is not mine, this I am not, this is not my

---

[6] See, for example, *Mahāpunnama Sutta* (MN 109.14): 'So it seems material form is not self, feeling is not self, perception is not self, volitions are not self, consciousness is not self. What self, then, will actions done by non-self affect?' See also Williams 2000: 89 *passim* for an extended discussion of the later *Abhidhamma* fine gradations of the five *khandha*.

self." He regards what is seen, heard, sensed, cognized, encountered, sought, mentally pondered thus: "This is not mine, this I am not, this is not my self." And this standpoint for views, namely, "That which is the self is the world; after death I shall be permanent, everlasting, eternal, not subject to change; I shall endure as long as eternity" – this too he regards thus: "This is not mine, this I am not, this is not my self."

(*Alagaddūpama Sutta*: 15 in MN: 1.136)

The mistake would be to see the Buddha's account as a type of 'non self'. This is as much an illusion as the essentialism of everyday thought, or as Peter Harvey puts it in 'The Selfless Mind' (1995), the denial of any kind of self, metaphysical or empirical is 'quite wrong' (1996: 7). We are therefore left with a sort of agnosticism towards selfhood. Therefore mindfulness as thus portrayed in its Buddhist context is generally seen as that which helps to sharpen our awareness of processes of the mind while generally remaining agnostic as to the nature of self in its essence. As the Buddha puts it in the *Sabbāsava Sutta,* both the view that 'self exists for me' and 'no self exists for me' are equally delusory:

This speculative view, bhikkus, is called the thicket of views, the contortion of views, the wilderness of views, the vacillation of views, the fetter of views.

(MN: 1.8)

With this Buddhist notion of the 'decentred agnostic self' revealed through mindfulness before us we now return to Teresa to see how she employs '*oración mental*' and '*contemplación*' in her works and whether, if at all, there are parallels with these Buddhist notions of mindfulness.

Teresa on Contemplation and Mindfulness

Teresa's first account of *oración mental* in her writings is an extended account in *The Life,* Chapters 8 to 10. Here she contrasts the peace she receives from this activity with the 'war so troublesome' where she would frequently 'fall and rise' (V: 8.2 *con estas caídas y con levantarme*) as her passions came and left her. Her mental prayer 'drew her to the harbour of salvation' (V: 8.4 *a puerto de salvación*). She refers to it here and later as her '*trato con Dios: Que no es otra cosa oración mental, a mi parecer, sino tratar de amistad, estando muchas veces tratando a solas con quien sabemos nos ama*' / 'For mental prayer is none other, it appears to me, than an association of friendship, frequently practised on an intimate basis, with the one we know loves us.'[7] The pivotal word '*Trato*' that Teresa uses to convey the intimacy and immediacy of mindfulness causes the most variation in translation. Allison Peers, in his usual robust fashion stays with 'intercourse', while Kavanaugh and Rodriguez opt for the 'intimate sharing between friends'. Of her older translators Matthew chose 'straight commerce with God', Woodhead 'conversing in prayer' and Cohen 'communion'.[8]

Where Teresa's method of prayer differs so clearly from the Buddhist mindfulness detailed above is the role that visualization and symbolic representation of Christ play in her meditations (see, for example, V: 9 1–4). Even though the *gustos* and *regalos* we discussed in Chapter 4 will be a necessary part of her mindfulness, the symbolic function discussed in the previous chapter plays an even more important role. However where Teresa's account of mindfulness converges with the Buddhist accounts above is the importance of drawing attention away from intellectual and mental activity to the location of what she calls 'the heart'. As we discussed in Chapter 6, this is not an anti-intellectual move but rather a consequence of the strategy of the medieval mystical theology to which she is heir. To overcome the whirring discourse of the intellect we will need to concentrate on the mindful '*trato*' with the beloved.

This is why I feel the term 'mental prayer' can be misleading and why I preference 'mindfulness' as a translation of *oración mental*. 'Mental' seems to have the contemporary association with the mind and intellectual activity whereas, I would suggest, Teresa is advocating something closer to the Buddhist practice of mindfulness outlined above, and certainly closer to the contemporary practice of mindfulness discussed by commentators such as Kabut-Zinn. As she says later in Chapter 13: '*Ansí que va mucho a los principios de comenzar oración a no amilanar los pensamientos, y créanme esto, porque lo tengo por espieriencia*' / 'Therefore it is of great importance, when we begin to practise prayer, not to be intimidated by thoughts, and believe you me, for I have had experience of this'

---

[7] Again, a tricky passage to translate and preserve the sense of intimacy Teresa wants to convey here. Allison Peers retains this sense with his translation: 'Mental prayer, in my view, is nothing but friendly intercourse, and frequent solitary converse, with Him Who we know loves us.' Kavanaugh and Rodriguez give a more distant: 'Mental prayer in my opinion is nothing less than an intimate sharing between friends; it means taking time frequently to be alone with Him who we know loves us.'

[8] Matthew, for example, translates the passage above with: 'For Mentall prayer, is no other thing, in my opinion, than a treatie, about making friendship with Almightie God; and a frequent and private Commerce, hand to hand, with him; by whome, we know, we are beloved.'

(V: 13.7).[9] Or as she later puts it in Chapter 17, rather poetically translated by Matthew, the thoughts are like 'unquiet little Gnatts, which buzze, and whizze by night, heer and there, for just so, are these Powers wont to goe, from one to another' (V: 17.6).[10]

As I argued earlier in this book, as Teresa's experience as a writer and pray-er progresses, she does not seem to alter the fundamental perceptions of the nature of the life as prayer as outlined in the early *Life*. What does change, however, is her ability to convey the exact subtle meaning regarding prayer-discourse in her writings. Indeed, as time goes on she seems to entrench the studied imprecision of *The Life*, enshrining in her writings the principle that the life of prayer/contemplation *by its very nature* most resist the hard edged analysing of the discursive intellect. In this respect, as I have argued here and elsewhere, her attempt to patrol the boundaries of the ineffable are as precise and subtle as any contemporary linguistic philosopher.

Her caution seems to stem from the essential core of 'unknowing' she feels that lies at the heart of prayer as the discursive intellect gives way to the subtler levels of mindfulness. As she writes in a letter to Gracián in mid-April 1579: '¡Oh, válame Dios, y cómo no nos conocemos!'/ 'Oh Good God! How true it is that we do not know ourselves!' She even goes so far, in a letter to the sisters of Seville, to counsel them against writing about prayer:

> I am not in favour of these sisters writing about prayer (*no estoy bien en que esas hermanas escrivan las cosas de oración*), for this has many drawbacks which I would like to tell you about. You should know that even though doing this amounts to nothing but a waste of time, it hinders the soul from walking in freedom and allows one to imagine all kinds of things (*y que es estorbo para andar el alma con libertad*).
>
> (Letter to Madre María de San José, 28 March 1578)

For we are talking about:

> Things of import never to be forgotten and if they are forgotten then there is no reason to talk of them (*Si son cosas de tomo, nunca se olvidan, y si se olvidan, ya no hay para qué*

---

[9] Matthew: 'It is therefore of great importance, for them, who beginn to hold Mentall Prayer, that they doe not subtilize too much, with their thoughts.' Kavanaugh: 'not to be intimidated by thoughts.' Allison Peers: 'not to let ourselves be frightened by our own thoughts.' Lewis: 'not to let our thoughts frighten us.'

[10] '*Que no parece sino de estas maripositas de las noches, importunas y desasosegadas: ansí anda de un cabo a otro.*' Teresa uses the key term *desasosegada* here which we discussed in Chapter 5.

las decir) … Because I understand the trouble they will run into from thinking about what they should write and from what the devil can put into their head I insist so much on this. (*Porque entiendo los inconvenientes que hay en andar pensando en qué han de escrivir y lo que las puede poner el demonio, pongo tanto en esto*) … It is better to praise the Lord, who gives these graces, and when they have passed to let them be, for it is the soul that will experience the benefit (*Y créame que es lo major alabar a el Señor que lo da; y pasado, pasarse por ello,*[11] *que el alma es la que ha de sentir la ganancia*).

(Letter to Madre María de San José, 28 March 1578)

The thrust of the advice being the necessity to 'let the soul be', not to over-intellectualize or analyse the process of meditation so that thereby the person comes to a position where awareness occurs naturally – 'organically', as it were. For prayer and contemplation, by their nature, cannot be measured or codified: 'in a short moment God often gives more than in a long time, one cannot measure His work in time.'[12]

Such prayer, as she goes on to say to her brother in the same letter:

Is certainly beyond what you can understand and the beginning of many blessings. It is a great affliction and pain that comes without one's knowing how, and most tasty (*sabrosísima*). And although, as a matter of fact, it is a wound caused by the love of God in the soul, one doesn't know where it comes from or how, or whether it is a wound or what it is, but it feels this tasty pain (*ese dolor sabrosa*) that makes it complain and so it says: 'Without wounding you cause pain, and without pain you wear away the love of Creatures' ('*Sin herir, dolor hacéis y sin dolor deshacéis el amor de las criaturas*').

(Letter to Don Lorenzo de Cepeda, 17 January 1577)

Later in *The Way of Perfection*, Teresa will write about a whole way of prayer (*todo el modo de oración*) which will include first principles, 'mental prayer', 'the prayer of quiet' and 'union': '*dende los principiantes a la oración mental, y de quietud y unión,*' all of which she will tell us can be contained within the simple

---

[11] On the phrase *pasarse por ello*, Allison Peers notes 'Not necessarily forget them, for some are unforgettable, but be resigned to their being over, and refrain from analyzing and in that way reliving them.' Allison Peers, *Letters of St Teresa of Jesus*.

[12] '*En un memento da Dios más, hartas veces, que con mucho tiempo; que no se miden sus obras por los tiempos.*' (Letter to Don Lorenzo de Cepeda, 2 January 1577)

words of the Lord's Prayer (CE: 37.1). Turning her attention to '*oración mental*' in particular in Chapter 25 of *The Way* (Escorial Codex) she states:

> I now want to explain – because some of you don't understand – what mental prayer/ mindfulness (*oración mental*) is, and please God we shall practise this as it ought to be practised. But I fear that mindfulness also involves much work if the virtues are not obtained, although it is not necessary that they be possessed in as high a degree as is required for the other (i.e. contemplation/ *contemplación*).
>
> (CE: 25.2)

Such mindfulness 'is not determined by whether or not the mouth is closed' (CE: 37), for 'if while speaking I am entirely aware that I speak with God with great *advertencia* (attention) in the words I speak then mental and vocal prayer are joined'.[13] Her sense of *advertencia* is central to her notion of mindfulness, Allison Peers gives 'clear realization and full consciousness' for his translation while Kavanaugh gives 'great awareness' (although both authors are translating CV not CE here).

Again, the sense of attention Teresa is conveying relates strongly to the Buddhist notions of mindfulness we began with (see also CE: 37.3). All this, she tells us, requires humility, not 'the talk of wise and learned men' (i.e. speculative theology) for God 'enjoys more these crudities of a humble shepherd, who He knows has more to say, than the most systematic (ordered, refined) theologies if they do not come with a certain humility' / '*Que gusta más de estas groserías de un pastorcito humilde que sabe si más le dijera, que de las teulogías muy ordenadas so no van con tanta humildad*' (CE: 37.4).

This mindfulness is in contrast to the speculative theology which she had heard described in Osuna's *Third Spiritual Alphabet* as a young woman. For such mindfulness, as she had stated in the *Life*, and now repeats, is in contrast to the *desasosiego* of those with a distracted soul:

> There are some souls and understandings so scattered that they are like wild horses that cannot be stopped. (*Hay unas almas y entendimientos tan desbaratados como unos caballos desbocados que no hay quien los haga parar*). Now they go this way, now that, always with lack of tranquillity (*siempre con desasosiego*) and although a skilled

---

[13] '*Sí, que no está la falta para no ser oración mental en tener cerrada la boca; si hablando estoy enteramente viendo que hablo con Dios con más advertencia que en las palabras que digo, junto está oración mental y vocal.*'

rider mounted on such a horse may not always be in danger – sometimes even he too
– and even if he is not concerned about his life there will always be the risk of doing
something untoward and so he must always proceed with great care.

(CE: 30.2)

Distractions and inner voices, the 'whizzing gnats' of *The Life*, still assault the
mind and prevent the tranquillity necessary for the practice of mindfulness:

You will hear some persons frequently making objections: 'there are dangers'; 'so and so
went astray by such means', 'this other one was deceived'; 'another who prayed a great
deal fell away'; 'it's harmful to virtue'; 'it's not for women, for they will be susceptible to
illusions'; 'it's better they stick to their sewing'; 'they don't need these delicacies' ; 'The
Our Father and the Hail Mary are sufficient.'

(CV: 21.2)

As if to counter these she spends the rest of the book giving mindful attention
to the words of the Lord's Prayer.

Turning to *The Foundations* it is no surprise to find Teresa describing the
shape and evolution of prayer in the terms of the earlier books. As before
in Chapter 5 of *The Foundations* she distinguishes prayer from thought
(*pensamiento*):

I have run into some for whom it seems the whole business lies in thinking (*el negocio
en el pensamiento*); and therefore if they are able to think a lot about God, no matter
what effort is exerted, they immediately think that they are spiritual (*parece que son
espirituales*); while, if they become distracted, and their efforts to think of good things
fail, they at once become greatly discouraged and suppose themselves to be lost … The
soul is not thought (*El alma no es el pensamiento*) … therefore the soul's profit consists
not in thinking much but in loving much (*el aprovechamiento del alma no está en pensar
mucho sino en amar mucho*).

(F: 5.2)

In summary then, from these passages I think a strong case can be made
to regard Teresa's 'mental prayer' as closer to the contemporary notion of
mindfulness than may at first sight be apparent. In the descriptions above what
clearly differentiates Teresa's approach is the necessary connection between her
own mindful prayer and attention in meditation to the person of Christ. Yet

where she comes close to the Buddhist masters is her challenge to the discursive power of the intellect and the necessary use of symbol and image to allow this power to be 'short-circuited' to allow direct awareness of self and indeed all creation around (in V: 9.5 she tells us that she extends her meditative awareness to 'fields or water or flowers: in these things I found a memory of the Creator').

In consequence I don't think it is far-fetched to talk of Teresa, in the early stages at least, as advocating a 'school of mindfulness' as she refashions and makes her own the tradition of *recogimiento* to which she is heir.

Having explored Teresa's writing on this aspect of the life of prayer I would like to conclude this chapter by tracing another aspect of Teresa's spiritual anthropology – how she conceives the notion of personhood. As stated at the beginning I propose to do this by relating Teresa's notion of 'the centre of the soul' with Buddhist notions of *anattā* or 'no-self'.

Descriptions of the Centre: *The Book of the Life* and *The Interior Castle*

When we look in *The Life* for descriptions of the 'centre of the soul' we should not be surprised to come across original and striking metaphors put across with passion and directness. In this respect, Teresa does not disappoint. However, when we study the accounts carefully both here, and in the *Spiritual Testimonies* presented for the *letrados* of Avila, Teresa is clearly aware of the difficulties involved in presenting the subject and remains circumspect.[14] Notwithstanding this circumspection, finally at the very end of *The Life* in Chapter 40 she presents her account.

As we would expect by now, and is typical of Teresa's 'apophatic' style, the account is couched in descriptions of unknowing and 'unsaying' with respect to the nature of the self/soul. The Divine Truth is presented 'without my knowing how or what' (V: 40.3), it is 'of a fashion I cannot describe' (V: 40.3), 'it appears to me (*Paréceme*), without my understanding how, the Lord gave me great tenderness (*ternura*), *regalo* and humility'. Finally, she presents her description of the 'centre':

---

[14] The *Testimonies* contain very little reference to the nature of the soul. Rather she cleverly concentrates on presenting the orthodoxy of her spiritual pedigree and the names of learned Dominicans, Franciscans and Jesuits who have approved of her accounts of the spiritual life.

Once, during the recitation of the Office with all the Sisters, my soul suddenly became recollected and it seemed to me to be like a totally clear mirror without having back, sides, top or bottom that weren't totally clear, and in the centre of it Christ Our Lord was represented to me, as I generally see Him. It seemed to me I saw Him in all parts of my soul, clear as a mirror, and also this mirror – I don't know how to say it – was engraved all over by the same Lord by a communication that I cannot explain but was very loving.[15]

What is striking in this text is the whole nature of destabilization that is occurring. There is no 'geographic centre' to the self. In fact, as we gaze into the self all we see are reflected surfaces – 'back, sides, top and bottom' which are unable to hold our gaze. Only an image of Christ remains, how 'I cannot describe', but it is felt 'most lovingly'. Although Teresa does not return to the mirror simile in later writings the overall spatial destabilization is one she will return to again. The mirror image is dropped, but the other simile she brings in later at V: 40.10 will return later:

Let us say, to make a comparison, that the Divinity is like a very clear diamond, much greater than all the world; or like a mirror … in so sublime a way that I wouldn't know how to do justice to it.

This diamond returns at the beginning of *The Interior Castle* where Teresa seems to consciously echo the end of the *Life*.[16] It certainly draws on the same strategies of unknowing and destabilization used in the earlier work to again leave the reader in no doubt that to look for 'a centre of the soul' would be a self-defeating task:

---

[15] 'Estando una vez en las Horas con todas, de presto se recogió mi alma, y parecióme ser como un espejo claro toda, sin haber espaldas ni lados ni alto ni bajo que no estuviese toda clara, y en el centro de ella se me representó Cristo nuestro Señor, como le suelo ver. Parecíame en todas las partes de mi alma le veía claro como en un espejo, y también este espejo – yo no sé decir cómo – se esculpía todo en el mismo Señor por una comunicación que yo no sabré decir, muy amorosa.'

A typically nightmarish piece of Teresa to translate. Kavanaugh gives:

'Once while I was reciting with all the Sisters the hours of the Divine Office, my soul suddenly became recollected; and it seemed to me to be like a brightly polished mirror, without any part on the back or sides or top or bottom that wasn't totally clear. In its center Christ, Our Lord, was shown to me, in the way I usually see Him. It seemed to me I saw Him clearly in every part of my soul, as though in a mirror. And this mirror also – I don't know how to explain it – was completely engraved upon the Lord Himself by means of a very loving communication I wouldn't know how to describe.'

[16] Teresa refers several times in the *Castle* to the *Life* which was, we may remember, at this point in the hands of the Inquisition (see Chapter 6).

While I was beseeching our Lord today to speak through me (*por mí*), as I was unable to find a thing to say (*no atinaba a cosa que decir*) or how to begin to comply with this obedience, what I will say now presented itself (*ofreció*) to begin with this starting point: that we consider our soul to be like a castle, totally of diamond or very clear crystal, where there are many abodes (*aposentos*), as in heaven there are many mansions. Now if we consider it carefully, sisters, the soul of a just person (*el alma del justo*) is nothing else but a paradise where He says he takes his delights (*El tiene sus deleites*). Well then, what do you think such an abode would be like where a King so powerful, so wise, so pure, so full of good things, takes his delight? I cannot find anything with which to compare the great beauty and capacity of the soul; and truly our intellects will no more be able to grasp this than they can comprehend God, no matter how keen they are, for He Himself said that He created us in his own image and likeness.

(M: 1.1.1)

The position presented here, where our intellects (*nuestros entendimientos*) cannot grasp that which we seek – whether it be the nature of God or the nature of the soul – seems close to the 'vision' described earlier in the *Book of the Life*, but now the convoluted (and frankly untranslatable) image of Christ, somehow etched onto a mirror without 'top, bottom, sides or back' is replaced by the slightly more concrete notion of the 'castle with many mansions'. Although this is clearly a literary masterstroke, and one for which Teresa will rightly be remembered, it seems as though she is also aware that as she offers it to her readers she will be also losing some of the uncertainty and unknowing so essential in the impact of the earlier, untranslatable *Vida* vision. As if to stress this point, whenever Teresa refers to a specific 'mansion/abode' she will usually qualify it by pointing out that the description should not be taken too literally. Her comments in the Epilogue are typical in this respect:

Although no more than seven abodes were discussed, in each of these there are many others, below and above and to the sides, with lovely gardens and fountains and labyrinths, such delightful things that you would want to be dissolved in praises of the great God who created the soul in His own image and likeness.

(M: Ep.3)[17]

---

[17] Paul Trafford adds: 'In Buddhism, it is said that human beings can access all realms. Thus in meditation, especially, they can travel to *deva* and *Brahma* realms – this can be direct or with the option to go "sideways" (taste some of the flowers) and then move on.' Communication to author, 2012.

Key in all her descriptions is that the 'castle' is not 'known' or 'understood' but 'enjoyed' (*se deleita*). The dialectic of affectivity lies at the heart of this epistemology. The true nature of ourselves, our relation to God, and God in God's self, are described in terms of affectivity and delight. In this respect, in both the prologue and epilogue to the *Castle* she makes, as we have seen, a clear allusion to the same passage from the Book of Proverbs (Proverbs 8.31) which we saw Francisco de Osuna referring to earlier in his account of the self. For Teresa, then, the soul is primarily a place 'wherein our Lord takes delight' rather than a space of knowledge or knowing. Knowledge, if it is to be obtained, comes from 'tasting' the delights of the *gustos*.

The 'interior matters of the soul', she constantly reminds us, are 'so obscure for our minds' (M: 1.2.7) that we must constantly rely on the experiential, especially the feelings of consolation and 'comfort' (*consuelo*).[18] For the self 'is capable of much more than we can imagine' (M: 1.2.8). Which is where Teresa introduces the following delightful phrase:

> It is very important for any soul that prays, whether little or much, that it doesn't tighten up (*apriete*) or squeeze itself into a corner (*arrincone*).
>
> (M: 1.2.8)[19]

This passage seems to sum up the expansiveness and openness with which Teresa sees the spiritual journey. It is also another example of her *grosería* – her coarse spiritual writing. *Arrincone* connotes 'being neglected', 'out in the cold', 'reclusive' while *Apriete* conjures up images of 'pinching', 'hurting' and 'tightening up'. As we have seen she once reminded her sisters, when speaking of spiritual things, that we must always be:

> Simple, frank and devout, rather like that of hermits and people who live in retirement. They must use none of the newfangled words – affectations, as I think people call them – which are current in a world always eager for new-fangled things. In all circumstances let them give preference to common expressions rather than to unusual ones.
>
> (ME in Peers CW: 3.251)

---

[18] Paul Trafford adds: 'In the *Dhammakaya* tradition, meditation instructions concerning visualization are often expressed in terms of feeling, as in finding a focal point that feels most comfortable, but also "feeling" the object of meditation.' Communication to author, 2012.

[19] *Esto importa mucho a cualquier alma que tenga oración, poca o mucha, que no la arrincone ni apriete.*

Literally, she is telling us here not to be 'uptight' about the spiritual journey, basically, 'to loosen up'. And this holds too for our conceptions of the 'centre of the soul'. Therefore, let the seeker, she continues, walk through the soul – 'the castle' – *arriba* and *abajo,* above and below and to the sides for God 'gives this to us for our dignity' (M: 1.2.8).

Into the Centre

As we have seen the style and tone set by the first Mansion – uncertainty, delight and spiritual freedom – continue throughout the rest of the Mansions. Similarly, as with the earlier passages in the *Life*, Teresa is loath to give us precise descriptions of 'the centre' but rather she prefers to concentrate on the effects of the life of prayer (in this she is pre-eminently a pastoral or practical theologian).

Thus, in Mansion Four, as we get closer to 'the centre': 'things get more delicate' and 'more obscure to the understanding' (M: 4.1.2) for 'the intellect is incapable of finding words to explain them'. The nearest she gets to 'explanation' is her analogy of the 'depths of the soul' (*una cosa mas profunda*) to 'deep waters', the same analogy she had used earlier in the *Life* (M: 4.2, c.f. V: 11). Whenever an analogy or symbol is presented in this Fourth Mansion, whether it is water, a fragrant smell or shepherd's pipe she always cautiously qualifies it with a phrase such as 'these are great secrets that we don't understand'. This continues in the Fifth Mansion where even when the 'Lord is united with the essence (*esencia*) of the soul' this is 'so secret' that it cannot be described (M: 5.1.5). The Sixth Mansion again gives no mention of the interior or centre, except for one reference in M: 6.11.2 to a 'fiery arrow' that pierces the 'deepest and most intimate (part) of the soul': *en lo muy hondo e intimo del alma* – the *entrañas* which we saw in Chapter Six are so intimately connected with the Transverberation passage from *The Life*.

So we come at last to the Seventh and last – most interior? – Mansion of the soul. Surely, here, if anywhere, Teresa will give us the description of the pole of the soul – the magnetic North, the motherlode. She calls it the '*muy muy interior*' / the 'most most interior'. However, again, she tells us it is a '*cosa muy honda que no sabe decir cómo es porque no tiene letras, siente en sí esta divina compañia*' / 'thing very deep that it doesn't know how to explain because it is not educated enough, for it feels within itself the companionship of the divine' (M: 7.1.7). The crucial thing Teresa tells us, and surely she is now employing her famous sense of humour and irony, is not to be obsessed with finding the 'centre of the soul' but in carrying out the work of God in the world:

> This may lead you to think that such a person will not remain in possession of her senses but will be so completely absorbed that she will be able to fix her mind upon nothing. But no: in all that belongs to the service of God she is more alert than before; and, when not otherwise occupied, she rests in that happy company.
>
> (M: 7.1.8)

> All its concern is taken up with how to please Him more and how or where it will show Him the love it bears Him. This is the reason for prayer, my daughters, the purpose of this spiritual marriage: the birth always of good works, good works.
>
> (M: 7.4.6)

Again, Teresa has thwarted expectations in a way only she could do. The intellectual, analytic or discriminating mind wants a 'centre' or 'essence' of the self or soul. Teresa just will not deliver it. Either it is a 'secret so great and a favour so sublime and a delight the soul experiences which is so extreme I don't know what to compare it to' (M: 7.2.3) or it is the call to good works in the world. However, there is the third explanation of the 'centre of the soul' which Teresa has already held up right at the beginning – that the centre is Christ Himself as revealed through the meeting in the Triune God. For at the centre of the soul is 'where God Himself is' for 'in my opinion there is no door for Him to enter' (M: 7.2.3). Of the nature of this union with God, however, 'one can say no more'.[20]

Conclusions: Christian and Buddhist 'No-Self' and Mindfulness

We are left after reading Teresa's *Interior Castle* with the feeling of having sat through a fascinating but ultimately baffling conjuring trick. What began in the *Life* with the Hall of Mirrors with Christ's face reflected wherever we looked has ended with a statement of apophasis and a call to 'good works'. She

---

[20] Interestingly enough John of the Cross comes to similar conclusions. See *The Living Flame of Love*: 1.10: 'Being a spirit, the soul does not have a height or a depth, neither deeper nor less deep within it as do quantitative bodies. As it has no parts, it doesn't have differences between the inner and outer, for all is of one manner and *it doesn't have a centre of depth and less depth quantitatively speaking*' (LF: 1.10).

will not be drawn as to the nature of the 'centre' except to say something 'very secret' happens there in our relationship with God. Juxtaposing Teresa with the Buddhist scholars with whom we began this chapter we are entitled to ask – is there a fixed self or 'centre of the soul' in Teresa? My conclusion from the above would be to reply: 'There is and there isn't.' There is certainly a pull to something, the divine, but this is a pull that is *felt* rather than *thought*. As the *entendimiento* is carefully distanced the self will primarily become known initially through *delight* and *gusto* and ultimately, for Teresa, it will be these, and the practice of good works, that will tell us if we are succeeding in our spiritual quest. As to where that track is leading, Teresa prefers to draw a discrete veil.

For Teresa's first readers this was surprising, shocking even. Alonso de la Fuente, speaking for the Inquisition, felt that when he read Teresa 'in effect the soul is not there' and felt the doctrine came from Tauler, with kinship to the early Marcellian heresy (see Llamas 1977: 398). Five hundred years later the respectability rightly accorded Teresa tends to blunt the 'shock and awe' which I hope to have demonstrated in this book lies at the heart of her writing.

I began this chapter by describing the relationship between mindfulness as understood in the Buddhist tradition and its link with providing insight into delusion and craving. It was suggested that the Buddha himself had resisted the urge to engage in metaphysical speculation about the nature of 'self' or 'non-self' but rather had insisted on the actual practice of mindfulness as a means to uncovering delusion.

My aim in this chapter has been to demonstrate how the process of contemplation in Teresa is every bit as radical in its 'deconstruction of self' as is the Buddhist tradition of contemplation of the self/non-self in mindfulness. Where the two traditions differ is, first, in the importance given to the personal Creative Deity by the Christian Teresa and secondly, in the Spanish school at least, the importance accorded to the role of desire as a *positive feature* in the search for the Beloved (however we noted at the beginning the Buddha's stress on the connection between mindfulness and ardency in the *Satipaṭṭhāna Sutta*).

Although I am not claiming that Teresa was an 'anonymous Buddhist', I feel it is not too far-fetched to claim that ontologically the process of deconstruction which is found in both traditions has much in common, perhaps more than we had hitherto thought.

However, phenomenologically Teresa's 'pedagogy of desire' gives a different nuance to the Buddhist resting in the 'selfless self' of mindfulness. With respect to the future development of mindfulness as a tool in, for example, the healthcare, education or psychological setting, I hope these considerations will force practitioners to give some thought as to 'what sort of mindfulness' they are pursuing and what is its role within the phenomenological sense of self hidden within the (sometimes confused and confusing) terms presently being deployed.

Epilogue – Teresa of Avila: Doctor of the Church, Doctor of the Soul

In 1970 Teresa of Avila, along with St Catherine of Siena, was declared a Doctor of the Universal Church by Pope Paul VI in Rome. According to the *New Catholic Encyclopedia* in 1967:

> No woman has been proclaimed (Doctor of the Church), although Teresa of Avila has popularly been given the title because of the influence of her spiritual teaching; it would seem that no woman is likely to be named because of the link between this title and the teaching office, which is limited to males.
>
> (Forshaw: 1967)

By conferring this honour upon her, the church demonstrated that Teresa's teaching had indeed become of age, yet it had waited several centuries before giving her this recognition. In light of the examination of her texts in this book this is perhaps unsurprising. As I have argued throughout, I believe that her writings remain as challenging today as they did five hundred years ago. What I hope to have demonstrated in this account is the intellectual rigour with which Teresa explores the landscape of the soul and how throughout she is alive to the nuances and subtleties of the language required to depict the encounter of the soul with the transcendent. As we have seen, this she does by using the tradition of *theologia mystica* to which she is heir but adapting it, almost playing with it, to forge a unique spiritual language as finely wrought as anything by a contemporary linguistic philosopher. By forging this provocative and challenging language she truly deserves to be called a 'Doctor of the Soul'.

I have concluded the book with a descriptive analysis of two aspects of the contemporary psycho-spiritual thought-world: the rediscovery of 'mindfulness' as a tool for clinical intervention and the long shadow cast by Carl Jung and his pioneering research into the nature of soul and psyche. In doing this I hope to have demonstrated how a re-reading of Teresa in the light of this context can challenge us to perceive our contemporary spiritual anthropology in new and surprising lights.

In the case of Jungian analytical psychology the questions raised by the challenges of Teresa's approach are ones not unfamiliar within the discipline itself. The second generation Jungian theorist, James Hillman (1926–2011), writing in the same year as the *Catholic Encyclopedia* was pronouncing on the legitimacy of the female teaching office, stated:

> Because the soul is lost – or at least temporarily mislaid or bewildered – ministers have been forced, upon meeting a pastoral problem, to go upstairs to its neighbour, the next closest thing to soul: the mind. So the churches turn to academic and clinical psychology, to psychodynamics and psychopathology and psychiatry, in attempts to understand the mind and its workings. This has led ministers to regards troubles of the soul as mental break-downs and cure of soul as psychotherapy. But the realm of the mind – perception, memory, mental diseases – is a realm of its own, another flat belonging to another owner who can tell us very little about the person whom the minister really wants to know, the soul.
>
> (Hillman 1967: 44)

Yet, shortly before his death in 2011, the same theorist voiced a sense of disillusionment with the direction that analytical psychology had taken in the past few years:

> I am critical of the whole analytic discipline ... It has become a kind of New Age substitute for life, on the one hand; a substitute for rigorous education in culture, philosophy and religion, on the other; and third, a 'helping profession' ... the whole thing has lost its way. Something is deeply missing.[1]

This 'something' he had described in somewhat cryptic terms in the earlier *Insearch*, in terms that Teresa would probably have concurred with:

> Besides the familiar reality of my mental activity (my introspection, worries, plans, observations, reflections, projects), and the worldly reality of objects, there can grow

---

[1] Interview with Jan Marlan, *International Association of Analytical Psychology Newsletter* 26: 2006.

a third realm, a sort of conscious unconscious. It is rather non-directed, non-ordered, non-object, non-subject, not quite a reality of a concrete kind … It is a realm for itself, neither object nor subject, yet both. This third reality is a psychic reality, a world of experiences, emotions, fantasies, moods, visions, dreams, dialogues, physical sensations, a large and open space, free and spontaneous.

(Hillman 1967: 66)

It is from this 'third position': 'the knowing unknowing' of the medieval *stulta sapientia*, that I have suggested Teresa's perspective on the soul arises, and it is from this third perspective that this book has been written. As we find ourselves in a world of rising materialism on the one hand and simplistic religious fundamentalism on the other, Teresa offers, I suggest, a light-footed path of desire that will lead us from the abyss into which we stare. Taken as a whole her writings provide a course in self-awareness and discovery, the aim of which is to lead us back into engagement with the world where our 'decentred' self may be nourished by the deep libidinal sources of grace that lie within us as our birthright.

Kristeva, with whom we began this book, sees in Teresa's phrase *Buscate in Mí* / 'Seek Yourself in Me' – heard in prayer sometime around 1576 (see VE), a rebuke to the western tradition of 'Know Thyself' and the Cartesian 'I think therefore I am'. She replaces the Socratic command with the Teresian *Connais-toi en Moi* – 'Know Thyself in Me' (Kristeva 2008:35). Is this, perhaps, Teresa's message to us today? She is the 'symbolic thinker' who taps into the deep subterranean libidinal sources upon which the roots of Western culture rests. As we listen to her gentle voice we realize that the wounded and disorientated postmodern soul is being called back to the ancient realities of the pre-modern self. For if we listen carefully we can just about make out the quiet song of a little girl singing in a cool courtyard high above the mountains of central Spain on a hot summer afternoon a long, long time ago. The breeze catches her song and we hear it again, now clear, now indistinct. Now, more than ever, the world once again needs to listen, and dance to, that song:

Alma, buscarte has en Mí,	*Soul, you must Seek Thyself in Me,*
Y a Mí, buscarme has en ti.	*And in Thyself Seek Me!*
De tal suerte pudo amor,	*With such fortune could love,*
Alma, en mí te retratar	*Soul, portray you in me*
Que ningún sabio pintor	*Such that no gifted painter*

Supiera con tal primor
Tal imagen estampar

Fuiste por amor criada
Hermosa, bella, y así
En mis entrañas pintada,
Si te perdieres, mi amada,
Alma, buscarte has en Mí

Que yo sé que te hallaras
En mi pecho retratada
Y tan al vivo sacada
Que si te ves te holgaras
Viéndote tan bien pintada.

Y si acaso no supieres
Donde me hallarás a Mí,
No andes de aquí para allí,
Sino, si hallarme quisieres
A Mí buscarme has en ti.

Porque tú eres mi aposento,
Eres me casa y morada,
Y así llamo en cualquier tiempo,
Si hallo en tu pensamiento
Estar la puerta cerrada.

Fuera de ti no hay buscarme
Porque para hallarme a Mí
Bastará solo llamarme,
Que a ti iré sin tardarme
Y a Mí buscarme has en ti.

Could portray that beauty
With which the image is engraved.

For love created you,
Precious, fair one,
Deep within me carved,
For if you lose me, love,
Soul, Seek Thyself in Me!

For I know that you will find
Yourself engraved in my heart
And so drawn from life
That when you see you will rejoice
To see yourself so well painted.

And if by chance you do not know
Where to find me,
Don't wander here and there,
For, if you want to find me,
In Thyself Seek Me!

For you are my refuge,
My home and my dwelling place,
And if I call at any time,
And find in the castle of your mind
The door is closed.

Do not look for me outside yourself
For, if you want to find me
All you need do is call me,
Then I shall come quickly
And in Thyself Seek Me!

Bibliography

ABBREVIATIONS

BAC = *Biblioteca de Autores Cristianos*

BMC = *Biblioteca Mística Carmelitana*

DNB = Dictionary of National Biography, Oxford University Press

DS = *Dictionnaire de Spiritualité Ascétique et Mystique Doctrine et Histoire.* M. Viller, F. Cavallera, J de Guibert, A. Rayez, A. Derville, P.Lamarche, A. Solignac (eds). 1937–present. Paris: Beauchesne

ICS = Institute of Carmelite Studies, Washington

MHCT = *Monumenta Historica Carmeli Teresiani.* Ed. Institutum Historicum Teresianum. Rome: Teresianum, 1973–present

OED = Oxford English Dictionary (Oxford: Oxford University Press)

PL = *Patrologiae Cursus Completus.* Series Latina. J.-P. Migne (ed.). Paris, 1844–64

PRIMARY SOURCES

TERESA OF AVILA

—(1611), *The Lyf of the mother Teresa of Iesus, foundresse of the monasteries of the discalced or bare-footed Carmelite nunnes and fryers, of the first rule. Written by herself, at the commmaundement of her ghostly father by W.M. of the Society of Jesus.* Trans. William Malone. Antwerp: Henry Iaye.

—(1623), *The Flaming Hart, or, the life of the gloriovs S. Teresa foundresse of the reformation of the order of the all-immaculate Virgin-Mother, our B. Lady, of Mount Carmel.* Trans. Tobie Matthew. Antwerp: Joannes Meursius.

—(1671), *The Life of the Holy Mother St Teresa, Foundress of the Reformation of the Discalceate Carmelites, according to the Primitive Rule.* Trans. Abraham Woodhead. England.

—(1851), *Life of Saint Teresa written by herself and Translated from the Spanish*. Trans. John Dalton. London: T. Jones.

—(1870), *The Life of Teresa of Avila by Herself*. Trans. David Lewis. London: Thomas Baker.

—(1882), *El Castillo Interior o Tratado de las Moradas Escrito por Santa Teresa de Jesus. Edición autografiada e impresa según el texto original propiedad de sus hijas las Religiosas Carmelitas Descalzas del Convento de San José de Esta Ciudad*. Publicado bajo la dirección del Cardenal Lluch, Arzobispo de Sevilla. Sevilla: Litografia de Juan Moyana.

—(1925), *The Way of Perfection*. Trans. the Benedictines of Stanbrook. London: Thomas Baker.

—(1930), *The Interior Castle or The Mansions*. Trans. a Benedictine of Stanbrook. London: Thomas Baker.

—(1946), *The Complete Works of St Teresa of Jesus*. Trans. E. Allison Peers. 3 Vols. London: Sheed and Ward (Allison Peers CW).

—(1951), *The Letters of St Teresa of Jesus*. Trans. E. Allison Peers (from the critical edition of P. Silverio de Santa Teresa). London: Burns, Oates and Washbourne Ltd. (Allison Peers LL).

—(1980–7), *The Collected Works of St Teresa of Avila*. Trans. K. Kavanaugh and O. Rodriguez. 3 Vols. Vol. 1: 2nd edn; Vols 2 and 3; 1st edn. Washington: Institute of Carmelite Studies (Kavanaugh and Rodriguez CW).

—(1997), *Obras Completas de Santa Teresa de Jésus*. Efrén de la Madre de Dios and Otger Steggink (eds), 9th edn. Madrid: Biblioteca de Autores Cristianos, (Steggink OC)

—(1998), *Santa Teresa Obras Completas*. T. Alvarez (ed.), 10th edn. Burgos: Editorial Monte Carmelo, (Alvarez OC)

—(2001), *The Collected Letters of St Teresa of Avila*. Trans. K. Kavanaugh. Washington: Institute of Carmelite Studies .(Kavanaugh LL).

WORKS OF TERESA AVILA

ABBREVIATIONS

C = *Meditaciones Sobre los Cantares / Meditations on the Song of Songs*
CC = *Cuentas de Conciencia / Spiritual Testimonies*
CE = *Camino de Perfección / The Way of Perfection*, Escorial Codex
CV = *Camino de Perfección / The Way of Perfection*, Valladolid Codex

CT = *Camino de Perfección* / *The Way of Perfection*, Toledo Codex
CO = *Constituciones* / *Constitutions*
Exc = *Exclamaciones* / *Exclamations*
F = *El Libro de las Fundaciones* / *The Book of the Foundations*
LL = *Epistolario* / *The Letters of St Teresa*
M = *Moradas del Castillo Interior* / *The Interior Castle*
ME = *Method for the Visitation of Discalced Nuns* / *Visita de Descalzas*
P = *Poetry*
V = *El Libro de La Vida* / *The Book of the Life*
VE = *Vejamen* / *Commentary on 'Seek Yourself in Me'*

JOHN OF THE CROSS

—(1929–31), *Obras de San Juan de La Cruz, Doctor de la Iglesia*. P. Silverio de Santa Teresa (ed.). Burgos: Biblioteca Mistica Carmelitana (5 Vols).
—(1943), *The Complete Works of Saint John of the Cross, Doctor of the Church Translated from the Critical Edition of P. Silverio de Santa Teresa, C.D.* Trans. E. Allison Peers. London: Burns Oates (3 Vols).
—(1979), *The Collected Works of St John of the Cross*. Trans. K. Kavanaugh and O. Rodriguez. Washington: Institute of Carmelite Studies.
—(2002), *San Juan de La Cruz: Obras Completas*. Lucinio Ruano de la Iglesia (ed.). Madrid: Biblioteca de Autores Cristianos.

ABBREVIATIONS (WORKS OF JOHN OF THE CROSS)

A = *Ascent of Mount Carmel*
DN = *Dark Night of the Soul*
LF = *The Living Flame of Love*
CA = *Spiritual Canticle* – Redaction A
CB = *Spiritual Canticle* – Redaction B

BUDDHIST TEXTS

MN = *The Middle Length Discourses of the Buddha* (Majjhima-nikāya). Trans. Bhikkhu Ñāṇamoli and Bhikkhu Bodhi. Oxford: Pali Text Society, 2002

BS = *The Connected Discourses of the Buddha* (Saṃyutta Nikāya). Trans. Bhikkhu Bodhi. Somerville: Wisdom, 2000

OTHER PRIMARY SOURCES

Anonymous (1964), *The Cloud of Unknowing : together with The epistle of privy counsel by an English mystic of the XIVth century.* J. McCann (ed.). London: Burn & Oates.

—(1981),*The Cloud of Unknowing.* J. J. Walsh (ed.). New York: Paulist.

Cassian, John (1997), *The Conferences.* Trans. B. Ramsey. New York: Newman.

Dionysius the Areopagite (1924), *Dionysius the Areopagite on the Divine Names and Mystical Theology* and *Denis Hid Divinity.* McCann (ed.). London: Burns and Oates.

—(1987), *Pseudo-Dionysius: The Complete Works.* Trans. C. Luibheid and P. Rorem. New York: Paulist.

Gerson, Jean (1958), *Ioannis Carlerii de Gerson De Mystica Theologia.* A Combes (ed.). Lugano: Thesaurus Mundi (GMT).

—(1998), *Jean Gerson: Early Works.* Trans. B. McGuire. New York: Paulist.

Gracián, Jerónimo (1932), *Obras del P. Jerónimo Gracián de la Madre de Dios.* P. Silverio de Santa Teresa (ed.). Burgos: El Monte Carmelo.

von Goethe, Johann Wolfgang (1808), *Faust: Eine Tragödie.* Tübingen: J. G. Cotta.

Hugh of St Victor, *On the Celestial Hierarchy* in PL CLXXV.

Jung, Carl Gustav (1963/1989), *Memories, Dreams, Reflections.* A. Jaffé (ed.). London: Vintage (Jung MDR).

—(1971/1999), *The Collected Works of C.G. Jung.* Trans. and revised by R. Hull and H. Baynes. London: Routledge (Jung CW).

—(2007), *The Jung-White Letters.* A. Conrad Lammers and A. Cunningham (eds). London: Routledge.

—(2009), *The Red Book: Liber Novus.* S. Shamdasani (ed.). London: Norton & Co. (Jung RB).

de Laredo, Bernado (1948), *Subida de monte Sión* in *Misticos Franciscanos Españoles.* Vol 2, J. Gomis (ed.). Madrid: Biblioteca de Autores Cristianos

—(1952), *The Ascent of Mount Sion.* Trans. E. Allison Peers. London: Faber and Faber.

Nicholas of France (1962), *Ignea Sagitta / The Flaming Arrow*. Trans. Bede
  Edwards, O. C. D. from the critical edition by Adrian Staring, O.Carm.
  Reproduced in *Carmelus* IX.

Nietzsche, Friedrich (1990), *Werke in Zwei Bänden*. Munich: Carl Hanser
  Verlag

de Osuna, Francisco (1981), *Francisco de Osuna: The Third Spiritual Alphabet*.
  Trans. M. Giles. New York: Paulist.

—(1998), *Tercer Abecedario Espiritual de Francisco de Osuna*. S. López
  Santidrián (ed.). Madrid: Biblioteca de Autores Cristianos (TA).

Scripture Quotations from the *New Revised Standard Version* (2007), London:
  Harper, 2007 with modifications as necessary.

Wittgenstein, Ludwig (1991), *Über Gewissheit* in *Werkausgabe*, Band 8.
  Frankfurt-am-Main: Suhrkamp, 1984. Translated as *On Certainty*. G. E. M.
  Anscombe and G. H. von Wright (eds). Oxford: Blackwell.

—(2000), *Wittgenstein's Nachlass: The Bergen Electronic Edition*. Oxford:
  Oxford University Press (BEE).

SECONDARY SOURCES

Ahlgren, G. (1996), *Teresa of Avila and the Politics of Sanctity*. Ithaca: Cornell
  University Press.

Alcalá, A. (ed.) (1987), *The Spanish Inquisition and the Inquisitorial Mind*.
  Boulder, Colorado: Columbia University Press.

Allison Peers, E. (1930), *Studies of the Spanish Mystics* (2 Vols). London:
  Sheldon Press.

—(1945), *Mother of Carmel: A Portrait of St Teresa of Jesus*. London: SCM.

—(1953), 'Saint Teresa's Style: A Tentative Appraisal' in *Saint Teresa of
  Jesus and Other Essays and Addresses*. London: Faber and Faber.

—(1954), *A Handbook to the Life and Times of St. Teresa and St John of the
  Cross*. London: Burns Oates.

Andrés Martín, M. (1975), *Los Recogidos: Nueva Vision de la Mistica Española
  (1500–1700)*. Madrid: Fundacion Universitaria Española, Seminario 'Suarez'.

—(1976), *La teología española en el siglo XVI*. Madrid: Biblioteca de Autores
  Cristianos.

—(1982), *Osuna (François de)* in DS, pp. 1037–51.

Bataillon, M. (1982), *Erasmo y España*. Mexico: Fondo de cultura económica.

Bell, A. (1925), *Luis de León*. Oxford: Clarendon.

Bethencourt, F. (2009), *The Inquisition: A Global History 1478–1834*. Cambridge: Cambridge University Press.

Bilinkoff, J. (1989), *The Avila of Saint Teresa: Religious Reform in a Sixteenth-Century City*. Ithaca, NY: Cornell University Press.

Bishop, P. (1995), *The Dionysian Self: C.G.Jung's Reception of Friedrich Nietzsche*. Berlin: Walter de Gruyter.

Chenu, M.-D. (1997), *Nature, Man and Society in the Twelfth Century*. Canada: Medieval Academy of America.

Crisógono de Jésus (1958), *Vida de San Juan de La Cruz*. Trans. as 'The Life of St John of the Cross' by K. Pond. London: Longmans.

Cunningham, B. (2004), *Malone, William* in DNB. Oxford: Oxford University Press.

De Certeau, M. (1992), *The Mystic Fable: Vol One, The Sixteenth and Seventeenth Centuries*. Trans. M. Smith. Chicago: University of Chicago Press.

De Foronda y Aguilera, M. (1913), 'Honras por Enrique IV y proclamación de Isabel la Católica en la ciudad de Avila' in *Boletín de la Academia de Historia*, pp. 427–34.

Davies, G. (1981), 'St Teresa and the Jewish Question' in *Teresa de Jésus and Her World*. M. Rees (ed.). Leeds: Trinity and All Saints College.

Dondaine, H. (1953), *Le Corpus dionysien de l'université de Paris au XIIIe siècle*. Rome: Edizioni di Storia et Letteratura.

Egido, Teófanes, (1980), 'The Historical Setting of St Teresa's Life' in *Carmelite Studies 1: Spiritual Direction*. Washington: ICS

—(1986), *El Linaje Judeoconverso de Santa Teresa (Pleito de Hidalguía de los Cepeda)*. Madrid: Editorial de Espiritualidad.

Efrén de la Madre de Dios (1951), *Tiempo y Vida de Santa Teresa*. Madrid: BAC.

Efrén de la Madre de Dios and Otto Steggink (1996), *Tiempo y Vida de Santa Teresa*. Rev. edn. Madrid: BAC.

Elliott, J. H. (2002), *Imperial Spain 1469–1716*. London: Penguin.

Flasche, H. (1983), 'El Problema de la Certeza en el "Castillo Interior"' in *Actas de Congreso Internacional Teresiano*. T. Egido Martínez, V. García de la Concha and O. Gonzalez de Caredal (eds). Salamanca: Universidad de Salamanca.

Florencio del Niño Jesús (1924), *El Monte Carmelo: Tradiciones e Historia de La Santa Montaña, de la Virgen del Carmen y De La Orden Carmelitana y la Luz do Los Monumentos y Documentos*. Madrid: Mensajero de Santa Teresa.

Forshaw, B. (1967), 'Doctor of the Church' in *The New Catholic Encyclopedia* 4:939. New York: McGraw Hill.

García Oro, J. (1992), *El Cardenal Cisneros: Vida y Empresas*. Madrid: Biblioteca de Autores Christianos.

—(1992), *La Iglesia de Toledo en tiempo del Cardenal Cisneros (1495–1517)*. Toledo: Publicaciones del Estudio Teológico de San Ildefonso.

Giordano, S. (1995), *Carmel in the Holy Land: From Its Beginnings to the Present Day*. Arenzano: Il Messaggero di Gesu Bambino.

González y González, N. (1976), *El Monasterio de la Encarnación de Ávila*. Avila: Caja Central de Ahorros y Préstamos

Green, D. (1989), *Gold in the Crucible: Teresa of Avila and the Western Mystical Tradition*. Shaftesbury: Element.

Hamilton, A. (1992) *Heresy and Mysticism in Sixteenth Century Spain: the Alumbrados*. Cambridge: James Clarke.

Harvey, P. (1995), *The Selfless Mind: Personality, Consciousness and Nirvana in Early Buddhism*. Richmond, Surrey: Curzon.

Haskins, C. H. (1957), *The Renaissance of the 12th Century*. New York: Meridian.

Hillman, J. (1975), *Re-Visioning Psychology*. New York: Harper.

—(1967), *Insearch: Psychology and Religion*. Woodstock, Connecticut: Spring Publications.

—(1983), *Inter Views* (with Laura Pozzo). Dallas, Texas: Spring Publications.

—(2006), Interview with Jan Marlan in *International Association of Analytical Psychology Newsletter* 26: 2006.

Hoeller, S. (1982),*The Gnostic Jung and the Seven Sermons to the Dead*. Wheaton, IL: Theosophical Publishing House.

Howells, E. (2002), *John of the Cross and Teresa of Avila: Mystical Knowing and Selfhood*. New York: Crossroad.

Kalupahana, D. (1992), *The Principles of Buddhist Psychology*. Delhi: Sri Satguru.

Knowles, M. D. (1962), *The Evolution of Medieval Thought*. London: Longmans.

Krishna, G. (1971), *Kundalini: the Evolutionary Energy in Man*. London: Robinson and Watkins.

Kristeva, J. (1984), *Revolution in Poetic Language*. Trans. M. Waller. New York: Columbia University Press.

—(2008), *Thérèse mon amour*. Paris: Fayard

—(2009), *This Incredible Need to Believe*. Trans. Beverley Bie Brahic. New York: Columbia University Press.

Llamas, E. (1977), *Santa Teresa y La Inquisición Española*. Madrid: Consejo Superior de Investigaciones Cientificas.

Llorca, B. (1949), *Bulario Pontificio de la Inquisición Española en Su Período Constitucional (1478-1525)*. Rome: Pontificia Università Gregoriana.

Loomie, A. (2004), *Matthew, Sir Toby* in DNB. Oxford: Oxford University Press.

López-Baralt, L. (1992), *Huellas del Islam in la literature española*. Trans. A. Hurley as *Islam in Spanish Literature From the Middle Ages to the Present*. Leiden: Brill.

MacCulloch, D. (2003), *Reformation: Europe's House Divided 1490-1700*. London: Allen Lane.

Márquez, A. (1980), *Los alumbrados: orígenes y filosofía (1525-1559)*. Madrid: Taurus.

Martínez De Bujanda, J. (ed.) (1984), *Index de L'Inquisition Espagnole 1551,1554,1559 /Index des Livres Interdit*. Sherbrooke, Geneve: Centre d'Etudes de la Renaissance.

Matthew, Sir Tobie (1904), *A True Historical Relation of the Conversion of Sir Tobie Matthew to the Holy Catholic Faith*. A. H. Matthew (ed.). London: Burns and Oates.

McGinn, B. (1991), *The Presence of God: A History of Western Christian Mysticism. Vol I: The Foundations of Mysticism*. London: SCM.

—(1994), *The Presence of God: A History of Western Christian Mysticism. Vol 2: Gregory the Great through the Twelfth Century*. London: SCM.

—(1998), *The Presence of God: A History of Western Christian Mysticism. Vol 3: The Flowering of Mysticism: Men and Women in the New Mysticism, 1200-1350*. London: SCM.

—(2005), *The Presence of God: A History of Western Christian Mysticism. Vol 4: The Harvest of Mysticism in Medieval Germany*. New York: Herder and Herder.

McGreal, W. (1999), *At the Fountain of Elijah: The Carmelite Tradition*. London: Darton, Longman and Todd.

Menéndez Pidal, R. (1942), 'El estilo de Santa Teresa' in *La lengua de Cristobál Colón*. Buenos Aires: Espasa.

Merton, T. (1990), *The Seven Storey Mountain*. London: SPCK.

—(1973) *Contemplative Prayer*. London: Darton, Longman and Todd.

Morris, C. (1972), *The Discovery of the Individual 1050-1200*. London: SPCK.

Namkhai Norbu (1986), *Crystal and the Way of Light - Sutra, Tantra and Dzogchen*. New York: Routledge.

Ortega y Gasset, J. (1957), *On Love: Aspects of a Single Theme*. Trans. T. Talbot. New York: Meridian.

Rhys Davids, T. W. (1881), *Buddhist Sutras*. Oxford: Clarendon.

Ribera, Francisco de (1908), *Vida de Santa Teresa de Jesús*. Jaime Pons (ed.). Barcelona: Gustavo Gili.

Rivers, E. (1984), 'The Vernacular Mind of St Teresa' in *Carmelite Studies*, 1984. Washington: ICS.

Rorem, P. (1993), *Pseudo-Dionysius. A Commentary on the Texts and an Introduction to their Influence*. Oxford: Oxford University Press.

Ros, Fidèle de, P. (1936), *Un maître de Sainte Thérèse: Le père François d'Osuna*. Paris: Beauchesne.

Roth, N. (1995), *Conversos, Inquisition and the Expulsion of the Jews from Spain*. Wisconsin: University of Wisconsin Press.

Ruiz, F. (ed.) (2000), *God Speaks in the Night*. Washington: ICS.

Rummel, E. (1999), *Jiménez de Cisneros: on the threshold of Spain's Golden Age*. Michigan: Arizona Center for Medieval and Renaissance Studies, the University of Michigan.

Safran, J. (ed.) (2003), *Psychoanalysis and Buddhism: An Unfolding Dialogue*. Somerville: Wisdom.

Samuel, G. (1993), *Civilised Shamans: Buddhism in Tibetan Societies*. Washington: Smithsonian Institute Press.

Segal, R. (1992), *The Gnostic Jung*. London: Routledge.

Slade, C. (1995), *Teresa of Avila – Author of a Heroic Life*. California: University of California Press.

Smet, J. (1988), *The Carmelites: A History of The Brothers of Our Lady of Mount Carmel* (3 Vols). Illinois: Carmelite Spiritual Center.

—(1997), 'The Carmelite Rule after 750 Years' in *Carmelus* 44:1.

Swietlicki, C. (1986), *Spanish Christian Cabala: the works of Luis de Léon, Santa Teresa de Jésus and San Juan de la Cruz*. Columbia: University of Missouri Press.

Tello, P. (1963), 'La Judería de Ávila durante el Reinado de los Reyes Católicos' in *Sefarad* 23:1.

Thanissaro Bhikkhu (2010), "Mindfulness Defined" in *Access to Insight*, http://www.accesstoinsight.org/lib/authors/thanissaro/mindfulnessdefined.html

Thomas, R. S. (2002), *Collected Poems 1945–1990*. A. Motion (ed.). London: Phoenix.

Thompson, C. (1988), *The Strife of Tongues: Fray Luis de León and the Golden Age of Spain*. Cambridge: Cambridge University Press.

Tyler, P. M. (1997), *The Way of Ecstasy: Praying with Teresa of Avila*. Norwich: Canterbury.

—(2010), *St John of the Cross: Outstanding Christian Thinker*. London: Continuum.

—(2010a), *Sources of Transformation: Revitilizing Christian Spirituality*. With E. Howells (ed.). London: Continuum.

—(2011), *The Return to the Mystical: Ludwig Wittgenstein, Teresa of Avila and the Christian Mystical Tradition*. London: Continuum.

—(2011a), 'The Roots of Desert Spirituality' in *The Pastoral Review*, September/October 2011.

—(2012), *The Bloomsbury Guide to Christian Spirituality*. with R. Woods (ed.). London: Bloomsbury.

Ulanov, A. and Dueck, A. (2008), *The Living God and Our Living Psyche: What Christians Can Learn from Carl Jung*. Grand Rapids: Eerdmans.

Von Franz, M-L. (1999), *Archetypal Dimensions of the Psyche*. London: Shambala.

Waaijman, K. (1999), *The Mystical Space of Carmel: A Commentary on the Carmelite Rule*. Leuven: Peeters.

Waldron, W. (2005), *The Buddhist Unconscious: The ālaya-vijñāna in the context of Indian Buddhist Thought*. London: Routledge.

Weber, A. (1990), *Teresa of Avila and the Rhetoric of Femininity*. Princeton, NJ: Princeton University Press.

Welch, J. (1982), *Spiritual Pilgrims: Carl Jung and Teresa of Avila*. New York: Paulist.

White, V. (1952), *God and the Unconcious* London: Harvill.

—(1960), *Soul and Psyche: An Enquiry into the Relationship of Psychotherapy and Religion*. London: Collins and Harvill.

Williams, P. (2000), *Buddhist Thought: A Complete Introduction to the Indian Tradition*. London: Routledge.

Wilson, C. (ed.) (2006), *The Heirs of St Teresa of Avila: Defenders and Disseminators of the Founding Mother's Legacy*. Carmelite Studes IX. Washington: ICS.

Zinn, G. A. (1979), *Richard of St Victor: The Twelve Patriarchs, The Mystical Ark, Book Three of the Trinity*. Trans. with Introduction. London: SPCK.

Index